# *419 Classic Recipes From Taste of Home's First Year!*

TRUTH BE TOLD, we *were* a bit skeptical back in 1999 when we produced a *Taste of Home Annual Recipes* volume featuring every single recipe from 1995. Would folks really want a book with timeless recipes that had first been published 4 years earlier? The answer from our loyal readers was a resounding "Yes!"

And that's not all—these everyday cooks wanted *even more* tried-and-true dishes to serve their families. So we did it again—in 2000 we created an edition featuring every single recipe from 1994.

We received many thank-you notes from happy readers, which made us happy, too. But a number of those dedicated country cooks added a P.S., "Now that you've done the 1994 recipes, will 1993 be coming, too?"

So here it is, the *1994 Taste of Home Annual Recipes* book featuring every single recipe from 1993—the first year we published *Taste of Home* magazine.

As you probably already know, *Taste of Home* has gone on to become the most popular cooking magazine in the world—and the main reason is wonderful readers like you. Our readers continue to share their best recipes with us, and we continue to pass them on to all our other readers.

With this *1994 Taste of Home Annual Recipes*, those cooks who told us they wanted every single recipe *ever* published in *Taste of Home* can now have a complete collection, including the premier year.

Here's why this volume will hold a place of honor on *your* bookshelf:

1. Its 240 pages are organized into 16 convenient chapters for easy reference.

2. Finding all of the 419 recipes is a snap with this book's *two different indexes*. One lists every dish by food category, major ingredient and/or cooking method. The other provides an alphabetical listing of each and every recipe.

3. The full-color pictures in this classic collection are *bigger* than ever, so you can plainly see what many of these dishes look like before you start preparing them.

4. We've used large print for easy reading while cooking. And each recipe is presented "all on-a-page", so you never have to turn pages back and forth while cooking.

5. This volume is printed on the highest quality coated paper, which means you can wipe away spatters easily.

6. The book lies open and *stays open* as you cook. Its durable hard cover will give you *years* of use.

But the real proof of this volume's value is in the tasting. Thumb through chapters such as "My Mom's Best Meal", Meals in Minutes and Editors' Meals. You'll find complete menus and accompanying photos that will make your mouth water.

Or browse chapters like Breakfast & Brunch, Cakes, Cookies & Candies or Pies & Desserts. The toughest part about making these recipes will be deciding which ones to try first. There are *so many* great choices!

We know you and your family will enjoy this cookbook and the tasty meals you'll share around your table. With 419 down-home dishes to choose from, you can enjoy delicious dining for many years to come!

### 🍴 🍴 🍴

## *1994 Taste of Home Annual Recipes*

**Editor:** Heidi Reuter Lloyd
**Art Director:** Kristin Bork
**Food Editor:** Janaan Cunningham
**Associate Editors:** Julie Schnittka,
Jean Steiner, Susan Uphill
**Food Photography Artists:**
Stephanie Marchese, Vicky Marie Moseley
**Assistant Art Director:** Linda Dzik
**Production:** Ellen Lloyd, Catherine Fletcher

## Taste of Home®

**Executive Editor:** Kathy Pohl
**Food Editor:** Janaan Cunningham
**Associate Food Editors:** Coleen Martin,
Diane Werner
**Senior Recipe Editor:** Sue A. Jurack
**Test Kitchen Director:** Karen Johnson
**Managing Editor:** Ann Kaiser
**Assistant Managing Editor:** Faithann Stoner
**Associate Editors:** Kristine Krueger, Sharon Selz
**Test Kitchen Home Economists:** Pat Schmeling,
Sue Draheim, Peggy Fleming, Julie Herzfeldt,
Joylyn Jans, Kristin Koepnick, Mark Morgan,
Wendy Stenman, Karen Wright
**Test Kitchen Assistants:** Kris Lehman,
Megan Taylor
**Editorial Assistants:** Barb Czysz,
Mary Ann Koebernik
**Design Director:** Jim Sibilski
**Art Director:** Emma Acevedo
**Food Photography:** Rob Hagen, Dan Roberts
**Food Photography Artists:** Stephanie Marchese,
Vicky Marie Moseley
**Photo Studio Manager:** Anne Schimmel
**Production:** Ellen Lloyd, Catherine Fletcher
**Publisher:** Roy Reiman

*Taste of Home* Books
©2001 Reiman Publications, LLC
5400 S. 60th St., Greendale WI 53129

International Standard Book Number:
0-89821-321-5
International Standard Serial Number:
1094-3463

**PICTURED AT RIGHT.** Clockwise from upper left: Berry Creme Parfaits (p. 125), Italian Pot Roast (p. 59), Smoked Turkey and Apple Salad (p. 24), Garlic-Buttered Green Beans (p. 178), Parsley Potatoes (p. 179), Old-Fashioned Pot Roast (p. 178) and Peach Bavarian (p. 179).

# Taste of Home 1994 Annual Recipes

**PICTURED ON FRONT COVER.** Clockwise from top: Emily's Spinach Salad (p. 22), Lemon Bars (p. 167) and Lemon Herbed Salmon (p. 73).

**PICTURED ON BACK COVER.** Top to bottom: Raspberry Trifle (p. 120) and Citrus Cheesecake (p. 124).

**FOR ADDITIONAL COPIES** of this book, write *Taste of Home* Books, P.O. Box 908, Greendale WI 53129.

To order by credit card, call toll-free 1-800/344-2560 or visit our Web site at www.reimanpub.com.

# Snacks & Beverages

*Turn to this chapter when you're looking for something different
to start a meal—such as an appealing appetizer or a delicious drink—
or you crave some memorable munchies.*

**SUPER STARTERS.** Clockwise from upper left:
BLT Bites (p. 14), Breakfast Wassail (p. 16), Mini
Apple Pizzas (p. 19), Cheesy Sun Crisps (p. 10),
Sweet Gingered Chicken Wings (p. 9) and Hot
Almond 'n' Cream Drink (p. 13).

## Cappuccino Mix
**(Pictured above)**

*One day, friends and I were swapping recipes for hot chocolate, and someone came up with this mix. I put it in jars as gifts for Christmas.* —Susan Prillhart
Rockledge, Florida

  1 cup powdered nondairy creamer
  1 cup instant chocolate drink mix
  2/3 cup instant coffee granules
  1/2 cup sugar
  1/2 teaspoon ground cinnamon
  1/4 teaspoon ground nutmeg

Combine all ingredients; mix well. Store in an airtight container. To prepare one serving, add 3 tablespoons mix to 6 ounces of boiling water; stir well. **Yield:** 3 cups dry mix.

## Pizza Cups

*My girls frequently have friends overnight, plus their big brother is always hungry. These miniature pizzas please everybody and don't take long to make.*
—Suzanne McKinley, Lyons, Georgia

  1 pound hot *or* mild pork sausage
  1 jar (14 ounces) pizza sauce
  2 tablespoons ketchup
  1/4 teaspoon garlic powder
  2 tubes (12 ounces *each*) refrigerated
    buttermilk biscuits, separated into 10
    biscuits

**Shredded mozzarella cheese**
**Grated Parmesan cheese**

In a skillet, cook the sausage over medium heat; drain. Stir in pizza sauce, ketchup and garlic powder; set aside. Press biscuits into 20 well-greased muffin cups. Spoon 1 or 2 tablespoons of the meat sauce into each biscuit; top with mozzarella cheese and sprinkle with Parmesan cheese. Bake at 350° for 10-15 minutes or until golden brown. (Refrigerate or freeze any remaining meat sauce.) **Yield:** 20 pizzas.

## Honey Granola

*This granola makes a sweet, healthy treat with only a touch of sugar. My son and daughter really like snacking on it.* —Sharon Mensing, Greenfield, Iowa

  1/4 cup honey
  1/4 cup butter *or* margarine, melted
  1 tablespoon brown sugar
  1/4 teaspoon ground cinnamon
  2 cups old-fashioned oats
  1/2 cup unprocessed bran*
  1/2 cup raisins, optional

In a 9-in. square baking pan, combine the honey, butter, brown sugar and cinnamon. Stir in the oats and bran. Bake at 350° for 25-30 minutes, stirring occasionally, until golden brown. Stir in the raisins if desired. Cool. Store in an airtight container. **Yield:** about 3 cups. **\*Editor's Note:** Unprocessed bran is available in health food stores and the health food aisle of some grocery stores.

## Sweet Minglers

*This snack mix is perfect for a late-night treat or a pick-me-up any time of the day. It's always eaten up quickly.* —Mary Obeilin, Selinsgrove, Pennsylvania

  1 cup (6 ounces) semisweet chocolate chips
  1/4 cup creamy peanut butter
  6 cups Corn *or* Rice Chex cereal
  1 cup confectioners' sugar

In a large microwave-safe bowl, melt chocolate chips on high for 1 minute. Stir; microwave 30 seconds longer or until the chips are melted. Stir in peanut butter. Gently stir in cereal until well coated; set aside. Place confectioners' sugar in a 2-gal. resealable plastic bag. Add cereal mixture and shake until well coated. Store in an airtight container in the refrigerator. **Yield:** about 6 cups.

## Stuffed Celery Snacks

*The creamy filling with each bite of crisp celery makes for a light satisfying snack that gets high marks from everyone in my family. It's also a simple appetizer for casual get-togethers.* —Patsy Faye Steenbock
Shoshoni, Wyoming

1 package (8 ounces) cream cheese,
  softened
1/3 cup shredded carrot
1-1/2 teaspoons dried parsley flakes
1/4 teaspoon dried thyme
1/4 teaspoon onion salt
Celery ribs, cut into 3-inch lengths

In a small bowl, combine cream cheese, carrot and seasonings. Stuff into celery. Cover and chill for at least 1 hour. **Yield:** about 2 dozen.

—— 🥄 🥄 🥄 ——

## Spicy Mint Tea

*In the old days, a steaming cup of mint tea was said to dispel headaches, heartburn and indigestion. I don't know about that, but I do know that this tea refreshes me every time.* —Ione Banks, Jefferson, Oregon

6 cups water
2 cinnamon sticks
4 whole cloves
4 whole allspice
2 cups fresh mint leaves
Honey, optional

Bring the water, cinnamon, cloves and allspice to a boil. Boil for 1 minute. Stir in the mint leaves. Remove from heat and steep for 5 minutes. Strain into cups. Sweeten with honey if desired. **Yield:** 4 servings.

—— 🥄 🥄 🥄 ——

## Zippy Horseradish Dip

*The area where I live produces a third of the country's supply of horseradish. Some of our fields are nearly 50 years old and were planted by my husband's parents, who homesteaded here. This dip is great with fresh veggies.* —Cathy Seus, Tulelake, California

1-1/2 teaspoons prepared horseradish
1/2 cup plain yogurt
1/2 cup sour cream
1 green onion, chopped
1/4 cup chopped peeled cucumber
1/4 teaspoon salt

1/4 teaspoon pepper
Fresh vegetables

In a small bowl, combine the first seven ingredients. Chill for at least 1 hour. Serve with vegetables. **Yield:** 1 cup.

—— 🥄 🥄 🥄 ——

## Creamy Green Onion Spread

### (Pictured below)

*Pineapple is a tasty surprise in this simple spread, which is great on crackers. You can make it without pineapple for a more traditional flavor, but once you've tried it with the fruit, you won't go back.*
—Sue Seymour, Valatie, New York

1 package (8 ounces) cream cheese,
  softened
2 tablespoons milk
2 green onions with tops, chopped
1/4 cup crushed pineapple, drained, optional
Assorted crackers

In a small bowl, beat cream cheese and milk until smooth. Stir in onions and pineapple if desired. Serve with crackers. **Yield:** 1 cup.

## Tomato Vegetable Juice
### (Pictured below)

*I've used this delicious recipe for many years, and it's always been a favorite. The tangy juice is refreshing on its own and also works great in any recipe calling for tomato juice. Because of all the vegetables, it's full of vitamins.*
—Sue Wille
Alexandria, Minnesota

✓ Uses less fat, sugar or salt. Includes Nutritional Analysis and Diabetic Exchanges.

    10 pounds tomatoes, peeled and chopped
       (about 8 quarts)
     3 garlic cloves, minced
     2 large onions, chopped
     2 large carrots, cut into 1/2-inch slices
     2 cups chopped celery
   1/2 cup chopped green pepper
   1/4 cup sugar
     1 tablespoon salt, optional
     1 teaspoon Worcestershire sauce
   1/2 teaspoon pepper
Lemon juice

Combine tomatoes, garlic, onions, carrots, celery and green pepper in a large Dutch oven. Bring to a boil; reduce heat and simmer for 20 minutes or until vegetables are tender. Cool. Press mixture through a food mill or fine sieve. Return juice to Dutch oven; add sugar, salt if desired, Worcestershire sauce and pepper. Bring to a boil. Ladle hot juice into hot sterilized quart jars, leaving 1/4-in. headspace. Add 2 tablespoons lemon juice to each jar. Adjust caps. Process for 40 minutes in a boiling-water bath. **Yield:** 56 servings (7 quarts). **Nutritional Analysis:** One 1/2-cup serving (prepared without salt) equals 46 calories, 15 mg sodium, 0 cholesterol, 10 gm carbohydrate, 2 gm protein, trace fat. **Diabetic Exchange:** 2 vegetable.

---

## Kid-Size Pizzas

*This is a recipe born out of desperation. One day I couldn't think of anything to serve the kids for lunch. Rummaging through the fridge, I came across some simple ingredients and prepared individual pizzas.*
—Polly Coumos, Mogadore, Ohio

     2 tubes (12 ounces *each*) refrigerated
       buttermilk biscuits
     1 can (8 ounces) tomato sauce
 1-1/2 teaspoons dried minced onion
     1 teaspoon dried oregano
     1 teaspoon dried basil
   1/8 teaspoon garlic powder
     2 cups (8 ounces) shredded mozzarella
       cheese

Roll or pat biscuits into 2-1/2-in. circles. Place on two greased baking sheets. In a small bowl, combine tomato sauce, onion, oregano, basil and garlic powder; spread over the biscuits. Sprinkle with cheese. Bake at 400° for 8-10 minutes. **Yield:** 20 mini pizzas.

---

## Mocha Fireside Coffee

*This is one of my absolute favorites around the holidays. It's quick and easy to fix, plus it makes a great gift that friends appreciate.*
—Gladys Goldstone
Nanaimbo, British Columbia

 2-1/2 cups powdered nondairy creamer
     2 cups hot cocoa mix
     1 cup instant coffee granules
     1 cup instant chocolate drink mix
   1/4 cup sugar
     2 teaspoons ground cinnamon
   1/2 teaspoon ground nutmeg

Combine all ingredients; mix well. Store in an airtight container. To prepare one serving, add 1 tablespoon mix to 3/4 cup boiling water. **Yield:** 6 cups dry mix.

## Crunchy Vegetable Spread

*I like to serve this with crackers at informal get-to-gethers. It's also super for a brown-bag sandwich on a crusty roll.* —Carolyn Griffin, Macon, Georgia

- 1 package (8 ounces) cream cheese, softened
- 1 tablespoon lemon juice
- 3/4 cup shredded carrots
- 1/4 cup finely chopped celery
- 1/4 cup finely chopped onion
- 1/4 cup diced green pepper
- 1/4 cup shredded seeded cucumber
- 1/4 teaspoon white pepper
- Assorted crackers *or* bread

In a small, beat cream cheese and lemon juice until smooth. Stir in vegetables and pepper. Serve with crackers or bread. **Yield:** about 2 cups.

— 🍺 🍺 🍺 —

## Stuffed Apple Treats

*Since we have apple trees right in our yard, I like to pack these nutritious and tasty treats in my children's school lunches.* —Margaret Slocum Ridgefield, Washington

- 2 tablespoons mayonnaise *or* softened cream cheese
- 2 tablespoons chopped nuts
- 2 tablespoons raisins, dried cranberries *or* dates
- 2 medium apples

Combine mayonnaise or cream cheese, nuts and raisins, cranberries or dates; set aside. Core each apple. Stuff cavity with mixture. **Yield:** 2 servings.

— 🍺 🍺 🍺 —

## Three-Herb Popcorn

*This popcorn is the No. 1 nighttime snack for my family. The herbs and nuts put a different spin on plain popcorn.* —Flo Burtnett, Gage, Oklahoma

- 6 quarts (24 cups) popped popcorn (about 1 cup kernels)
- Salt to taste
- 1/2 cup butter *or* margarine
- 1 teaspoon dried basil
- 1 teaspoon dried chervil
- 1/2 teaspoon dried thyme
- 1 can (12 ounces) mixed nuts, optional

Place popcorn in a large container or oven roasting pan. Salt to taste and set aside. Melt butter in a small saucepan. Remove from heat; stir in basil,

chervil and thyme. Drizzle butter mixture over popcorn and toss lightly to coat evenly. Stir in the nuts if desired. **Yield:** about 20 cups.

## Sweet Gingered Chicken Wings

**(Pictured above and on page 4)**

*I first tasted this delicious chicken dish years ago when I attended a class on using honey in cooking. When I prepare this recipe for a party, it's always one of the first dishes to disappear.* —Debbie Dougal Roseville, California

- 1 cup all-purpose flour
- 2 teaspoons salt
- 2 teaspoons paprika
- 1/4 teaspoon pepper
- 24 chicken wings
- SAUCE:
- 1/4 cup honey
- 1/4 cup frozen orange juice concentrate, thawed
- 1/2 teaspoon ground ginger
- Snipped fresh parsley, optional

In a bowl, combine flour, salt, paprika and pepper. Coat chicken wings in flour mixture; shake off excess. Place wings on a large greased baking sheet. Bake at 350° for 30 minutes. Remove from the oven and drain. Combine honey, orange juice concentrate and ginger; brush generously over chicken wings. Reduce heat to 325°. Bake for 30-40 minutes or until chicken tests done, basting occasionally with more sauce. Sprinkle with parsley before serving if desired. **Yield:** 2 dozen.

## Cinnamon-Raisin Granola

*This granola recipe makes a great after-school or late-night snack. I like it best teamed with a glass of cold milk. I also like that it's nutritious. This makes it an especially appropriate mix for kids to munch on.*
—Tammy Neubauer, Ida Grove, Iowa

- 4 cups old-fashioned oats
- 1 cup flaked coconut
- 1/4 cup packed brown sugar
- 1/4 cup vegetable oil
- 1/4 cup honey
- 1 teaspoon ground cinnamon
- 1-1/2 teaspoons vanilla extract
- 1 cup raisins

In a large bowl, combine oats and coconut; set aside. In a saucepan, combine brown sugar, oil, honey and cinnamon; bring to a boil. Remove from the heat and stir in vanilla. Pour over oat mixture; stir to coat. Spread in a large shallow baking pan. Bake at 350° for 15-20 minutes, stirring occasionally. Cool. Add the raisins. Store in an airtight container. **Yield:** 6 cups.

— 🍷 🍷 🍷 —

## Fresh Vegetable Dip
### (Pictured below left)

*This cool and creamy dip is a real family favorite for snacking, especially when paired with fresh-from-the-garden vegetables. Making this dip a day ahead and refrigerating it nicely enhances the flavors.*
—Denise Goedeken, Platte Center, Nebraska

- 1-1/2 cups (12 ounces) sour cream
- 3/4 cup mayonnaise
- 1 tablespoon dried minced onion
- 1 teaspoon dill weed
- 1 teaspoon dried parsley flakes
- 1 teaspoon garlic salt
- Dash Worcestershire sauce
- Fresh vegetables

In a small bowl, combine sour cream, mayonnaise, onion, dill, parsley, garlic salt and Worcestershire sauce. Chill for at least 1 hour. Serve with vegetables. **Yield:** 2 cups.

— 🍷 🍷 🍷 —

**SNACKS** like Fresh Vegetable Dip and Cheesy Sun Crisps (shown above, top to bottom) are nice for nibbling when the urge strikes.

## Cheesy Sun Crisps
### (Pictured at left and on page 4)

*Oats and sunflower kernels give these homemade crackers a hearty flavor. Serve them with dip or slices of cheese and sausage. Although this recipe makes a big batch, they won't last long.*
—Mary Detweiler
Farmington, Ohio

- 2 cups (8 ounces) shredded cheddar cheese
- 1/2 cup grated Parmesan cheese
- 1/2 cup butter *or* margarine, softened
- 3 tablespoons water
- 1 cup all-purpose flour
- 1/4 teaspoon salt
- 1 cup quick-cooking oats
- 2/3 cup roasted salted sunflower kernels

In a mixing bowl, combine the cheddar and Parmesan cheeses, butter and water until well mixed. Combine the flour and salt; add to the cheese mixture. Stir in the oats and sunflower kernels. Knead the dough until it holds together. Shape into a 12-in. roll. Cover with plastic wrap; chill for 4 hours or overnight. Allow to stand at room temperature for 10 minutes before cutting into 1/8-in. slices. Place on greased foil-lined baking sheets. Bake at 400° for 8-10 minutes or until edges are golden brown. Slide crackers and foil off baking sheets to wire racks to cool. **Yield:** 8 dozen.

— ♖ ♖ ♖ —

## Creamy Hot Beef Dip

*I got this zesty recipe from a dear neighbor years ago. Served with crackers and fresh vegetables, it makes a great snack. I also serve it on crusty bread with a salad for a light meal.* —Susan Wolfe, Olathe, Kansas

   1 **package (8 ounces) cream cheese, softened**
   1 **cup (8 ounces) sour cream**
   3 **ounces dried beef, rinsed and finely chopped**
   2 **tablespoons chopped green pepper**
1-1/2 **tablespoons dried minced onion**
  1/2 **teaspoon garlic powder**
**Pepper to taste**
   1 **teaspoon dried green pepper flakes, optional**
**Fresh vegetables *or* assorted crackers**

Combine the first seven ingredients and the green pepper flakes if desired in a 1-qt. baking dish. Bake at 375°, uncovered, for 30 minutes or until hot and bubbly. Serve with vegetables or crackers. **Yield:** about 2 cups.

— ♖ ♖ ♖ —

## Chewy Bread Pretzels

*I used this simple pretzel recipe to introduce my grandsons to baking. The boys took turns measuring and mixing. They enjoyed kneading the dough and shaping their pretzels any way they wanted.*
   —Marilyn Strickland, Williamson, New York

   1 **package (1/4 ounce) active dry yeast**
1-1/2 **cups warm water (110° to 115°)**
   1 **tablespoon sugar**
   2 **teaspoons salt**
   4 **cups all-purpose flour**
   1 **egg, beaten**
**Coarse salt, optional**

In a large bowl, dissolve yeast in water. Add sugar and salt. Blend in flour, 1 cup at a time, to form a soft dough. Turn out onto a floured surface; knead until smooth and elastic, about 5 minutes. Place dough in a greased bowl, turning once to grease

top. Cover and let rise in a warm place until doubled, about 1 hour. Punch dough down and divide into 15 equal portions. Roll each portion into a 14-in. rope. Shape into the traditional pretzel shape and place on a greased baking sheet. Brush pretzels with egg and sprinkle with salt if desired. Cover and let rise 15 minutes. Bake at 425° for 15 minutes. **Yield:** 15 servings.

— ♖ ♖ ♖ —

## Fried Cactus Strips

*This fun recipe makes a tasty, crunchy treat that uses a wild resource so abundant here in the Southwest. Many people don't know cactus is edible—and tasty! If cactus don't grow where you live, your grocery store may carry cactus pads in the produce section.*
   —Nema Lu Parker, Eastland, Texas

  4 **to 6 large cactus pads (about 8 inches x 4 inches)**
   1 **cup all-purpose flour**
1-1/2 **teaspoons salt, *divided***
  1/4 **teaspoon pepper**
   3 **eggs**
  1/2 **cup milk**
   1 **cup soft bread crumbs**
  3/4 **cup crushed saltines**
1-1/2 **teaspoons chili powder**
1-1/2 **teaspoons cayenne pepper**
**Vegetable oil for deep-fat frying**
**Picante sauce**

Remove all needles and spines from cactus pads. Slice into 1/2-in.-wide strips. Wash thoroughly; drain and pat dry. Set aside. In a shallow bowl, combine flour, 1/2 teaspoon salt and pepper. In another bowl, lightly beat eggs and milk. Combine the bread and cracker crumbs, chili powder, cayenne pepper and remaining salt; set aside. Dredge cactus strips in flour mixture; shake off excess. Dip in egg mixture, then coat with crumb mixture. In a deep-fat fryer, heat oil to 375°. Fry strips until golden brown, about 1-2 minutes. Drain on paper towels. Serve with picante sauce. **Yield:** 3-4 dozen.

---

### *Pretty Pretzels*

In a microwave-safe bowl or heavy saucepan, melt 12 ounces of white or dark chocolate and 1 tablespoon vegetable oil. Dip miniature pretzel twists (about 6 ounces) into chocolate; place on waxed paper. Sprinkle with jimmies. Refrigerate until set.

## Honey-Glazed Snack Mix

### (Pictured below)

*This slightly sweet snack is a nice change of pace from more costly packaged snack mixes. I've even put it in decorative canisters and given it as gifts.*
—Cindy Kolberg, Syracuse, Indiana

    4 cups Rice Chex, Corn Chex *or* Crispix
      cereal
1-1/2 cups miniature pretzel twists
    1 cup pecan halves
1/3 cup butter *or* margarine
1/4 cup honey

In a large mixing bowl, combine cereal, pretzels and pecans; set aside. In a saucepan, melt butter; stir in honey and blend well. Pour over cereal mixture and stir to coat evenly. Spread in a jelly roll pan. Bake at 350° for 12-15 minutes or until mixture is lightly glazed, stirring occasionally. Remove from oven and cool slightly. Spread on waxed paper to cool completely. **Yield:** about 6-1/2 cups.

## Marshmallow Delights

*When you bake these snacks, the marshmallow inside disappears and creates a sweet, gooey, cinnamon roll. They're a favorite treat for kids of all ages.*
—Diane Hixon, Niceville, Florida

    1 tube (8 ounces) refrigerated crescent rolls
1/4 cup sugar
    1 tablespoon ground cinnamon
    8 large marshmallows
1/4 cup butter *or* margarine, melted

Separate rolls into eight triangles. Combine sugar and cinnamon. Dip each marshmallow into butter, roll in cinnamon-sugar and place on a triangle. Pinch dough around marshmallow, sealing all edges. Dip tops of dough into the remaining butter and cinnamon-sugar. Place with sugar side up in greased muffin cups. Bake at 375° for 13-15 minutes. Serve warm. **Yield:** 8 servings.

—— ▼ ▼ ▼ ——

## Spiced Tea

*Simply by simmering together spices, tea and fruit juices, you can prepare a concoction that gives extra zip to holiday parties. It's easy to fix and warms up guests coming in from the cold. For a nice touch, I put cinnamon stick "stirrers" in the cups before serving.*
—Janine Connelley, Mountain City, Nevada

    3 quarts water, *divided*
    4 tea bags
  18 whole cloves
    2 cinnamon sticks
    1 can (12 ounces) frozen orange juice
      concentrate, thawed
    1 can (12 ounces) frozen lemonade
      concentrate, thawed
    1 cup sugar

In a large kettle or Dutch oven over medium heat, bring 1 qt. of water to a boil. Remove from the heat; add tea bags. Cover and steep for 5 minutes. Remove tea bags. Place cloves and cinnamon sticks in a double thickness of cheesecloth; bring up corners of cloth and tie with a string (or, if desired, place loose spices in pan and strain tea before serving). Place the cheesecloth bag in pan; add concentrates, sugar, tea and remaining water. Bring to a boil. Boil, uncovered, for 6 minutes. Serve hot. **Yield:** 3-1/2 quarts.

—— ▼ ▼ ▼ ——

## Fireside Clam Logs

*These snacks taste great after a frolic in the snow. What's more, I've found a way to make them even easier: After shaping them, I cover and refrigerate them until ready to bake. They're yummy right from the oven.* —Mrs. Chester Forwood, Merced, California

3 cans (6-1/2 ounces *each*) minced clams, rinsed and drained
1/2 cup mayonnaise
1/3 cup sliced green onions
1/3 cup grated Parmesan cheese
1 teaspoon Worcestershire sauce
3/4 teaspoon garlic powder
1/2 teaspoon hot pepper sauce
24 thin slices sandwich bread, crusts removed
1/3 cup butter *or* margarine, melted

In a medium bowl, combine the first seven ingredients; mix well. Chill until serving. Flatten each slice of bread with a rolling pin; spread with 1 tablespoon of clam mixture. Roll up jelly-roll style and cut in half. Place 1 in. apart on a greased baking sheet; brush with butter. Bake at 425° for 10-12 minutes or until lightly browned. Serve immediately. **Yield:** 4 dozen.

---

## Individual Cheese Balls

*With their creamy, nutty flavor, these small cheese balls work great in a bag lunch. It's a fun idea that really hits the spot when you're hungry.* —Mildred Sherrer Bay City, Texas

2 packages (8 ounces *each*) cream cheese, softened
1 cup (4 ounces) shredded cheddar cheese
1 to 2 tablespoons chopped onion
1 to 2 tablespoons chopped fresh parsley
1 to 2 teaspoons lemon juice
1 to 2 teaspoons Worcestershire sauce
1-1/2 to 2 cups ground walnuts
Assorted crackers

In a small bowl, combine the first six ingredients; mix well. Shape into 1-1/2-in. balls. Roll in nuts. Chill thoroughly. Serve with crackers. **Yield:** 20 servings.

---

## Spiced Pecans

*These pecans are a treat to munch on anytime, plus they're nice to serve when you have company.* —Miriam Hershberger, Holmesville, Ohio

1 egg white
1 teaspoon cold water
1 pound (4 cups) pecan halves
1/2 cup sugar
1/4 teaspoon salt
1/2 teaspoon ground cinnamon

In a mixing bowl, beat egg white lightly. Add water; beat until frothy but not stiff. Add pecans; stir until well coated. Combine sugar, salt and cinnamon. Sprinkle over pecans; toss to mix. Spread in a 15-in. x 10-in. x 1-in. greased baking pan. Bake at 250° for 1 hour, stirring occasionally. **Yield:** about 4 cups.

## Hot Almond 'n' Cream Drink

**(Pictured above and on page 4)**

*Just a few sips of this drink, with its rich almond flavor, will warm you up in a hurry. I'm the food service manager for a Christian camp, and it's a favorite each year at our Christmas party. It wouldn't be a party without it.* —Kaye Kirsch, Bailey, Colorado

1 cup butter *or* margarine
1 cup sugar
1 cup packed brown sugar
2 cups vanilla ice cream, softened
2 teaspoons almond extract
Ground nutmeg

In a saucepan over low heat, cook and stir the butter and sugars for 12-15 minutes or until the butter is melted. Pour into a large mixing bowl; add the ice cream and extract. Beat on medium speed for 1-2 minutes or until smooth, scraping the bowl often. **Yield:** 4 cups mix (16 servings). **To make one serving:** Spoon 1/4 cup mix into a mug; add 3/4 cup boiling water and stir well. Sprinkle with nutmeg. Serve immediately. **Editor's Note:** Mix can be stored in a covered container in the refrigerator up to 1 week.

## BLT Bites

**(Pictured above and on page 4)**

*These quick hors d'oeuvres may be mini, but their bacon and tomato flavor is full-size. I serve them at parties, brunches and picnics, and they're always a hit...even my kids love them.* —Kellie Remmen
*Detroit Lakes, Minnesota*

  **16 to 20 cherry tomatoes**
   **1 pound bacon, cooked and crumbled**
**1/2 cup mayonnaise *or* salad dressing**
**1/3 cup chopped green onions**
   **3 tablespoons grated Parmesan cheese**
   **2 tablespoons snipped fresh parsley**

Cut a thin slice off each tomato top. Scoop out and discard pulp. Invert the tomatoes on a paper towel to drain. In a small bowl, combine all remaining ingredients; mix well. Spoon into tomatoes. Refrigerate for several hours. **Yield:** 16-20 servings.

— 🛒 🛒 🛒 —

## Pecan Logs

*This is a favorite snack for me and my great-grandson because it tastes good and we can make it together. It has a hearty pecan taste without being too sweet. Their cool, soft texture makes the logs a nice alternative to cookies, and they slice nicely.*
—Ruby Williams, Bogalusa, Louisiana

  **1 package (12 ounces) vanilla wafers, crushed**
**3-3/4 cups finely chopped pecans**
  **1 can (14 ounces) sweetened condensed milk**

In a mixing bowl, combine all ingredients; mix well. Divide mixture in half. Between sheets of waxed paper, roll out each half into a 9-in. x 2-in. log. Tightly wrap each log in foil. Chill well. Cut into 1/4-in. slices. Store leftovers in the refrigerator. **Yield:** 50 servings.

— 🛒 🛒 🛒 —

## Spicy Snack Mix

*This snack mix is my family's favorite. I like it because it travels well without making a mess of the car! The nuts help satisfy "the hungries", and you can make the mix more or less spicy to suit your family's taste.* —Betty Sitzman, Wray, Colorado

**1/2 cup butter *or* margarine**
  **1 tablespoon seasoned salt**
  **1 tablespoon Worcestershire sauce**
**1/2 to 1 teaspoon garlic powder**
**1/2 to 1 teaspoon hot pepper sauce**
  **7 cups Rice Chex cereal**
  **6 cups Cheerios cereal**
  **5 cups Wheat Chex cereal**
  **1 can (12 ounces) mixed nuts**

In a small saucepan, melt butter. Add seasoned salt, Worcestershire sauce, garlic powder and hot pepper sauce; set aside. In a large mixing bowl, combine cereals and nuts; mix well. Stir in butter mixture until well blended. Spread into two 15-in. x 10-in. x 1-in. baking pans. Bake at 250° for 1 hour, stirring every 15 minutes. **Yield:** 20 cups.

— 🛒 🛒 🛒 —

## Dill Dip

*Be prepared—you'll likely need to make a double batch of this delightful dip. My family has found that one is never enough when we have a get-together. It tastes great with just about any vegetable, so you can use whatever you have on hand as dippers.*
—Kathy Beldorth, Three Oaks, Michigan

✓ Uses less fat, sugar or salt. Includes Nutritional Analysis and Diabetic Exchanges.

  **1 cup mayonnaise**
  **1 cup (8 ounces) sour cream**
  **2 tablespoons dried parsley flakes**
  **1 tablespoon dried minced onion**

2 teaspoons dill weed
1-1/2 teaspoons seasoned salt
1 teaspoon sugar
**Fresh vegetables *or* assorted crackers**

In a small bowl, combine the first seven ingredients. Chill for at least 1 hour. Serve with vegetables or crackers. **Yield:** 2 cups. **Nutritional Analysis:** One 2-tablespoon serving (prepared with fat-free mayonnaise and light sour cream) equals 34 calories, 236 mg sodium, 6 mg cholesterol, 4 gm carbohydrate, trace protein, 2 gm fat. **Diabetic Exchange:** 1/2 fat.

— 🍷 🍷 🍷 —

## Frosty Pineapple Nog

*You'll want to find a big shade tree to sit under while you sip this summertime thirst quencher. Pineapple adds a tropical flair to honey-sweetened buttermilk in this recipe provided by the United Dairy Industry Association and the Wisconsin Milk Marketing Board.*

3 cups buttermilk
1 can (8 ounces) crushed pineapple, undrained, chilled
1/4 cup sugar *or* honey
1 teaspoon vanilla extract
1/4 teaspoon salt
5 ice cubes
**Fresh mint sprigs, optional**

In a blender container, combine the buttermilk, pineapple, sugar, vanilla and salt. Cover and blend about 30 seconds or until combined. With blender running, add ice cubes, one at a time, through the opening in the lid. Blend until the mixture is nearly smooth and frothy. Pour into chilled glasses. If desired, garnish with a sprig of fresh mint. **Yield:** 6 servings.

— 🍷 🍷 🍷 —

## Thick Chocolate Shake

*Sometimes I crave an old-fashioned shake like ice cream parlors used to serve: thick, creamy and chocolaty. This recipe is so simple and yet it tastes just like the ones I remember. I can make it in my own kitchen.*
—*Bonnie Rueter, Englewood, Florida*

1 cup milk
1/2 cup instant chocolate drink mix
3 cups vanilla ice cream

Place all ingredients in a blender container; cover and process on high until smooth. Pour into glasses. Refrigerate any leftovers. **Yield:** 3-4 servings.

— 🍷 🍷 🍷 —

## 'I Wish I Had That Recipe...'

ONION BLOSSOMS—whole onions cut to resemble a flower and then deep-fried—were the talk of the town when served at a popular local festival in northwestern Louisiana.

Jeanne Bennett of Minden, Louisiana helped track down the recipe at its source—Liar's Pub in Bossier City, which is just outside Shreveport.

Owner Steve Watkins shared his restaurant-sized recipe, and the *Taste of Home* test kitchen staff reduced it to family proportions.

### Onion Blossoms

2 large sweet onions, unpeeled
1/2 cup mayonnaise
1/2 cup sour cream
1 tablespoon chili powder
2-1/2 teaspoons Cajun seasoning, *divided*
1-1/4 cups all-purpose flour
1 cup milk
**Vegetable oil for deep-fat frying**

Leaving the root ends intact, peel the outer skin of the onions. Cut a small slice off the tops. Starting at the tops of the onions and on one side, make a cut downward toward the root ends, stopping 1/2 in. from the bottom. Make additional cuts 1/8 in. from the first until there are cuts completely across the tops of the onions. Turn the onions a quarter turn so the slices are horizontal to you. Repeat the cuts 1/8 in. apart from each other until there is a checkerboard pattern across the tops of the onions. In a small bowl, make the dip by combining the mayonnaise, sour cream, chili powder and 1-1/2 teaspoons Cajun seasoning. Mix well and set aside. In a 1-gal. resealable plastic bag, combine the flour and remaining Cajun seasoning. Place milk in a small, deep bowl. Coat the cut onions in flour, then dip into milk and back into the flour mixture. In a deep-fat fryer, heat oil to 375°. Fry onions for 5 minutes or until golden, turning once. Remove from the oil; place on a serving plate. Discard the very center of the fried onion blossoms. Place a few spoonfuls of dip into the center of blossoms and serve immediately. **Yield:** 4 servings.

— 🍷 🍷 🍷 —

## Breakfast Wassail

### (Pictured below and on page 4)

*This fruity beverage is great all year-round, and tasty hot or chilled. I got the recipe from a co-worker and made it one Christmas for a family gathering. Now whenever we get together for the holidays, I'm the designated wassail maker.* —Amy Holtsclaw
Carbondale, Illinois

 1 bottle (64 ounces) cranberry juice
 1 bottle (32 ounces) apple juice
 1 can (12 ounces) frozen pineapple juice
   concentrate, undiluted
 1 can (12 ounces) frozen lemonade
   concentrate, undiluted
 3 to 4 cinnamon sticks
 1 quart water, optional

In a large saucepan or Dutch oven, combine juices, lemonade and cinnamon sticks. Bring to a boil. Reduce heat; cover and simmer for 1 hour. Add water if desired. Serve hot or cold. **Yield:** about 4 quarts.

## Mustard Egg Dip

*For a delicious surprise, try this zesty dip with a selection of fresh vegetables. Although we prefer it with sliced sweet peppers, it's just as good with tamer veggies such as celery.* —Janice Carr, Fort Davis, Texas

 6 hard-cooked eggs, finely chopped
 1/3 cup mayonnaise
 1 tablespoon butter *or* margarine, softened
 2 teaspoons lemon juice
 1 teaspoon prepared mustard
 1 teaspoon Worcestershire sauce
 3/4 teaspoon liquid smoke, optional
 1/2 teaspoon salt
 1/4 teaspoon pepper
**Hot pepper sauce to taste**
**Green *or* sweet red peppers and other fresh
  vegetables**

In a bowl, combine the first 10 ingredients; mix until smooth. Serve with sliced peppers and other vegetables, or, if desired, cut peppers in half lengthwise and fill with dip. **Yield:** 1-3/4 cups.

---

## Chili Cheese Dip

*This hearty snack is easy to prepare and is always a big hit at get-togethers, especially when you want to serve something more than plain chips. Use medium or hot salsa, depending on your family's taste.*
—Miriam Hershberger, Holmesville, Ohio

 1 package (8 ounces) cream cheese,
   softened
 1 can (15 ounces) chili con carne
 1 can (4 ounces) chopped green chilies
 1/2 cup salsa
 1 cup (4 ounces) shredded cheddar cheese
**Tortilla chips**

Spread cream cheese in the bottom of an 8-in. square baking dish. Layer with chili, green chilies and salsa. Sprinkle with shredded cheese. Bake at 350° for 5 minutes or until cheese is melted and dip is warmed. Serve with tortilla chips. **Yield:** 8-10 servings.

---

## Sugar-Free Cocoa Mix

*When the holidays roll around, it can be difficult to come up with something special for the friend who needs a sugar-free gift from the kitchen. The folks at Equal provided this classic recipe, which has a tasty hint of cinnamon.*

☑ Uses less fat, sugar or salt. Includes Nutritional Analysis and Diabetic Exchanges.

 2 cups nonfat dry milk powder
 1/2 cup low-fat powdered nondairy creamer
 1/2 cup baking cocoa

10 packets Equal sweetener *or* 1 tablespoon
   Equal for Recipes
3/4 teaspoon ground cinnamon, optional

Combine the milk powder, nondairy creamer, cocoa, Equal and cinnamon if desired. Store in an airtight container. To prepare one serving, add 3/4 cup boiling water to 1/3 cup cocoa mix; stir to dissolve. **Yield:** 2-2/3 cups mix (8 servings). **Nutritional Analysis:** One one-third cup (dry mix) serving equals 104 calories, 93 mg sodium, 3 mg cholesterol, 17 gm carbohydrate, 8 gm protein, 2 gm fat. **Diabetic Exchange:** 1 milk.

———  🍴 🍴 🍴  ———

## Egg Salad Cheese Spread

*The addition of cheese makes this version of egg salad deliciously different from others. Serve it on crackers for a snack or on bread for a light lunch with a steaming bowl of soup.* —Denise Goedeken
*Platte Center, Nebraska*

   2 cups shredded process cheese
   4 hard-cooked eggs, chopped
1/2 cup mayonnaise *or* salad dressing
1/4 cup sweet pickle relish
   1 teaspoon prepared mustard
Salt and pepper to taste
Assorted crackers *or* bread

Combine first five ingredients in a mixing bowl; season with salt and pepper. Serve on crackers or bread. **Yield:** about 3 cups.

———  🍴 🍴 🍴  ———

## Russian Tea Mix

*This tea mix is sweet, citrusy and gently spiced. It's a fabulous warm-up on a cold day. It also makes a great holiday gift to give or receive. It's especially aromatic and comforting when the spices are freshly ground.*
   —Mary Ann Kosmas, Minneapolis, Minnesota

   2 cups instant orange drink mix
   1 cup instant unflavored tea
   1 cup sugar
   6 tablespoons sugar-sweetened lemonade
     mix
   1 teaspoon ground cinnamon
1/2 teaspoon ground cloves

Combine all ingredients; mix well. Store in an airtight container. To prepare one serving, add 2 tablespoons mix to 3/4 cup boiling water; stir. **Yield:** 36 servings (4-1/2 cups mix).

## Peanutty Party Mix

**(Pictured above)**

*The secret to this munchable mixture, which will quickly disappear when you serve it to family and friends, is in the flavor. It's so inviting that folks can't stop with just one bite! It's a fun, nutty snack for a Halloween party. I've also given decorated jars of the mix as gifts.*
   —Kitty Henderson, Hazelhurst, Georgia

   25 whole graham crackers, broken into
      bite-size pieces
    3 cups salted peanuts
2-1/2 cups raisins
    1 pound confectioners' sugar, *divided*
    2 cups (12 ounces) semisweet chocolate
      chips
    1 jar (18 ounces) crunchy peanut butter

In a large bowl, combine the graham crackers, peanuts and raisins; set aside. Divide confectioners' sugar between two gallon-size resealable plastic bags; set aside. In a heavy saucepan over low heat, cook and stir the chocolate chips and peanut butter until melted. Pour over the graham cracker mixture; stir until well coated. Immediately divide the mixture between the two bags; seal and shake well. Store in an airtight container in the refrigerator. **Yield:** 13 cups.

---

### *Peanut Butter Pointer*

An unopened jar of peanut butter can be stored in a cool, dry place for at least 1 year. Once opened, it will stay fresh about 3 months. After that, the jar should be refrigerated to keep the oil from spoiling. Natural peanut butter must be refrigerated and will keep about 6 months.

## Pineapple Smoothie

*I first came across this recipe more than 20 years ago. I've tried many diabetic recipes over time, and this is still one of the best.* —*Margery Bryan Royal City, Washington*

✓ Uses less fat, sugar or salt. Includes Nutritional Analysis and Diabetic Exchanges.

**1 can (20 ounces) unsweetened pineapple chunks**
**1 cup buttermilk**
**2 teaspoons vanilla extract**
**Sugar substitute equivalent to 1/3 cup sugar**
**Mint leaves, optional**

Drain pineapple, reserving 1/2 cup juice. Freeze pineapple chunks. Place juice, buttermilk, vanilla, sugar substitute and frozen pineapple into a blender container. Blend until smooth. Pour into glasses and garnish with mint if desired. Serve immediately. **Yield:** 5 servings. **Nutritional Analysis:** One serving equals 74 calories, 52 mg sodium, 2 mg cholesterol, 16 gm carbohydrate, 2 gm protein, 1 gm fat. **Diabetic Exchanges:** 1/2 milk, 1/2 fruit.

— 🏆 🏆 🏆 —

## Buttery Onion Pretzels

*If you like the taste of onion, you'll love these zesty pretzels. They're so crunchy and yummy, they disappear fast! They're great to munch while watching football games or other sporting events on television.* —*Betty Claycomb, Alverton, Pennsylvania*

**1-1/4 cups butter *or* margarine**
**1 envelope onion soup mix**
**1 package (16 ounces) chunky pretzels, broken into pieces**

In a skillet, melt butter. Stir in soup mix. Heat and stir until well mixed. Add pretzels; toss to coat. Spread pretzel mixture in a baking pan. Bake at 250° for 1-1/2 hours, stirring every 15 minutes. Cool. Store in an airtight container. **Yield:** 6 cups.

— 🏆 🏆 🏆 —

## Presidential Cinnamon-Glazed Almonds

*For his 1993 inauguration, President Bill Clinton ordered a half ton of these sweet and crunchy almonds! They were nicknamed the president's snack of choice, so many people tried them. You and your family will likely find them irresistible as well.*
—*Crescent Dragonwagon, Eureka Springs, Arkansas*

**1/3 cup butter *or* margarine**
**2 egg whites**
**Pinch salt**
**1 cup sugar**
**4 teaspoons ground cinnamon**
**3 cups whole almonds**

Place butter in a 15-in. x 10-in. x 1-in. baking pan. Bake at 325° until melted, about 5-7 minutes. Meanwhile, in a mixing bowl, beat the egg whites with salt until soft peaks form. Gradually add sugar, beating until stiff peaks form. Fold in cinnamon and almonds; pour over butter and toss to coat. Bake at 325° for 40 minutes, turning every 10 minutes, or until almonds are crisp. **Yield:** 3 cups.

— 🏆 🏆 🏆 —

## Make-Ahead S'mores

*When you want the around-the-campfire taste without all the fuss, these s'mores are easy. I make them ahead of time, and then we can enjoy them as a light dessert with lunch or dinner.* —*Anne Sherman Orangeburg, South Carolina*

**8 ounces semisweet chocolate**
**1 can (14 ounces) sweetened condensed milk**
**1 teaspoon vanilla extract**
**1 package (16 ounces) graham crackers**
**2 cups miniature marshmallows**

In a heavy saucepan, melt chocolate over low heat. Stir in milk and vanilla; cook and stir until smooth. Making one s'more at a time, spread 1 tablespoon each of chocolate mixture on two whole graham crackers. Place 5-6 marshmallows on one cracker; gently press the other cracker on top. Repeat with remaining chocolate, crackers and marshmallows. Wrap with plastic wrap; store at room temperature. **Yield:** 16 servings.

— 🏆 🏆 🏆 —

## Berry Slush

*This colorful slush is perfect for patriotic potlucks, barbecues or any fun fair-weather event. It's a breeze to freeze a batch ahead of time, then pack it for a picnic later.* —*Ruth Seitz, Columbus Junction, Iowa*

**1 package (3 ounces) berry blue *or* raspberry gelatin**
**2 cups boiling water**
**2 cups sugar**
**1 can (46 ounces) pineapple juice**
**2 liters ginger ale**

4-1/2 cups cold water
1 cup lemon juice
**Blue *or* red liquid food coloring, optional**
**Fresh raspberries, blueberries and starfruit,
optional**

In a large container, dissolve gelatin in boiling water; stir in sugar until dissolved. Add pineapple juice, ginger ale, cold water and lemon juice. Add food coloring if desired. Freeze for 8 hours or overnight. Remove from freezer 20 minutes before serving. Stir so that mixture will be slushy. If desired, thread fruit on wooden skewers and use to garnish glasses. **Yield:** 5 quarts.

— ☕ ☕ ☕ —

## Mini Apple Pizzas

### (Pictured below and on page 4)

*My four children are now grown, but they still enjoy snacking on these sweet little pizzas...and so do my grandchildren. We use fresh apples from the small orchard on our dairy farm. The pizzas are so easy to make. The warm cinnamon flavor and light crust make them delicious!* —Helen Lamb, Seymour, Missouri

1 tube (12 ounces) refrigerated biscuits, separated into 10 biscuits
1/2 cup packed brown sugar
2 tablespoons all-purpose flour
1 teaspoon ground cinnamon
2 medium tart apples, peeled, cored and shredded
1 cup (4 ounces) shredded cheddar cheese, optional

Roll or pat biscuits into 3-1/2-in. circles; place on a lightly greased baking sheet. In a mixing bowl, combine brown sugar, flour and cinnamon; mix well. Add apples and mix well; spoon rounded tablespoonfuls onto biscuits. Bake at 350° for 15-20 minutes or until edges begin to brown. If desired, sprinkle each pizza with 1 tablespoon cheese. Serve warm. **Yield:** 10 servings.

— ☕ ☕ ☕ —

## Fruit Punch

*We had a diabetic child in our church youth group many years ago and tried to fix snacks that would be within his restrictions but enjoyable for the other kids as well. This punch really fills the bill.*
—Ruth Tacoma, Falmouth, Michigan

☑ Uses less fat, sugar or salt. Includes Nutritional Analysis and Diabetic Exchanges.

1 envelope (.35 ounce) sugar-free tropical punch soft drink mix
4-3/4 cups water
1 can (12 ounces) unsweetened frozen orange juice concentrate, thawed
4 quarts diet lemon-lime soda

In a large pitcher, combine soft drink mix and water; mix well. Add orange juice concentrate; mix well. When ready to serve, pour into punch bowl and add the white soda. **Yield:** 20 servings (5 quarts). **Nutritional Analysis:** One serving equals 38 calories, 3 mg sodium, 0 cholesterol, 9 gm carbohydrate, trace protein, trace fat. **Diabetic Exchange:** 1/2 fruit.

# Salads

**Salads offer unbeatable refreshment, whether as a cool and creamy first course or a warm and tangy main dish.**

**SCRUMPTIOUS SALADS.** Clockwise from upper left: Zesty Potato Salad (p. 30), Cranberry Pineapple Salad (p. 25), Chinese Chicken Salad (p. 28), California Pasta Salad (p. 27) and Tomato Bread Salad (p. 28).

## Emily's Spinach Salad

**(Pictured below and on front cover)**

*I've always loved spinach—it's grown here in our area. When I saw an announcement of a spinach cooking contest, I made up this recipe to enter. I was delighted when my colorful, tangy salad took the grand prize!*
*—Emily Fields, Santa Ana, California*

  2/3 cup vegetable oil
  1/4 cup cider *or* red wine vinegar
    2 teaspoons lemon juice
    2 teaspoons soy sauce
    1 teaspoon sugar
    1 teaspoon ground mustard
  1/2 teaspoon curry powder
  1/2 teaspoon salt
  1/2 teaspoon seasoned pepper
  1/4 teaspoon garlic powder
    1 package (10 ounces) fresh spinach, torn
    5 bacon strips, cooked and crumbled
    2 hard-cooked eggs, sliced

In a jar with a tight-fitting lid, combine the first 10 ingredients; mix well. Set aside. Place the spinach in a large salad bowl. Just before serving, pour the dressing over the spinach and toss gently. Garnish with the crumbled bacon and egg slices. **Yield:** 6-8 servings.

## Fiddlehead Shrimp Salad

*Fiddleheads are young, tightly curled fronds from bracken, ostrich and cinnamon ferns that sprout in moist fields and open wooded areas. Each spring, fiddleheads are prepared in dozens of ways—from soups to cakes—at the Fiddlehead Festival in my home state.*
*—Wilma Johnson, Thorndike, Maine*

    3 cups fiddlehead ferns *or* sliced fresh asparagus
    1 cup cooked shell macaroni
  1/2 cup diced unpeeled apple
  1/4 cup chopped celery
    1 cup diced cooked shrimp
  1/4 to 1/2 cup mayonnaise
    1 tablespoon lemon juice
    1 teaspoon grated lemon peel
Salt and pepper to taste

Cook ferns in a small amount of water until tender. Drain. Toss with all remaining ingredients. Chill. **Yield:** 4 servings. **Editor's Note:** As with any wild ingredient, be certain of what you're picking and that it's edible. If you're unsure, check with your county Extension agent.

— ▽ ▽ ▽ —

## Green and Red Tomato Salad

*This recipe is especially appreciated at the tail end of tomato season—when there are plenty of green tomatoes to use up. It's a colorful Southern favorite that's nicely seasoned.* *—Pauline Forrester, Titus, Alabama*

✓ Uses less fat, sugar or salt. Includes Nutritional Analysis and Diabetic Exchanges.

  1/2 cup olive *or* vegetable oil
    3 tablespoons cider *or* red wine vinegar
    2 tablespoons lemon juice
    1 garlic clove, minced
  1/2 teaspoon ground cumin
  1/8 teaspoon pepper
    3 medium red tomatoes, diced
    3 medium green tomatoes, diced
    1 medium red onion, thinly sliced into rings
    3 tablespoons minced fresh basil *or* 1 tablespoon dried basil

In a small bowl or jar with a tight-fitting lid, combine oil, vinegar, lemon juice, garlic, cumin and pepper; mix well. Refrigerate. In a large salad bowl, combine the tomatoes, onion and basil. About 30 minutes before serving, add the dressing and toss. **Yield:** 18 servings. **Nutritional Analysis:** One 1/2-cup serving equals 63 calories, 4 mg sodium, 0 cholesterol, 3 gm carbohydrate, 1 gm protein, 6 gm fat. **Diabetic Exchanges:** 1 vegetable, 1 fat.

## Frozen Fruit Salad

_I use this recipe to add a healthy twist to brown-bag lunches. I'm always in a hurry in the morning, so having a ready-made salad is a great help. Cool fruit is a great noon-hour pick-me-up._ —Virginia Powell
Eureka, Kansas

- 1 **can (16 ounces) apricots in light syrup, drained**
- 1 **package (16 ounces) frozen sweetened sliced strawberries, thawed and drained**
- 1 **can (8 ounces) pineapple tidbits, drained**
- 3 **medium firm bananas, sliced**
- 1 **can (6 ounces) frozen orange juice concentrate, thawed**
- 1 **juice can water**

In a food processor, chop the apricots. In a pitcher or bowl, combine the apricots, strawberries, pineapple, bananas, orange juice and water. Pour or ladle into muffin cups that have been coated with nonstick cooking spray. Freeze. When frozen, quickly remove the salads to freezer bags or tightly covered storage containers. When packing a lunch, place salad in individual storage container in a thermal lunch bag, and it will thaw by lunchtime. **Yield:** 22-24 servings.

## Wilted Dandelion Greens Salad

_If you can't beat 'em, eat 'em. That's my motto. Dandelions are much more than a seasonal lawn annoyance. In addition to salads, dandelions make good jelly, wine, coffee and salad. Remember, though, to never pick dandelions in areas that have been sprayed with weed killer._ —Naomi Giddis, Grawn, Michigan

- 6 **cups dandelion greens***
- 2 **bacon strips, diced**
- 2 **hard-cooked eggs, chopped**
**DRESSING:**
- 2 **eggs**
- 2 **tablespoons vinegar**
- 1 **tablespoon sugar**
**Water**

Wash dandelion greens thoroughly; drain and place in a large salad bowl. Chill. Meanwhile, in a skillet, fry bacon until crisp. Remove and drain on paper towels. Discard all but 2 tablespoons of drippings. For dressing, combine eggs, vinegar, sugar and enough water to make 1 cup. Beat well; pour into the skillet. Cook over medium heat, stirring constantly, until mixture thickens and coats the back of a spoon. Pour over greens and toss well.

Sprinkle with chopped eggs and crumbled bacon; toss lightly. Serve immediately. **Yield:** 4-6 servings. **\*Editor's Note:** When dandelions aren't in season, you can substitute fresh spinach for the dandelion greens.

## German Potato Salad

**(Pictured above)**

_I'd always loved my German grandmother's potato salad. So when I married a potato farmer—and had spuds in abundance—I played with several recipes that sounded similar and came up with this salad, which reminds me of hers._ —Sue Hartman, Parma, Idaho

- 5 **bacon strips**
- 3/4 **cup chopped onion**
- 2 **tablespoons all-purpose flour**
- 2/3 **cup cider vinegar**
- 1-1/3 **cups water**
- 1/4 **cup sugar**
- 1 **teaspoon salt**
- 1/8 **teaspoon pepper**
- 6 **cups sliced cooked peeled potatoes**

In a large skillet, fry bacon until crisp; remove and set aside. Drain all but 2-3 tablespoons of drippings; cook onion until tender. Stir in flour; blend well. Add vinegar and water; cook and stir until bubbly and slightly thick. Add sugar and stir until it dissolves. Crumble bacon; gently stir in bacon and potatoes. Heat through, stirring lightly to coat potato slices. Serve warm. **Yield:** 6-8 servings.

## Smoked Turkey and Apple Salad

### (Pictured below)

*An eye-catching dish, this refreshing salad is a great main course for a summer lunch or light dinner. The dressing's Dijon flavor goes nicely with the turkey, and the apples add crunch.* —Carolyn Popwell
Lacey, Washington

✓ Uses less fat, sugar or salt. Includes Nutritional Analysis and Diabetic Exchanges.

**DRESSING:**
    2 tablespoons cider vinegar
    5 tablespoons olive *or* vegetable oil
    1 tablespoon Dijon mustard
    1 teaspoon lemon-pepper seasoning
  1/2 teaspoon salt, optional
**SALAD:**
    1 bunch watercress *or* romaine, torn into
       bite-size pieces
    1 medium carrot, julienned
  10 cherry tomatoes, halved
    8 ounces smoked turkey, julienned
    4 medium unpeeled apples, sliced
  1/3 cup chopped walnuts, toasted

Whisk together dressing ingredients and set aside. Just before serving, arrange salad greens on a platter or individual plates. Top with carrot, tomatoes, turkey and apples. Drizzle dressing over salad and sprinkle with walnuts. **Yield:** 8 servings. **Nutritional Analysis:** One serving (prepared with romaine and without added salt) equals 195 calories, 267 mg sodium, 8 mg cholesterol, 10 gm carbohydrate, 6 gm protein, 16 gm fat. **Diabetic Exchanges:** 2 fat, 1-1/2 vegetable, 1 meat.

—— 🍷 🍷 🍷 ——

## Ranch Salad

*A blend of blue cheese and ranch salad dressings gives the vegetables in this salad a tangy taste. It makes a big batch, so I often take it to potlucks.*
—Marlene Thompson, Winchester, Ohio

  1 medium head cauliflower, broken into
    florets (4 cups)
  1 bunch broccoli, broken into florets (3
    cups)
4 to 6 small tomatoes, quartered
  4 medium carrots, thinly sliced
  4 green onions with tops, thinly sliced
  1 cup chopped celery
  6 bacon strips, cooked and crumbled *or* 1/2
    cup bacon bits
  1 cup (4 ounces) shredded cheddar cheese
  1 bottle (8 ounces) blue cheese salad
    dressing
  1 bottle (8 ounces) ranch salad dressing

Combine vegetables, bacon and cheese in a large salad bowl. Combine salad dressings; pour over salad and toss to mix. Chill. **Yield:** 16-20 servings.

—— 🍷 🍷 🍷 ——

## Freezer Coleslaw

*I like this slaw because it's both practical and flavorful. It's crispy with a sweet-and-sour dressing—and you just take it out of the freezer when you want some.*
—Connie Wilkinson, Napanee, Ontario

    1 medium head cabbage (3 pounds),
      shredded
  1/2 medium green pepper, chopped
  1/2 cup shredded carrot
    1 small onion, chopped
    1 teaspoon salt
**DRESSING:**
    1 cup sugar
    1 cup vinegar
  1/4 cup water
    1 teaspoon salt
  1/2 teaspoon celery seed
  1/2 teaspoon mustard seed

In a large bowl, combine the first five ingredients. Let stand 1 hour. Drain. In a saucepan, bring all dressing ingredients to a boil; simmer 2-3 minutes. Cool. Pour over cabbage. Pack in freezer containers; freeze. **Yield:** about 4 pints.

out added salt) equals 58 calories, 4 . 3 mg cholesterol, 12 gm carbohydrate, 2 g tein, 1 gm fat. **Diabetic Exchanges:** 1 vegetable, starch.

🍵 🍵 🍵

## Cranberry Pineapple Salad

### (Pictured below and on page 21)

*A refreshing salad or side dish, this recipe impresses family and guests with its striking rosy color. It's a delightfully different alternative to traditional cranberry sauce. The nuts add a tasty crunch.*
—Dorothy Angley, Carver, Massachusetts

1 package (6 ounces) raspberry gelatin
1-3/4 cups boiling water
1 can (16 ounces) jellied cranberry sauce
1 can (8 ounces) crushed pineapple, undrained
3/4 cup orange juice
1 tablespoon lemon juice
1/2 cup chopped walnuts
**Lettuce leaves**
**Mayonnaise *or* salad dressing**

In a bowl, dissolve gelatin in boiling water. Break up and stir in cranberry sauce. Add pineapple, orange juice and lemon juice. Chill until partially set. Stir in nuts. Pour into an 11-in. x 7-in. x 2-in. dish. Chill until firm. Cut into squares; serve each on a lettuce leaf and top with a dollop of mayonnaise. **Yield:** 12 servings.

## Quick Vegetable Salad

### (Pictured above)

*This recipe was given to me many years ago by a dear friend, and I still make it often. The entire family likes it. In fact, whenever we have a get-together, I'm asked to bring this salad.* —Priscilla Witthar Marshall, Missouri

✓ Uses less fat, sugar or salt. Includes Nutritional Analysis and Diabetic Exchanges.

1 can (16 ounces) whole kernel corn, drained
1 large tomato, seeded and chopped
1/2 cup chopped celery
1/2 cup chopped cucumber
1/3 cup finely chopped green pepper
1/4 cup finely chopped onion
1/4 cup sour cream
2 tablespoons mayonnaise
1 tablespoon cider vinegar
1/4 teaspoon salt, optional
1/4 teaspoon celery seed
1/8 teaspoon pepper

In a large salad bowl, combine the corn, tomato, celery, cucumber, green pepper and onion. In a small bowl, combine the remaining ingredients; gently blend into the salad. Serve immediately. **Yield:** 8 servings. **Nutritional Analysis:** One 1/2-cup serving (prepared with no-salt-added corn, light sour cream and fat-free mayonnaise and with-

3 medium oranges, peeled and sectioned
2 cups cauliflowerets
1/4 cup chopped green pepper
2 cups torn fresh spinach
**DRESSING:**
1 can (12 ounces) evaporated fat-free milk
1 can (6 ounces) frozen orange juice concentrate, thawed

In a large salad bowl, combine orange segments, cauliflower, green pepper and spinach. Place dressing ingredients in a jar with a tight-fitting lid; shake until well mixed. Add desired amount of dressing to salad and toss. Refrigerate the leftover dressing. **Yield:** 6 servings (2 cups dressing). **Nutritional Analysis:** One serving (with 1 tablespoon of dressing) equals 62 calories, 47 mg sodium, trace cholesterol, 13 gm carbohydrate, 3 gm protein, trace fat. **Diabetic Exchanges:** 1 vegetable, 1/2 fruit.

— 🍷 🍷 🍷 —

## Creamy Sliced Tomatoes

### (Pictured above)

*This is a family favorite that's also popular with friends. It's a pretty presentation—perfect as a side dish. The basil and cool, creamy dressing make the dish tasty and refreshing.*
—Doris Smith
Woodbury, New Jersey

1 cup mayonnaise
1/2 cup half-and-half cream
3/4 teaspoon dried basil *or* 1-1/2 teaspoons chopped fresh basil, *divided*
**Lettuce leaves**
6 medium tomatoes, sliced
1 medium red onion, thinly sliced into rings

In a small bowl, combine mayonnaise, cream and half of the basil; mix well. Refrigerate. Just before serving, arrange lettuce, tomatoes and onions on individual salad plates. Drizzle dressing over. Sprinkle with remaining basil. **Yield:** 12 servings.

— 🍷 🍷 🍷 —

## Orange Blossom Salad

*This lively salad can be made year-round. I make it for everyday dinners as well as entertaining. It fits nicely into a "hurry-up" meal.*
—Dorothy Anderson
Ottawa, Kansas

✓ Uses less fat, sugar or salt. Includes Nutritional Analysis and Diabetic Exchanges.

## Classic Cobb Salad

### (Pictured below)

*Complementary flavors make this salad taste so good. Preparing it is a lot like putting in a garden. That's because I "plant" everything in nice, neat sections, just like I do in my vegetable garden.*
—Patty Kile
Greentown, Pennsylvania

6 cups torn lettuce
2 medium tomatoes, chopped
1 avocado, chopped
3/4 cup diced fully cooked ham

2 hard-cooked eggs, chopped
3/4 cup diced cooked turkey
1-1/4 cups sliced fresh mushrooms
1/2 cup crumbled blue cheese
Red onion rings, lemon wedges and sliced ripe
   olives, optional
Salad dressing

Arrange the lettuce in a large bowl. Place chopped tomatoes across the center, dividing the bowl in half. On one half, arrange the avocado, ham and eggs in sections. On the other half, arrange the turkey, mushrooms and blue cheese. Garnish with onion, lemon and olives if desired. Top with the salad dressing of your choice. **Yield:** 12-14 servings.

## California Pasta Salad

**(Pictured on page 21)**

_Fresh vegetables, which are abundant in California, make this salad crunchy and healthy. Although the recipe makes a large bowl, it's always quick to empty. It's a sure hit at family get-togethers and church potlucks._
—_Jeanette Krembas_
_Laguna Niguel, California_

1 pound thin spaghetti _or_ vermicelli, broken
   into 1-inch pieces, cooked
3 large tomatoes, diced
2 medium zucchini, diced
1 large cucumber, diced
1 medium green pepper, diced
1 medium sweet red pepper, diced
1 large red onion, diced
2 cans (2-1/4 ounces _each_) sliced ripe
   olives, drained
1 bottle (16 ounces) Italian salad dressing
1/4 cup grated Parmesan _or_ Romano cheese
1 tablespoon sesame seeds
2 teaspoons poppy seeds
1 teaspoon paprika
1/2 teaspoon celery seed
1/4 teaspoon garlic powder

Combine all of the ingredients in a large bowl; cover and refrigerate overnight to blend flavors. **Yield:** 10-15 servings.

### Taste Twist

For a new twist on an old standby salad dressing, substitute an ingredient with a slightly different flavor. For example, use fresh lime juice instead of lemon or use fruit-flavored vinegar for regular.

## Wild Rice Salad

**(Pictured above)**

_Since I spend part of my summers in northern Minnesota near the wild rice fields, I have tried many recipes featuring this delicious, nutty-flavored grain in the past 40-plus years. This salad is often requested by family and friends._
—_Florence Jacoby_
_Granite Falls, Minnesota_

✓ Uses less fat, sugar or salt. Includes Nutritional Analysis and Diabetic Exchanges.

1 cup uncooked wild rice
Seasoned salt, optional
2 cups diced cooked chicken
1-1/2 cups halved green grapes
1 cup sliced water chestnuts, drained
3/4 cup reduced-fat mayonnaise
1 cup cashews, optional
Lettuce leaves

Cook rice according to package directions, omitting salt or substituting seasoned salt if desired. Drain well; cool to room temperature. Spoon into a large bowl; add chicken, grapes, water chestnuts and mayonnaise. Toss gently with a fork. Cover and chill. Just before serving, add cashews if desired. Serve on lettuce leaves or line a bowl with lettuce leaves and fill with salad. **Yield:** 6 servings. **Nutritional Analysis:** One serving (prepared without cashews or additional salt) equals 318 calories, 229 mg sodium, 38 mg cholesterol, 40 gm carbohydrate, 19 gm protein, 10 gm fat. **Diabetic Exchanges:** 2 lean meat, 1 starch, 1 fruit, 1 vegetable, 1 fat.

## Tomato Bread Salad

**(Pictured below and on page 20)**

*We look forward to tomato season each year so we can make this unique and tasty recipe. It's a super dish for lunch, especially on warm summer days, and a great way to use your garden onions, cucumbers and tomatoes. It also makes a good appetizer.*
*—Dodi Hardcastle, Harlingen, Texas*

✓ Uses less fat, sugar or salt. Includes Nutritional Analysis and Diabetic Exchanges.

- 3 **large tomatoes, finely chopped and seeded**
- 1 **medium cucumber, finely chopped and seeded**
- 1/2 **large sweet onion, finely chopped**
- 1 **cup loosely packed fresh basil, minced**
- 1/4 **cup olive *or* vegetable oil**
- 1 **tablespoon cider vinegar**
- 1 **garlic clove, minced**
- 1/2 **teaspoon salt**
- 1/4 **teaspoon pepper**
- 1 **large loaf white *or* French bread**

In a large bowl, combine tomatoes, cucumber and onion. In a small bowl, combine basil, oil, vinegar, garlic, salt and pepper. Pour over tomatoes and toss. Refrigerate for at least 1 hour. Before serving, allow salad to come to room temperature. Cut bread into thick slices; toast under broiler until lightly browned. Top with salad. Serve immediately. **Yield:** 18 servings. **Nutritional Analysis:** One serving (with a 1-inch slice of white bread) equals 188 calories, 262 mg sodium, 0 cholesterol, 28 gm carbohydrate, 5 gm protein, 7 gm fat. **Diabetic Exchanges:** 1-1/2 starch, 1 vegetable, 1 fat.

## Chinese Chicken Salad

**(Pictured above and on page 21)**

*This salad is a cool, easy entree perfect for steamy summer days! You can do most of the preparation for this dish ahead of time and just mix it together before serving. The crispy lettuce and wonton skins keep this dish light, while the chicken and dressing give it wonderful flavor.*
*—Shirley Smith*
*Yorba Linda, California*

- 1/2 **package wonton skins, cut into 1/4-inch strips***
- **Vegetable oil for deep-fat frying**
- 3 **cups cubed cooked chicken**
- 1 **head lettuce, shredded**
- 4 **green onions with tops, sliced**
- 4 **tablespoons sesame seeds, toasted**
- **DRESSING:**
- 1/3 **cup cider *or* white wine vinegar**
- 1/4 **cup sugar**
- 3 **tablespoons vegetable oil**
- 2 **tablespoons sesame oil**
- 1 **teaspoon salt**
- 1/2 **teaspoon pepper**

Deep-fry wonton skins in oil until brown and crisp. Drain on paper towels; set aside. In a large salad bowl, combine chicken, lettuce, green onions and sesame seeds; mix gently. In a small bowl, whisk together all dressing ingredients. Just before serving, add fried wonton skins to salad; pour dressing over and toss to coat. **Yield:** 6-8 servings. ***Editor's Note:** For faster preparation, a can of chow mein noodles can be substituted for the wonton skins.

## Crisp Potato Salad

*Adding crisp veggies was all it took to transform one of my time-worn recipes into a sensational new potato salad. This dish tastes like it's fresh from the garden, and, at our house, it often is! The dressing I developed gives the salad a nice zip, too.*
*—Lucy Meyring, Walden, Colorado*

- 1/2 **pound fresh green beans, cut into 1-inch pieces**
- 2 **medium carrots, sliced 1/8 inch thick**
- 1 **medium zucchini, sliced 1/4 inch thick**
- 6 **medium potatoes (about 2 pounds), cooked and peeled**
- 1/3 **cup mayonnaise**
- 1/3 **cup plain yogurt**
- 1 **tablespoon lemon juice**
- 1/2 **cup finely chopped onion**
- 2 **tablespoons minced fresh parsley**
- 1-1/2 **teaspoons minced fresh dill**
- 3/4 **teaspoon salt**
- 1/4 **teaspoon pepper**

In a large kettle, cook beans and carrots in enough water to cover for 5 minutes. Add zucchini and cook for 2 minutes; drain and rinse in cold water. Cool; transfer to a large bowl. Cut potatoes into 1/2-in. cubes; add to vegetables. In a small bowl, combine remaining ingredients. Pour over salad and toss to coat. Cover and chill for at least 1 hour before serving. **Yield:** 12 servings.

## Light Cabbage Slaw

*The crunch, texture and taste of coleslaw are preserved, but the fat and calories are reduced in this light version of traditional slaw. I've been making it for years, and everyone who tastes it comments on how good it is. This recipe is a keeper.* *—Carol Scovel Baton Rouge, Louisiana*

✓ Uses less fat, sugar or salt. Includes Nutritional Analysis and Diabetic Exchanges.

- 6 **cups chopped cabbage**
- 2 **large carrots, chopped**
- 1 **medium green pepper, chopped**
- 1 **celery rib, chopped**
- 2 **medium dill pickles, chopped**
- 3/4 to 1 **cup light Italian salad dressing**

In a large bowl, toss first five ingredients. Add enough salad dressing to moisten. **Yield:** 12 servings. **Nutritional Analysis:** One serving equals 25 calories, 261 mg sodium, 1 mg cholesterol, 5 gm carbohydrate, 1 gm protein, 1 gm fat. **Diabetic Exchange:** 1 vegetable.

# 'I Wish I Had That Recipe...'

"WHILE visiting historic Amana, Iowa, we had one of the best salads I've ever eaten," says Helen DoBell of Albuquerque, New Mexico.

"It was a wonderful chilled sauerkraut salad served at the Brick Haus Restaurant as part of a hearty family-style meal. I'd love to have the recipe… can *Taste of Home* help?"

We certainly can, Helen! We phoned Florence Schuerer, who operates this friendly dining room with husband Walter and their family. She was quick to share her recipe for you and others to try.

"The recipe for our popular, easy-to-make Sauerkraut Salad was handed down in my husband's family," Florence shares. "You most often think of tangy sauerkraut served warm with a meat dish, but this chilled version has a sweet taste that makes it different and refreshing.

"The peppers add flavor, but they're mainly for color. You can use canned peppers if fresh are not available."

Both of the Schuerers' mothers and grandmothers cooked in the old-time community kitchens of the Amana colonies, which were founded by German, Swiss and Alsatian settlers.

"We have some interesting old photos of Sauerkraut Days in the 1920s, when the folks would cut cabbage for hundreds of gallons of kraut, a staple food over the winter months," says Florence.

You'll find the Schuerers' Brick Haus Restaurant in Amana on Highway 220, just west of U.S. 151. Phone 1-319/622-3278 or 1-319/622-3471.

## Brick Haus Sauerkraut Salad

- 1 **cup sugar**
- 1/2 **cup vegetable oil**
- 1 **jar (32 ounces) sauerkraut, rinsed and drained**
- 1 **cup chopped celery**
- 1 **medium green *or* sweet red pepper, chopped**
- 1/2 **cup chopped onion**

In a large bowl, combine sugar and oil; mix well. Add all remaining ingredients. Chill several hours or overnight. **Yield:** 6-8 servings.

## Pork and Spinach Salad

**(Pictured above)**

*My family enjoys picnics any time of year—especially in the spring. To get in the mood for warmer weather, I serve this hearty main-dish salad. You just can't beat a salad that tastes great and is good for you, too.*
*—Marian Platt, Sequim, Washington*

> ✓ Uses less fat, sugar or salt. Includes Nutritional Analysis and Diabetic Exchanges.

  10 ounces fresh spinach, washed and stems removed
   1 can (16 ounces) black-eyed peas, rinsed and drained
 1/3 cup Italian *or* low-fat Italian dressing
 1/4 cup sliced green onions
 1/2 cup sliced fresh mushrooms
 1/4 cup sliced celery
   1 jar (2 ounces) sliced pimientos, drained
   2 to 3 tablespoons sliced ripe olives
   2 garlic cloves, minced
   1 tablespoon olive *or* vegetable oil
 1/2 pound pork tenderloin, cut into thin strips

Line four plates with spinach leaves; set aside. In a bowl, combine the peas, Italian dressing, green onions, mushrooms, celery, pimientos and olives; set aside. In a medium skillet, saute the garlic in oil for 30 seconds. Add the pork and stir-fry for 2-3 minutes or until no pink remains. Remove from the heat; add the vegetable mixture and mix well. Di-

vide among the four spinach-lined plates. Serve immediately. **Yield:** 4 servings. **Nutritional Analysis:** One serving (prepared with low-fat dressing) equals 317 calories, 758 mg sodium, 56 mg cholesterol, 24 gm carbohydrate, 27 gm protein, 13 gm fat. **Diabetic Exchanges:** 3 vegetable, 1-1/2 lean meat, 1 starch, 1 fat.

---

## Celebration Salad

*No matter what size your celebration is, this salad will fit right in. This has been my standby for family gatherings, church functions and other special occasions for more than 30 years.*
*—Barbara Berger*
*Breckenridge, Colorado*

  16 cups torn salad greens
   1 package (16 ounces) frozen peas, thawed
   1 large red onion, thinly sliced into rings
   4 celery ribs, thinly sliced
   1 block (12 ounces) cheddar *or* Swiss cheese, julienned
  12 bacon strips, cooked and crumbled
 1/2 cup sour cream
 1/2 cup mayonnaise
   3 teaspoons Dijon mustard
   2 teaspoons sugar
 1/2 teaspoon ground nutmeg
 1/2 teaspoon salt
 1/4 teaspoon pepper

In a large salad bowl, toss the greens, peas, onion, celery, cheese and crumbled bacon. In a small bowl, combine the remaining ingredients; pour over salad and toss to coat. Serve immediately. **Yield:** 16 servings.

---

## Zesty Potato Salad

**(Pictured on page 20)**

*A new, zippy version of the old favorite, this refreshing potato salad is sure to please! Horseradish gives it a delightfully different flavor. Try it for your next family gathering or picnic.*
*—Aney Chatterton*
*Soda Springs, Idaho*

   2 pounds red potatoes
 1/2 cup mayonnaise
 1/2 cup sour cream
   2 tablespoons prepared horseradish
   1 tablespoon chopped fresh parsley
 1/2 teaspoon salt
 1/2 teaspoon pepper
   3 bacon strips, cooked and crumbled

**4 hard-cooked eggs, chopped**
**2 green onions, sliced**

Peel potatoes; cook in boiling salted water for 20 minutes or until tender. Drain and cool. Cut potatoes into cubes. In a large bowl, combine mayonnaise, sour cream, horseradish, parsley, salt and pepper; mix until smooth. Stir in potatoes, bacon, eggs and onions. Cover and chill up to 24 hours. **Yield:** 6 servings.

—— 🍵 🍵 🍵 ——

## Cheese Ball Salad

*You'll have a ball with this dish! To fix it, you top a standard salad with crafty little cheese nuggets you make yourself. I was bored with the ordinary salad I'd been serving for years, so I added the cheese balls. They sure spiced it up.* —Elaine Arnold
*Chatham, Ontario*

**1 package (3 ounces) cream cheese,**
**softened**
**1-1/2 cups (6 ounces) shredded cheddar cheese**
**1/4 cup sour cream**
**1/4 cup finely chopped fresh chives *or* green**
**onions**
**1/2 teaspoon Worcestershire sauce**
**1 cup finely chopped walnuts**
**8 to 10 cups torn salad greens**
**1 medium cucumber, sliced**
**4 radishes, sliced**
**Italian salad dressing**

In a small bowl, combine the first five ingredients; mix well. Chill for at least 30 minutes. Shape into 1/2-in. balls; roll in walnuts. Just before serving, combine greens, cucumber and radishes in a large salad bowl. Add dressing and toss; top with cheese balls. **Yield:** 8-10 servings.

—— 🍵 🍵 🍵 ——

## Marinated Tomatoes

*When the tomatoes are ripe and fresh from the garden, this salad just can't be beat. Basil and lemon-pepper make a fine seasoning combination.* —Monica Wilcott
*Sturgis, Saskatchewan*

**3 medium tomatoes, thickly sliced**
**2 tablespoons chopped fresh basil**
**2 tablespoons olive *or* vegetable oil**
**2 tablespoons lemon juice**
**1/2 teaspoon sugar**
**1/8 teaspoon lemon-pepper seasoning**

Place the tomato slices in a shallow serving dish; sprinkle with the basil. In a small bowl, combine the remaining ingredients; pour over the tomatoes. Let stand at room temperature for 1 hour before serving. **Yield:** 6 servings.

—— 🍵 🍵 🍵 ——

## Orange Carrot Salad

**(Pictured below)**

*This is a colorful salad that puts a spark in dinner, especially for special occasions. I use oranges grown right here in my home state.* —Nancy Schmidt
*Delhi, California*

**3 cups shredded carrots**
**2 medium oranges, peeled**
**3 tablespoons lemon juice**
**1 tablespoon sugar**
**1 teaspoon ground cinnamon**
**Dash salt**

Place carrots in a medium bowl. Section oranges into the bowl to catch juices. Add remaining ingredients and mix well. Cover and chill for several hours. **Yield:** 4-6 servings.

### Keeping Carrots

Store carrots in a plastic bag in the refrigerator for up to 2 weeks. As they age, they lose flavor and firmness. Rinse and/or peel before using.

# Soups & Sandwiches

***The combination of soup and a sandwich is a classic. With 24 hearty choices, you can mix and match to form your own dynamic duo.***

**PERFECTLY PAIRED.** Clockwise from upper left: Ham Buns (p. 38), Scotch Broth (p. 40), Cornish Pasties (p. 36), Creamy Vegetable Soup (p. 39) and Cajun Corn Soup (p. 34).

thinner chili is desired, add additional water. **Yield:** 11 servings. **Nutritional Analysis:** One serving (1 cup) equals 191 calories, 616 mg sodium, 0 cholesterol, 38 gm carbohydrate, 7 gm protein, 2 gm fat. **Diabetic Exchanges:** 2 starch, 2 vegetable.

— 🍲 🍲 🍲 —

## Cajun Corn Soup

**(Pictured on page 32)**

*I found this recipe years ago and substituted Cajun stewed tomatoes for a bolder taste. Now I prepare this dish for out-of-state guests who want to taste some real Cajun food. Everyone who tries it gives it high marks. Plus, it's easy to prepare.* —Sue Fontenot
Kinder, Louisiana

    1 cup chopped onion
    1 cup chopped green pepper
    6 green onions, sliced
  1/2 cup vegetable oil
  1/2 cup all-purpose flour
    3 cups water
    1 can (14-1/2 ounces) Cajun-style stewed
      tomatoes
    2 cups chopped peeled tomatoes
    1 can (6 ounces) tomato paste
    2 packages (16 ounces *each*) frozen whole
      kernel corn
    3 cups cubed fully cooked ham
1-1/2 pounds fully cooked smoked sausage,
      sliced
  1/8 teaspoon cayenne pepper *or* to taste
Salt to taste
Hot pepper sauce to taste

In a large soup kettle or Dutch oven, saute the onion, green pepper and green onions in oil until tender, about 5 minutes. Add flour and cook until bubbly. Add water, tomatoes and tomato paste; mix well. Stir in the corn, ham, sausage, cayenne pepper, salt and hot pepper sauce. Bring to a boil, stirring frequently. Reduce heat; simmer, uncovered, for 1 hour, stirring occasionally. **Yield:** 12-14 servings.

## Chunky Vegetarian Chili

**(Pictured above)**

*This robust chili from the USA Rice Federation teams rice and kidney and pinto beans with a variety of colorful vegetables for a hearty meatless meal that's great tasting and good for you.*

☑ Uses less fat, sugar or salt. Includes Nutritional Analysis and Diabetic Exchanges.

    1 medium green pepper, chopped
    1 medium onion, chopped
    3 garlic cloves, minced
    1 tablespoon vegetable oil
    2 cans (14-1/2 ounces *each*) Mexican-style
      stewed tomatoes, undrained
    1 can (16 ounces) kidney beans, rinsed
      and drained
    1 can (15 ounces) pinto beans, rinsed
      and drained
    1 can (11 ounces) whole kernel corn,
      drained
2-1/2 cups water
    1 cup uncooked long grain rice
    1 to 2 tablespoons chili powder
1-1/2 teaspoons ground cumin

In a large soup kettle or Dutch oven, saute the green pepper, onion and garlic in oil until tender. Stir in all remaining ingredients; bring to a boil. Reduce the heat; cover and simmer for 25-30 minutes or until the rice is cooked, stirring occasionally. If

---

### *Soup Flavor to Savor*

Browning meats and vegetables gives soup a richer flavor. Try adding 1 teaspoon of sugar to the fat, then heat, stirring often, until the fat is hot, before browning the meat and vegetables. The sugar carmelizes and gives everything a beautiful color and flavor. The added sweetness is so slight it won't be noticed.

## Creamed Cabbage Soup

**(Pictured below)**

*Although we live in town, we have a big garden, which I love spending time in—even pulling the weeds. Honestly! This soup is especially good with garden-fresh vegetables. Everyone who tries it seems to agree, because they always ask for seconds.*
—Laurie Harms, Grinnell, Iowa

    2 cans (14-1/2 ounces *each*) chicken broth
    2 celery ribs, chopped
    1 medium head cabbage, shredded (about
      3 pounds)
    1 medium onion, chopped
    1 medium carrot, chopped
  1/4 cup butter *or* margarine
    3 tablespoons all-purpose flour
    1 teaspoon salt
  1/4 teaspoon pepper
    2 cups half-and-half cream
    1 cup milk
    2 cups cubed fully cooked ham
  1/2 teaspoon dried thyme
**Chopped fresh parsley**

In a large soup kettle or Dutch oven, combine the broth, celery, cabbage, onion and carrot; bring to a boil. Reduce the heat; cover and simmer for 15-20 minutes or until the vegetables are tender. Meanwhile, melt the butter in a medium saucepan. Add the flour, salt and pepper; stir to form a smooth paste. Combine the cream and milk; gradually add to flour mixture, stirring constantly. Cook and stir until thickened; continue cooking 1 minute longer. Gradually stir into the vegetable mixture. Add the ham and thyme and heat through. Garnish with parsley. **Yield:** 8-10 servings.

## Cheesy Chicken Chowder

**(Pictured above)**

*I like to serve this hearty chowder with garlic bread and a salad. It's a wonderful dish to prepare when company drops in. The rich, mild flavor and tender chicken and vegetables appeal even to children and picky eaters.*      —Hazel Fritchie, Palestine, Illinois

    3 cups chicken broth
    2 cups diced peeled potatoes
    1 cup diced carrots
    1 cup diced celery
  1/2 cup diced onion
1-1/2 teaspoons salt
  1/4 teaspoon pepper
  1/4 cup butter *or* margarine
  1/3 cup all-purpose flour
    2 cups milk
    2 cups (8 ounces) shredded cheddar cheese
    2 cups diced cooked chicken

In a 4-qt. saucepan, bring chicken broth to a boil. Reduce heat; add potatoes, carrots, celery, onion, salt and pepper. Cover and simmer for 15 minutes or until vegetables are tender. Meanwhile, melt butter in a medium saucepan; add flour and mix well. Gradually stir in milk; cook over low heat until slightly thickened. Stir in cheese and cook until melted; add to broth along with chicken. Cook and stir over low heat until heated through. **Yield:** 6-8 servings.

## Cornish Pasties

**(Pictured below and on page 33)**

*Years ago, when bakeries in my Midwestern hometown made pasties, people scrambled to get there before they were all gone. Now I make my own. Filled with meat, potatoes and vegetables, they make a complete meal and are great for picnics or potlucks.*
—*Gayle Lewis, Yucaipa, California*

**FILLING:**
- 1 pound boneless top round steak, cut into 1/2-inch pieces
- 2 to 3 medium potatoes, peeled and cut into 1/2-inch cubes
- 1 cup chopped carrots
- 1/2 cup finely chopped onion
- 2 tablespoons chopped fresh parsley
- 1 teaspoon salt
- 1/2 teaspoon pepper
- 1/4 cup butter *or* margarine, melted

**PASTRY:**
- 3 cups all-purpose flour
- 1 teaspoon salt
- 1 cup shortening
- 8 to 9 tablespoons ice water
- 1 egg, beaten, optional

In a bowl, combine round steak, potatoes, carrots, onion, parsley, salt and pepper; mix well. Add butter and toss to coat; set aside. For pastry, combine flour and salt in a mixing bowl. Cut in shortening until mixture is crumbly. Sprinkle with water, 1 tablespoon at a time. Toss lightly with a fork until dough forms a ball. Do not overmix. Divide dough into fourths. Roll out one portion into a 9-in. circle; transfer to a greased baking sheet. Mound about 1-1/4 cups of meat filling on half of circle. Moisten edges with water; fold dough over mixture and press edges with fork to seal. Repeat with remaining pastry and filling. Cut slits in the top of each pasty. Brush with beaten egg if desired. Bake at 375° for 50-60 minutes or until golden brown. **Yield:** 4 servings.

— 🍷 🍷 🍷 —

## Olive Sandwich Spread

*People may be a bit skeptical to see green olives in this mixture, but after one bite, they'll agree it is tasty and unique.* —*Dorothy Warren, Toulon, Illinois*

- 2 packages (3 ounces *each*) cream cheese, softened
- 1/2 cup mayonnaise
- 1/2 cup chopped green olives
- 1/2 cup chopped pecans
- 1 tablespoon olive juice

**Bread *or* assorted crackers**

In a small bowl, combine first five ingredients. Spread on bread or crackers. **Yield:** 1-1/2 cups.

— 🍷 🍷 🍷 —

## Special Ham and Cheese Sandwiches

*When I tire of ordinary meat and cheese sandwiches for my brown-bag lunch, I try creative alternatives. I love these ham and cheese sandwiches because they're so convenient and a little different.* —*Mattie Cheek Lawrenceburg, Kentucky*

- 1 package (3 ounces) cream cheese, softened
- 1/2 cup shredded cheddar cheese
- 2 tablespoons pickle relish
- 2 teaspoons Dijon mustard
- 2 ounces fully cooked ham, finely chopped
- 6 slices bread

In a small bowl, combine cream cheese, cheddar cheese, relish and mustard. Add ham. Divide mixture among three slices of bread; top with remaining bread to make sandwiches. Wrap and freeze. Remove from the freezer in the morning and sandwich will thaw by lunch. **Yield:** 3 servings.

ally. Remove spices. Add tomatoes and heat through. **Yield:** 14 servings (3-1/2 quarts) per batch. **Nutritional Analysis:** One serving (1 cup) equals 191 calories, 293 mg sodium, 0 mg cholesterol, 35 gm carbohydrate, 13 gm protein, 1 gm fat. **Diabetic Exchanges:** 2 starch, 1 vegetable, 1/2 meat.

---

### Hearty Potato Soup

**(Pictured below)**

*Having grown up on a dairy farm in Holland, I love our country life here in Idaho's "potato country". My favorite potato soup originally called for whipping cream and bacon fat, but I've trimmed down the recipe.*
—*Gladys DeBoer, Castleford, Idaho*

    6 medium potatoes, peeled and sliced
    2 medium carrots, diced
    6 celery ribs, diced
    2 quarts water
    1 medium onion, chopped
    6 tablespoons butter *or* margarine
    6 tablespoons all-purpose flour
    1 teaspoon salt
  1/2 teaspoon pepper
1-1/2 cups milk

In a large soup kettle or Dutch oven, cook potatoes, carrots and celery in water until tender, about 20 minutes. Drain, reserving liquid and setting vegetables aside. In the same kettle, saute onion in butter until tender. Stir in flour, salt and pepper; gradually add milk, stirring constantly until thickened. Gently stir in cooked vegetables. Add 1 cup or more of reserved cooking liquid until soup is desired consistency. **Yield:** 8-10 servings (about 2-1/2 quarts).

### Five-Bean Soup

**(Pictured above)**

*One of my family's favorite soups, this tasty recipe was one I discovered years ago. Served with a salad and bread or rolls, it makes a savory supper. Sometimes we like to grate mozzarella cheese over the individual bowls just before serving.* —*Lynne Dodd Mentor, Ohio*

☑ Uses less fat, sugar or salt. Includes Nutritional Analysis and Diabetic Exchanges.

    5 packages (16 ounces *each*) dry lima beans,
      great northern beans, kidney beans,
      pinto beans and split peas
ADDITIONAL INGREDIENTS:
    3 tablespoons dried chives
    1 teaspoon dried savory
    1 teaspoon salt, optional
  1/2 teaspoon ground cumin
  1/2 teaspoon pepper
    1 bay leaf
    3 beef bouillon cubes
2-1/2 quarts water
    1 can (14-1/2 ounces) stewed tomatoes

Combine beans. Store in an airtight container in a cool dry place for up to 1 year. **Yield:** 4 batches (15 cups total). **To prepare soup:** Wash 3-3/4 cups of beans. Place in a large kettle; add enough water to cover. Bring to a boil; cook for 3-4 minutes. Remove from heat; cover and let stand 1 hour. Tie spices in a cheesecloth bag. Drain and rinse beans. Return to kettle; add bouillon, spices and water. Bring to boil. Reduce heat; cover and simmer 1-1/2 hours or until beans are tender, stirring occasion-

### Chicken Chili with Black Beans

**(Pictured above)**

*Because it looks different than traditional chili, my family was a little hesitant to try this dish at first. But thanks to a full, hearty flavor, it's become a real favorite around our house. I serve it with warm corn bread.* —Jeanette Urbom, Overland Park, Kansas

> ✓ Uses less fat, sugar or salt. Includes Nutritional Analysis and Diabetic Exchanges.

  3 whole boneless skinless chicken breasts
      (about 1-3/4 pounds), cubed
  2 medium sweet red peppers, chopped
  1 large onion, chopped
  4 garlic cloves, minced
  3 tablespoons olive *or* vegetable oil
  1 can (4 ounces) chopped green chilies
  2 tablespoons chili powder
  2 teaspoons ground cumin
  1 teaspoon ground coriander
  2 cans (15 ounces *each*) black beans,
      rinsed and drained
  1 can (28 ounces) Italian plum tomatoes,
      undrained, chopped
  1 cup chicken broth *or* beer

In a large soup kettle or Dutch oven, saute chicken, red peppers, onion and garlic in oil for 5 minutes or until chicken is no longer pink. Add green chilies, chili powder, cumin and coriander; cook for 3 minutes. Stir in beans, tomatoes and broth; bring to a boil. Reduce heat and simmer, uncovered, for 15 minutes, stirring often. **Yield:** 10 servings (3 quarts). **Nutritional Analysis:** One serving (prepared with chicken broth) equals 149 calories, 172 mg sodium, 33 mg cholesterol, 12 gm carbohydrate, 16 gm protein, 4 gm fat. **Diabetic Exchanges:** 1 meat, 1 vegetable, 1/2 starch.

───── 🏆 🏆 🏆 ─────

### Ham Buns

**(Pictured below and on page 32)**

*These tasty sandwiches are a great way to use left-over ham. Friends with whom I've shared the recipe tell me the meat-filled buns disappear fast at potlucks. Use mini buns and make ahead for an easy meal or snack.* —Esther Shank, Harrisonburg, Virginia

  1/2 cup butter *or* margarine, softened
  1 small onion, grated
  1 tablespoon poppy seed
  2 teaspoons Worcestershire sauce
  2 teaspoons prepared mustard
1-1/4 cups finely chopped fully cooked ham
      (about 8 ounces)
  1 cup (4 ounces) shredded Swiss cheese
  6 to 8 hamburger buns *or* 16 to 20 mini
      buns, split

In a bowl, mix butter, onion, poppy seed, Worcestershire sauce and mustard until well blended. Add ham and cheese; mix well. Divide evenly among buns. Place in a shallow baking pan and cover with foil. Bake at 350° for 15-20 minutes or until hot. **Yield:** 6-8 main dish or 16-20 appetizer servings.

## Brown-Bag Burritos

_For a change from sandwiches, we like burritos—something many people don't consider in a brown-bag lunch. They're good cold but are easy to heat if a microwave's available. Just remember to take off the foil wrapper._ —Rhonda Cliett, Barton, Texas

    1 **pound lean ground beef**
    1 **can (16 ounces) refried beans**
  2/3 **cup enchilada sauce**
  1/4 **cup water**
    3 **tablespoons minced onion**
1-1/2 **tablespoons chili powder**
1-1/2 **teaspoons garlic powder**
  3/4 **teaspoon salt**
  1/2 **teaspoon dried oregano**
  15 **to 20 flour tortillas (7 inches)**
1-1/2 **to 2-1/2 cups (6 to 10 ounces) shredded cheddar cheese**

In a large skillet, brown the ground beef; drain. Add the next eight ingredients; bring to a boil. Reduce heat; cover and simmer for 20 minutes. Heat 3-4 tortillas in a microwave until warm, about 45 seconds. Spoon 3-4 tablespoons of the beef mixture down the center of each tortilla. Top with 2-3 tablespoons of cheese. Roll up. Wrap each burrito in paper towel, then in foil. Repeat with the remaining ingredients. Refrigerate. Eat the burritos cold, or remove foil and heat paper towel-wrapped burrito in a microwave on high for about 1 minute. **Yield:** 15-20 burritos.

## Basil Burgers

_Chopped fresh basil leaves add a welcome spark to these hamburgers and wonderfully capture the taste of summer. Grilling brings out the best flavors in the ground beef as well as the basil. They're a pleasant surprise at a family cookout._ —Jennie Wilburn
Long Creek, Oregon

1/4 **cup beef broth _or_ red wine**
1/4 **cup seasoned bread crumbs**
1/4 **cup minced red onion**
1/4 **to 1/2 cup fresh basil leaves, minced**
  1 **to 2 teaspoons garlic salt**
  2 **pounds lean ground beef**
  8 **hamburger buns, split**
**Monterey Jack cheese slices, optional**

In a large bowl, combine first five ingredients. Add beef and mix well. Shape into eight patties. Grill over medium-hot heat until burgers reach desired doneness. Serve on hamburger buns; top with cheese slices if desired. **Yield:** 8 servings.

## Creamy Vegetable Soup

**(Pictured above and on page 32)**

_I tasted this delicious soup in a restaurant, and when I couldn't persuade the chef to share the recipe, I began to experiment on my own. Finally, I came up with this blend, which is very close to what I'd tasted. The secret ingredient, I think, is sweet potatoes!_ —Audrey Nemeth, Mount Vernon, Maine

  1 **large onion, chopped**
1/4 **cup butter _or_ margarine**
  3 **medium sweet potatoes, peeled and chopped**
  3 **medium zucchini, chopped**
  1 **bunch broccoli, chopped**
  2 **quarts chicken broth**
  2 **medium potatoes, peeled and shredded**
  1 **teaspoon celery seed**
  1 **to 2 teaspoons ground cumin**
  2 **teaspoons salt**
  1 **teaspoon pepper**
  2 **cups half-and-half cream**

In a large soup kettle or Dutch oven, saute onion in butter until transparent but not browned. Add the sweet potatoes, zucchini and broccoli; saute lightly for 5 minutes or until crisp-tender. Stir in broth; simmer for a few minutes. Add potatoes and seasonings; cook another 10 minutes or until vegetables are tender. Stir in cream and heat through. **Yield:** 12-16 servings (4 quarts).

## Cucumber Potato Soup

**(Pictured below)**

*Served hot or cold, this soup never fails to delight the taste buds! It's simple to make, has a nice dill flavor and is a great way to use a few potatoes and a garden cucumber. It's one of my favorites.* —Robert Breno
Strongsville, Ohio

 Uses less fat, sugar or salt. Includes Nutritional Analysis and Diabetic Exchanges.

      4 **medium potatoes, peeled and diced**
      1 **teaspoon salt**
      2 **cups water**
      1 **medium cucumber, peeled, diced and seeded**
  1/4 **teaspoon white pepper**
      1 **cup whipping cream *or* milk**
  1/2 **cup milk**
      1 **green onion, sliced**
      1 **teaspoon dill weed *or* 1 tablespoon chopped fresh dill**
**Additional salt and pepper to taste**

In a large saucepan, cook potatoes in salted water until tender. Place sieve over a large bowl. Pour potatoes and liquid into sieve and force potatoes through. Return to saucepan. Stir in cucumber, pepper, cream, milk and onion. Simmer gently for about 5 minutes or until cucumber is tender. Add dill, salt and pepper. Serve hot or cold. **Yield:** 4 servings. **Nutritional Analysis:** One serving (prepared with fat-free milk) equals 131 calories, 631 mg sodium, 2 mg cholesterol, 27 gm carbohydrate, 6 gm protein, trace fat. **Diabetic Exchanges:** 1 starch, 1/2 skim milk, 1 vegetable.

## Scotch Broth

**(Pictured above and on page 33)**

*Early in winter, I make up big pots of this hearty soup to freeze in plastic containers. Then I can bring out one or two containers at a time. I heat the frozen soup in a saucepan on low all morning. By lunchtime, it's hot and ready to serve my hungry family!* —Ann Main
Moorefield, Ontario

      2 **pounds meaty beef soup bones**
      2 **quarts water**
      6 **whole peppercorns**
  1-1/2 **teaspoons salt**
      1 **cup chopped carrots**
      1 **cup chopped turnips**
      1 **cup chopped celery**
  1/2 **cup chopped onion**
  1/4 **cup medium pearl barley**

In a large soup kettle or Dutch oven, combine soup bones, water, peppercorns and salt. Cover and simmer for 2-1/2 hours or until the meat comes easily off the bones. Remove bones. Strain broth; cool and chill. Skim off fat. Remove meat from bones; dice and return to broth along with remaining ingredients. Bring to a boil. Reduce heat; cover and simmer about 1 hour or until vegetables and barley are tender. **Yield:** 6-8 servings (2 quarts).

## Perky Tuna Salad Sandwiches

*The crunch of celery, onion and carrot really livens up tuna salad in this tasty recipe.* —Paula Pelis
*Rocky Point, New York*

- 1 can (6 ounces) tuna, drained and flaked
- 2 hard-cooked eggs, chopped
- 1 celery rib, chopped
- 1 small onion, chopped
- 1 small carrot, shredded
- 8 medium pitted ripe olives, chopped
- 3 tablespoons mayonnaise
- 1/2 teaspoon salt
- 1/4 teaspoon pepper
- Bread *or* assorted crackers

Combine first nine ingredients in a small bowl. Spread on bread or crackers. **Yield:** 2 cups.

— 🏺 🏺 🏺 —

## Rosemary Split Pea Soup

*This zesty soup is great served with warm rolls or bread. The meatballs are a tasty twist to ordinary split pea soup.* —Diane Hixon, Niceville, Florida

✓ Uses less fat, sugar or salt. Includes Nutritional Analysis and Diabetic Exchanges.

- 3 celery ribs, finely chopped
- 1 cup finely chopped onion
- 1 garlic clove, minced
- 1 tablespoon fresh rosemary, minced *or* 1 teaspoon dried rosemary, crushed
- 3 tablespoons butter *or* margarine
- 6 cups chicken broth
- 1-1/4 cups dried split peas, rinsed
- 1 teaspoon salt, optional

**MEATBALLS:**
- 1/2 pound ground pork *or* turkey
- 1-1/2 teaspoons fresh rosemary, minced *or* 1/2 teaspoon dried rosemary, crushed
- 1/4 teaspoon pepper

In a large soup kettle or Dutch oven, saute celery, onion, garlic and rosemary in butter until tender. Add broth, peas and salt if desired; bring to a boil. Reduce heat; cover and simmer for 1-1/2 hours or until peas are tender. Remove from the heat and allow to cool. For meatballs, combine pork, rosemary and pepper. Shape into 1/2-in. balls. In a skillet, brown meatballs until no pink remains, about 5-10 minutes. Ladle half of cooled soup into a blender or food processor; puree. Return soup to the kettle along with meatballs and heat through. **Yield:** 5 servings. **Nutritional Analysis:** One serving (prepared with margarine and ground turkey and without added salt) equals 359 calories, 1,064 mg sodium, 24 mg cholesterol, 37 gm carbohydrate, 26 gm protein, 13 gm fat. **Diabetic Exchanges:** 2 lean meat, 2 starch, 1 vegetable, 1/2 fat.

— 🏺 🏺 🏺 —

## U.S. Senate Bean Soup

**(Pictured below)**

*Chock-full of ham, beans and celery, this hearty soup makes a wonderful meal any time of the year. Freeze the bone from a holiday ham until you're ready to make soup. Plus, once prepared, it freezes well for a great make-ahead supper!* —Rosemarie Forcum
*White Stone, Virginia*

- 1 pound dried great northern beans
- 1 meaty ham bone *or* 2 smoked ham hocks
- 3 medium onions, chopped
- 3 garlic cloves, minced
- 3 celery ribs, chopped
- 1/4 cup chopped fresh parsley
- 1 cup mashed potatoes *or* 1/3 cup instant potato flakes
- Salt and pepper to taste
- Parsley *or* chives for garnish

Place beans and enough water to cover in a saucepan; bring to a boil and boil for 2 minutes. Remove from the heat and soak for 1 hour. Drain and rinse beans. In a large soup kettle or Dutch oven, place beans, ham bone and 3 qts. water. Bring to a boil. Reduce heat; cover and simmer for 2 hours. Skim fat if necessary. Add onions, garlic, celery, parsley, potatoes, salt and pepper; simmer 1 hour longer. Remove meat and bones from the soup. Remove meat from the bones; dice and return to kettle. Heat through. Garnish with parsley or chives. **Yield:** 8-10 servings (2-1/2 quarts).

## Easy Low-Fat Chili

**(Pictured above)**

*Family and friends agree that this zesty chili hits the spot, especially on cool days. It has wonderful flavor, so no one misses the meat!* —Janet Moore
Ogdensburg, New York

✓ Uses less fat, sugar or salt. Includes Nutritional Analysis and Diabetic Exchanges.

- **1 medium onion, chopped**
- **1/4 cup chopped green pepper**
- **2 cups water, *divided***
- **1 can (15 to 16 ounces) great northern beans, rinsed and drained**
- **1 can (15 ounces) navy beans, rinsed and drained**
- **1 can (6 ounces) no-salt-added tomato paste**
- **1 can (14-1/2 ounces) no-salt-added tomatoes, undrained and diced**
- **2 to 4 teaspoons chili powder**
- **1 teaspoon salt, optional**
- **1/2 teaspoon pepper**

In a large saucepan, cook the onion and green pepper in 1/2 cup water until tender. Add beans, tomato paste and tomatoes. Stir in chili powder, salt if desired, pepper and remaining water; bring to a boil. Reduce heat; cover and simmer for 20 minutes. **Yield:** 7 servings. **Nutritional Analysis:** One 1-cup serving (prepared without added salt) equals 198 calories, 295 mg sodium, 0 cholesterol, 38 gm carbohydrate, 11 gm protein, 1 gm fat. **Diabetic Exchanges:** 2 starch, 1-1/2 vegetable.

## Cabbage Chowder

*Because it starts with canned condensed soup, this recipe goes together in just a few minutes. The cabbage and sausage give it fabulous flavor, and it's rich and creamy. You'd think it was from scratch.*
—Doris Ratcliff, Fillmore, Indiana

- **2 cups diagonally sliced carrots**
- **1/4 teaspoon caraway seeds**
- **2 tablespoons butter *or* margarine**
- **2 cans (10-3/4 ounces *each*) condensed cream of celery soup, undiluted**
- **1 soup can milk**
- **1 soup can water**
- **3 cups shredded cabbage**
- **1 pound fully cooked smoked sausage, cut into 1/2-inch diagonal slices**

In a large soup kettle or Dutch oven, cook the carrots and caraway seeds in butter over low heat until the carrots are crisp-tender, about 5 minutes. Add soup, milk, water, cabbage and sausage. Bring to boil; reduce heat and cook until cabbage is tender, about 15 minutes. **Yield:** 6-8 servings (2 qts.).

— 🞜 🞜 🞜 —

## German Potato Soup

*For as long as I can remember, this comforting concoction has been a family favorite. Some of my fondest memories are centered on the soup kettle. This recipe came from my mom. It's been enjoyed by several generations over the years.* —Mary Beth Jung
Deep River, Connecticut

- **6 cups cubed peeled potatoes**
- **1-1/4 cups sliced celery**
- **1/2 cup chopped onion**
- **5 cups water**
- **1/2 teaspoon salt**
- **1/8 teaspoon pepper**
- **DROP DUMPLINGS:**
  - **1 egg, beaten**
  - **1/3 cup water**
  - **1/2 teaspoon salt**
  - **3/4 cup all-purpose flour**
- **Butter *or* margarine**
- **Chopped parsley**

In a soup kettle, combine the potatoes, celery, onion, water, salt and pepper; bring to a boil. Reduce the heat and simmer until the vegetables are tender, about 1 hour. With a potato masher, puree most of the vegetables. For the dumplings, combine the egg, water, salt and flour. Stir until smooth and stiff. Drop by teaspoonfuls into the boiling soup.

Cover and simmer until the dumplings are cooked through, about 10-15 minutes. Serve with a pat of butter and sprinkle with parsley. **Yield:** 6 servings.

—— 🥄 🥄 🥄 ——

## Barbecued Pork Sandwiches

**(Pictured below)**

*Spirits will rise with every bite of these sandwiches! The seasoning has lots of flavor. That's what friends tell me they like best when I bring these to our get-togethers.* —Mrs. Jerome Privitera, Geneva, Ohio

- **3 medium onions, chopped**
- **4 cups ketchup**
- **2 cups water**
- **2 tablespoons Worcestershire sauce**
- **1-1/2 teaspoons vinegar**
- **2-1/2 teaspoons pepper**
- **1 teaspoon salt**
- **1 teaspoon *each* paprika and chili powder**
- **1/2 teaspoon cayenne pepper**
- **1 boneless pork shoulder roast (3-1/2 to 4 pounds)**
- **12 to 16 sandwich buns, split**

In a bowl, combine the onions, ketchup, water, Worcestershire sauce, vinegar and seasonings. Place pork in a large roasting pan or Dutch oven; pour sauce over pork. Cover and bake at 325° for 6 hours. Remove roast and cool for 20 minutes; shred with a fork. Return to sauce in pan and heat through. Fill buns using a slotted spoon. **Yield:** 12-16 servings.

## Tomato Dill Bisque

**(Pictured above)**

*My family really enjoys this soup when we make it from our garden tomatoes. When those tomatoes are plentiful, I make a big batch (without mayonnaise) and freeze it. Then we can enjoy it even after the garden is gone for the season.* —Susan Breckbill Lincoln University, Pennsylvania

✓ Uses less fat, sugar or salt. Includes Nutritional Analysis and Diabetic Exchanges.

- **2 medium onions, chopped**
- **1 garlic clove, minced**
- **2 tablespoons butter *or* margarine**
- **2 pounds tomatoes, peeled and chopped**
- **1/2 cup water**
- **1 chicken bouillon cube**
- **1 teaspoon sugar**
- **1 teaspoon dill weed**
- **1/2 teaspoon salt**
- **1/4 teaspoon pepper**
- **1/2 cup mayonnaise, optional**

In a large saucepan, saute onions and garlic in butter until tender. Add tomatoes, water, bouillon, sugar and seasonings. Cover and simmer 10 minutes or until tomatoes are tender. Remove from heat; cool. Puree in a blender or food processor. Return to saucepan. If a creamy soup is desired, stir in mayonnaise. Cook and stir over low heat until heated through. Serve warm. **Yield:** 5 servings (5 cups). **Nutritional Analysis:** One serving (prepared with margarine and without mayonnaise) equals 108 calories, 572 mg sodium, 0 cholesterol, 14 gm carbohydrate, 3 gm protein, 5 gm fat. **Diabetic Exchanges:** 2 vegetable, 1 fat.

# Side Dishes

*These delicious dishes will complement your main courses and garner a big batch of compliments for you, too.*

**SATISFYING SIDE DISHES.** Clockwise from upper left: Hot Fruit Compote (p. 50), Tomato Dumplings (p. 51), Spinach-Topped Tomatoes (p. 50) and Continental Zucchini (p. 48).

## Confetti Scalloped Potatoes

### (Pictured below)

*The first time I tasted this casserole was at a church supper, and I immediately asked around to find out who had made it. The cook shared her recipe, and it has become one of my family's most requested dishes.*
—*Frances Anderson, Boise, Idaho*

  1/2 **cup butter *or* margarine**
  1/2 **cup chopped onion**
    1 **package (16 ounces) frozen hash brown potatoes**
    1 **can (10-3/4 ounces) condensed cream of mushroom soup, undiluted**
    1 **soup can milk**
    1 **cup (4 ounces) shredded cheddar cheese**
    1 **small green pepper, cut into strips**
    2 **tablespoons chopped pimientos**
**Dash pepper**
    1 **cup cheese cracker crumbs, *divided***

In a skillet, melt butter over medium heat. Saute onion until tender. Stir in potatoes, soup and milk. Add cheese, green pepper, pimientos, pepper and 1/2 cup of the crumbs. Pour into a shallow casserole; top with remaining crumbs. Bake at 375° for 35-40 minutes. **Yield:** 6-8 servings.

## Broccoli Bake

*This tasty side dish is always a big hit when my son, daughter-in-law and granddaughter come for dinner or when I'm hosting a shower or party. At Easter, it's a great way to use up hard-cooked eggs!*
—*Carolyn Griffin, Macon, Georgia*

    2 **packages (10 ounces *each*) frozen broccoli cuts**
  1/2 **cup chopped onion**
    1 **tablespoon butter *or* margarine**
    1 **can (10-3/4 ounces) condensed cream of mushroom soup, undiluted**
  1/2 **teaspoon ground mustard**
  1/2 **teaspoon salt**
    4 **hard-cooked eggs, chopped**
1-1/2 **cups (6 ounces) shredded cheddar cheese**
    1 **can (2.8 ounces) french-fried onions**

Cook broccoli according to package directions; drain and set aside. In a skillet, saute onion in butter until tender. Stir in soup, mustard and salt; heat until bubbly. In a 1-1/2-qt. casserole, arrange half of broccoli; top with half of the eggs, half of the cheese and half of the mushroom sauce. Repeat layers. Bake at 350° for 20 minutes. Sprinkle onions on top; bake 5 minutes more. **Yield:** 6 servings.

— 🥤 🥤 🥤 —

## Boston Baked Corn

*My family enjoys this recipe, which I received from my sister-in-law. It's a nice side dish with many meals.*
—*Mrs. Willard Wilson, Woodsfield, Ohio*

    1 **cup ketchup**
    2 **tablespoons brown sugar**
    1 **teaspoon ground mustard**
  1/2 **teaspoon salt**
    1 **small onion, chopped**
    3 **cups fresh corn**
    3 **bacon strips, diced**

Combine ketchup, brown sugar, mustard and salt in a bowl; stir in onion and corn and mix thoroughly. Pour into a greased 1-1/2-qt. casserole. Top with bacon. Bake, uncovered, at 350° for 40 minutes or until bacon is cooked and dish is heated through. **Yield:** 6-8 servings.

— 🥤 🥤 🥤 —

## Italian Zucchini

*I make this hot vegetable dish quite often in summer when zucchini is abundant. Garden-fresh sliced onion and tomato add a tasty touch.* —*Christopher Gordon Springfield, Missouri*

☑ Uses less fat, sugar or salt. Includes Nutritional Analysis and Diabetic Exchanges.

    4 **cups sliced zucchini**
    1 **medium onion, sliced into rings**
    2 **medium tomatoes, sliced**
    1 **lemon, quartered**

1-1/2 teaspoons Italian seasoning
3/4 teaspoon red pepper flakes
1 tablespoon butter *or* margarine

In a greased 2-1/2-qt. casserole, layer one-third of the zucchini, onion and tomatoes. Squeeze one lemon quarter over all. Sprinkle with one-third of Italian seasoning and red pepper flakes. Repeat layers two more times. Dot with butter. Squeeze remaining lemon over all. Cover and bake at 350° for 1 hour or until vegetables are tender. Serve immediately. **Yield:** 4 servings. **Nutritional Analysis:** One serving (prepared with margarine) equals 64 calories, 35 mg sodium, 0 cholesterol, 9 gm carbohydrate, 2 gm protein, 3 gm fat. **Diabetic Exchanges:** 1-1/2 vegetable, 1/2 fat.

---

## Crunchy Sweet Potato Casserole

*I adapted this pumpkin recipe to use sweet potatoes instead, with great results.* —Virginia Slater
*West Sunbury, Pennsylvania*

2 cups mashed sweet potatoes
1/2 cup butter *or* margarine, melted
1/4 cup sugar
1/4 cup packed brown sugar
2 eggs, beaten
1/2 cup milk
1 teaspoon ground cinnamon
1/2 teaspoon ground nutmeg
TOPPING:
1 cup crushed cornflakes
1/2 cup chopped walnuts
1/4 cup packed brown sugar
1/4 cup butter *or* margarine

In a large bowl, combine the first eight ingredients and mix well. Spoon into a greased 1-1/2-qt. casserole. Bake, uncovered, at 375° for 20 minutes. Combine topping ingredients; sprinkle over potatoes. Bake 5-10 minutes longer or until the topping is lightly browned. **Yield:** 6 servings.

---

## Candy-Coated Carrots

*Getting my kids to eat vegetables was a problem for me...until I came up with this recipe that easily dresses up carrots with a sweet, tangy glaze.*
—Lavonne Hartel, Williston, North Dakota

1 package (16 ounces) fresh baby carrots
1/4 cup butter *or* margarine
1/4 cup packed brown sugar
1 teaspoon lemon juice

1/8 to 1/4 teaspoon hot pepper sauce
1/8 teaspoon salt

In a saucepan, cook carrots in a small amount of water until crisp-tender; drain and keep warm. In the same saucepan, cook butter and brown sugar until bubbly. Stir in lemon juice, hot pepper sauce and salt. Return carrots to pan and heat through. **Yield:** 4-6 servings.

## Company Brussels Sprouts

### (Pictured above)

*Want to serve an extra-special vegetable side dish? This tempting recipe might just do the trick. The combination of flavorful ingredients dresses up ordinary brussels sprouts.*
—Donald Roberts
*Amherst, New Hampshire*

4 bacon strips, diced
12 brussels sprouts, trimmed and halved
1 medium onion, chopped
2 tablespoons snipped fresh chives
1 medium carrot, thinly sliced
10 stuffed green olives, sliced
1/2 teaspoon dried basil
1/3 cup chicken broth *or* dry white wine
1 teaspoon olive *or* vegetable oil
1/2 teaspoon pepper
Pinch salt

In a skillet, fry bacon just until cooked. Drain, reserving 2 tablespoons drippings. Add remaining ingredients; cook and stir over medium-high heat for 10-15 minutes or until brussels sprouts are crisp-tender. **Yield:** 4 servings.

## Continental Zucchini

**(Pictured above and on page 44)**

*Zucchini are big and plentiful here, and people often joke about using them up before they multiply! Sharing zucchini—and zucchini recipes—is a good-neighbor policy. This easy recipe wins raves at church gatherings.  —Martha Fehl, Brookville, Indiana*

☑ Uses less fat, sugar or salt. Includes Nutritional Analysis and Diabetic Exchanges.

- 1 tablespoon vegetable oil
- 1 pound zucchini (about 3 small), cubed
- 1 to 2 garlic cloves, minced
- 1 jar (2 ounces) chopped pimientos, drained
- 1 can (15-1/2 ounces) whole kernel corn, drained
- 1 teaspoon salt, optional
- 1/4 teaspoon lemon-pepper seasoning
- 1/2 cup shredded mozzarella cheese

Heat oil in a large skillet. Saute zucchini and garlic for 3-4 minutes. Add pimientos, corn, salt if desired and lemon-pepper; cook and stir for 2-3 minutes or until zucchini is tender. Sprinkle with cheese and heat until cheese is melted. **Yield:** 6 servings. **Nutritional Analysis:** One serving (prepared with low-fat mozzarella cheese and without added salt) equals 131 calories, 107 mg sodium, 10 mg cholesterol, 15 gm carbohydrate, 8 gm protein, 6 gm fat. **Diabetic Exchanges:** 1 vegetable, 1 meat, 1/2 starch.

## Best Broccoli Casserole

*I'm a home economics teacher, and finding vegetable recipes my students enjoy preparing and eating really puts me to the test. Many kids who say they don't like broccoli actually ask for second helpings of this one!  —Cindy Kolberg, Syracuse, Indiana*

- 1 cup water
- 1/2 teaspoon salt
- 1 cup instant rice
- 1/4 cup butter *or* margarine
- 1/4 cup chopped onion
- 1/4 cup chopped celery
- 1 can (10-3/4 ounces) condensed cream of mushroom soup, undiluted
- 1 can (10-3/4 ounces) condensed cream of celery soup, undiluted
- 1 package (10 ounces) frozen chopped broccoli, thawed
- 1/2 cup diced process American cheese

Bring the water and salt to a boil. Add the rice; cover and remove from the heat. Let sit for 5 minutes. Melt the butter in a skillet; saute the onion and celery until tender. In a large mixing bowl, combine the rice, celery and onion with remaining ingredients. Pour into a greased 1-1/2-qt. casserole. Bake at 350° for 1 hour. **Yield:** 6 servings.

— 🛒 🛒 🛒 —

## Roasted Potatoes

*With just five ingredients, I can assemble this dish in no time, pop it in the oven and forget about it.  —Christopher Gordon, Springfield, Missouri*

- 5 large potatoes, peeled and sliced
- 1 cup chicken broth
- 1 teaspoon garlic powder
- Pepper to taste
- 4 tablespoons butter *or* margarine

Place potatoes in a greased 13-in. x 9-in. x 2-in. baking pan. Combine chicken broth, garlic powder and pepper; pour over potatoes. Dot with butter. Cover and bake at 400° for 1 hour and 15 minutes. Remove cover during last 15 minutes to brown. **Yield:** 4-6 servings.

— 🛒 🛒 🛒 —

## Broccoli with Red Pepper

*The crisp snap of water chestnuts adds to the great taste of this colorful dish.  —Karen Davis Wanipigow, Manitoba*

☑ Uses less fat, sugar or salt. Includes Nutritional Analysis and Diabetic Exchanges.

2 tablespoons vegetable oil
4 cups broccoli florets
1/2 teaspoon ground ginger *or* 2 teaspoons minced fresh gingerroot
2 garlic cloves, minced
1 medium sweet red pepper, cut into strips
1 can (8 ounces) sliced water chestnuts, drained

In a skillet, heat oil over high. Stir-fry broccoli, ginger and garlic until broccoli is crisp-tender, about 2 minutes. Add red pepper and water chestnuts; stir-fry just until heated through. Serve immediately. **Yield:** 4 servings. **Nutritional Analysis:** One serving equals 117 calories, 28 mg sodium, 0 mg cholesterol, 17 gm carbohydrates, 3 gm protein, 7 gm fat. **Diabetic Exchanges:** 2 vegetable, 1-1/2 fat.

## Autumn Casserole

### (Pictured below)

*My family often requests this dish for Sunday dinners as well as Thanksgiving.* —Shirley Brownell
*Amsterdam, New York*

3 cups sliced unpeeled tart apples
3 cups sliced carrots, cooked
1/2 cup packed brown sugar
2 tablespoons all-purpose flour
1 teaspoon ground cinnamon
1/2 teaspoon salt
1 tablespoon cold butter *or* margarine
3/4 cup orange juice

Place half the apples in a greased 2-qt. casserole. Cover with half the carrots. In a bowl, combine brown sugar, flour, cinnamon and salt. Cut in butter until crumbly; sprinkle half over apples and carrots. Repeat layers. Pour orange juice over all. Bake, uncovered, at 350° for 30-35 minutes. **Yield:** 6 servings.

## Irish Herbed Potatoes

### (Pictured above)

*St. Patrick's Day is one of my favorite holidays because everything is so festive, especially the food. It wouldn't be St. Patty's Day without these potatoes.*
—Connie Lou Blommers, Pella, Iowa

2-1/2 pounds potatoes, peeled and cut into wedges
1/2 cup butter *or* margarine, melted
1 tablespoon lemon juice
1/4 cup chopped fresh parsley
3 tablespoons chopped fresh *or* dried chives
3 tablespoons chopped fresh dill *or* 3 teaspoons dill weed
1/8 teaspoon salt
1/8 teaspoon pepper

In a saucepan, cook potatoes in boiling salted water until tender; drain. Combine remaining ingredients; pour over potatoes and toss to coat. Serve immediately. **Yield:** 8-10 servings.

the tomato halves, cut side up, in a shallow baking dish. Divide the spinach mixture over the tomatoes. Sprinkle with shredded Parmesan cheese if desired. Bake at 350° for about 15 minutes or until heated through. **Yield:** 6 servings.

## Hot Fruit Compote

**(Pictured below and on page 44)**

*This simple-to-prepare compote is a tasty way to get fruit into your meal when fresh fruit is not plentiful. Perfect with ham, pork, chicken or turkey, this dish can also help to stretch a meal when guests pop in.*
—Judy Kimball, Haverhill, Massachusetts

  1 **can (12 ounces) frozen orange juice concentrate, thawed**
  2 **tablespoons cornstarch**
  2 **pounds apples, peeled, cored and sliced**
  1 **can (8 ounces) pineapple chunks, drained**
  1 **can (16-1/2 ounces) pitted Bing cherries, drained**
1-1/2 **cups fresh *or* frozen cranberries**
  1 **package (6 ounces) dried apricots, cooked and drained**
1/4 **cup white wine, optional**

In a large bowl, combine orange juice concentrate and cornstarch; stir until smooth. Add fruit; stir to coat. Pour into a buttered 3-qt. casserole. If desired, pour wine over all. Cover and bake at 350° for 50-60 minutes or until hot and bubbly. **Yield:** 12 servings.

## Spinach-Topped Tomatoes

**(Pictured above and on page 45)**

*The perfect taste of summer, this colorful side dish is sure to please. The spinach and tomato, combined with the Parmesan cheese, give it a fabulous flavor. My daughter especially loves this dish, which I make for her often.* —Ila Alderman, Galax, Virginia

  1 **package (10 ounces) frozen chopped spinach**
  2 **chicken bouillon cubes**
**Salt**
  3 **large tomatoes, halved**
  1 **cup soft bread crumbs**
1/2 **cup grated Parmesan cheese**
1/2 **cup chopped onion**
1/2 **cup butter *or* margarine, melted**
  1 **egg, beaten**
  1 **garlic clove, minced**
1/4 **teaspoon pepper**
1/8 **teaspoon cayenne pepper**
**Shredded Parmesan cheese, optional**

In a saucepan, cook the spinach according to package directions with the bouillon cubes added to the water. Drain well. Cool slightly; press out the excess liquid. Lightly salt the tomato halves; place with cut side down on a paper towel for 15 minutes to absorb the excess moisture. Meanwhile, in a small bowl, combine the spinach with the bread crumbs, Parmesan cheese, onion, butter, egg, garlic, pepper and cayenne pepper. Mix well. Place

## Squash and Potatoes

*My German grandmother taught me to cook, and she used bacon drippings in almost every recipe, even cookies! I happened upon this concoction one summer afternoon when our neighbors gave us a bumper crop of vegetables from their garden. Naturally I started with Grandma's favorite ingredient...bacon!*
—Lillian Child, Omaha, Nebraska

      6  bacon strips, diced
      1  large potato, peeled and diced
      1  small onion, diced
      1  medium zucchini, diced
      1  medium yellow summer squash, diced
      1  tablespoon minced fresh dill *or* 1
         teaspoon dill weed
   1/2  teaspoon salt
   1/8  teaspoon pepper

In large skillet, cook bacon until crisp. Remove bacon; drain, discarding all but 2 tablespoons drippings. Add potato; cook and stir until lightly browned, about 5 minutes. Add onion, zucchini and yellow squash; cook until tender, about 8 minutes. Return bacon to skillet; sprinkle with dill, salt and pepper. Cook and stir for about 1 minute. **Yield:** 4-6 servings.

———— 🍴 🍴 🍴 ————

## Tomato Dumplings

**(Pictured at right and on page 45)**

*The wonderful fresh tomato taste of the sauce complements these light savory dumplings. They make a super side dish, especially for a meal with beef. My family loves them.*   —Lucille Tucker, Clinton, Illinois

   1/2  cup finely chopped onion
   1/4  cup finely chopped green pepper
   1/4  cup finely chopped celery
   1/4  cup butter *or* margarine
      1  bay leaf
      1  can (28 ounces) diced tomatoes, undrained
      1  tablespoon brown sugar
   1/2  teaspoon dried basil
   1/2  teaspoon salt
   1/4  teaspoon pepper
DUMPLINGS:
      1  cup all-purpose flour
 1-1/2  teaspoons baking powder
   1/2  teaspoon salt
      1  tablespoon cold butter *or* margarine
      1  tablespoon snipped fresh parsley
   2/3  cup milk

In a medium skillet, saute the onion, green pepper and celery in butter until tender. Add the bay leaf, tomatoes, brown sugar, basil, salt and pepper; cover and simmer for 5-10 minutes. Meanwhile, for the dumplings, combine the flour, baking powder and salt in a bowl. Cut in butter until crumbly. Add the parsley and milk; stir just until mixed. Drop by tablespoonfuls into six mounds onto bubbling tomato mixture; cover tightly and simmer for 12-15 minutes or until a toothpick inserted into dumpling comes out clean. Remove and discard the bay leaf. Serve immediately. **Yield:** 6 servings.

---

### *Tomato Taste Tips*

- Never cook tomatoes or tomato-based sauce in an aluminum pan. The tomatoes will lose their bright color and gain a bitter taste.
- Don't refrigerate tomatoes. Cold temperatures make the flesh pulpy and destroy the flavor.
- Ripen tomatoes by putting them and an apple in a paper bag with a few tiny holes punched in it. Let them stand at room temperature for 2 to 3 days.

# Main Dishes

*Whether you're in the mood for meat, fish, fowl or pasta,*
*the selection here offers plenty to satisfy your family.*

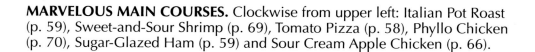

**MARVELOUS MAIN COURSES.** Clockwise from upper left: Italian Pot Roast (p. 59), Sweet-and-Sour Shrimp (p. 69), Tomato Pizza (p. 58), Phyllo Chicken (p. 70), Sugar-Glazed Ham (p. 59) and Sour Cream Apple Chicken (p. 66).

## Vegetable Beef Casserole

### (Pictured above)

*This easy one-dish recipe has been a family favorite ever since it was handed down to me 35 years ago from my husband's aunt. Add whatever vegetables you have on hand. A simple salad goes nicely with this dish.*
—*Evangeline Rew, Manassas, Virginia*

- 3 **medium unpeeled potatoes, sliced**
- 3 **medium carrots, sliced**
- 3 **celery ribs, sliced**
- 2 **cups fresh *or* frozen green beans**
- 1 **medium onion, chopped**
- 1 **pound lean ground beef**
- 1 **teaspoon dried thyme**
- 1 **teaspoon salt**
- 1 **teaspoon pepper**
- 4 **medium tomatoes, peeled, seeded and chopped**
- 1 **cup (4 ounces) shredded cheddar cheese**

In a 3-qt. casserole, layer half of the potatoes, carrots, celery, green beans and onion. Crumble half of the uncooked beef over vegetables. Sprinkle with 1/2 teaspoon each of the thyme, salt and pepper. Repeat layers. Top with the tomatoes. Cover and bake at 400° for 15 minutes. Reduce heat to 350°; bake about 1 hour longer or until the vegetables are tender and the meat is done. Sprinkle with cheese; cover and let stand until the cheese is melted. **Yield:** 6-8 servings.

## Chicken and Sausage Stew

*I enjoy cooking for family and friends, but I don't want to break the bank. That's why I frequently rely on delicious one-pot meals like this.* —*Ernest Foster Climax, New York*

- 1 **broiler/fryer chicken (3 to 4 pounds)**
- 2 **quarts water**
- 2 **pounds hot Italian sausage links**
- 6 **bacon strips**
- 2 **garlic cloves, minced**
- 1 **tablespoon chopped fresh parsley**
- 1 **teaspoon dried oregano**
- 1 **can (16 ounces) crushed tomatoes**
- 1 **can (8 ounces) tomato sauce**
- 8 **ounces elbow macaroni, cooked and drained**

**Salt and pepper to taste**

Place chicken and water in a large kettle; bring to a boil. Reduce heat; cover and simmer until chicken nearly falls from the bones. Remove chicken from stock. Chill stock. Remove chicken from bones and cube; set aside. Puncture skins of sausages; cover with water in a small saucepan and boil until fully cooked, 20-30 minutes. Drain; pan-fry sausages until browned. Cool and cut into bite-size pieces; set aside. In a Dutch oven, cook bacon until crisp. Drain, reserving 1 teaspoon drippings. Cool and crumble bacon; set aside. In the drippings, saute garlic. Skim fat from the chicken stock; add 5 cups to Dutch oven. Add chicken, sausage, bacon, parsley and oregano. Cover and simmer for 10-15 minutes. Add tomatoes, tomato sauce, macaroni, salt and pepper; simmer 10 minutes more. **Yield:** 8-10 servings.

———— 🍴 🍴 🍴 ————

## Turkey Minute Steaks

*Many people think of eating turkey around the holidays, but these quick steaks are delightful any time of the year.* —*Barbara Powell, Laramie, Wyoming*

- 3/4 **cup seasoned bread crumbs**
- 1/4 **cup grated Parmesan cheese**
- 1/2 **teaspoon dried basil**

**Salt and pepper to taste**

- 1-1/2 **pounds uncooked sliced turkey breast**
- 1 **egg, beaten**
- 3 **tablespoons butter *or* margarine**

In a shallow bowl, combine the bread crumbs, Parmesan cheese, basil, salt and pepper; mix well. Dip turkey in egg, then in crumbs, coating both sides. Melt butter in a skillet over medium-high heat. Cook turkey for 2-3 minutes on each side or until golden brown and juices run clear. **Yield:** 6-8 servings.

———— 🍷 🍷 🍷 ————

## Zesty Pork Ribs

*My family has enjoyed these ribs for years; we especially like them with sauerkraut. A friend from Texas gave me the recipe years ago.* —Carolyn Lloyd
Somerset, Kentucky

   4 **pounds pork spareribs *or* pork loin**
      **back ribs**
3/4 **cup soy sauce**
1/4 **cup water**
   1 **cup crabapple jelly, melted and cooled**
   1 **large onion, chopped**
   1 **garlic clove, minced**
   1 **cup chili sauce**
1/2 **teaspoon salt**
1/4 **teaspoon pepper**

Cut ribs into serving-size pieces; place in a large resealable plastic bag and set aside. Combine remaining ingredients; reserve 1 cup. Pour remaining marinade into bag; seal and turn to coat ribs. Refrigerate for 6-24 hours, turning bag occasionally. Drain ribs, discarding marinade; place on a rack in a large shallow roasting pan. Cover and bake at 350° for 1-1/2 hours. Remove ribs and rack from pan; discard fat. Place ribs back into the roasting pan; pour reserved marinade over ribs. Bake, uncovered, for 45-60 minutes or until meat is tender, basting occasionally. **Yield:** 4 servings.

———— 🍷 🍷 🍷 ————

## Lemon-Lime Chicken

*Every time I make this dish for my husband, he says, "This is the best chicken I've ever had."*
—Dana Fulton, Stone Mountain, Georgia

   6 **boneless skinless chicken breast halves**
1/2 **cup packed brown sugar**
1/4 **cup cider vinegar**
   3 **tablespoons *each* lemon juice and**
      **lime juice**
   3 **tablespoons Dijon mustard**
3/4 **teaspoon garlic powder**
1/4 **teaspoon pepper**
1/2 **teaspoon salt**

Place chicken in a shallow glass dish. Combine remaining ingredients; pour over chicken. Cover and refrigerate at least 4 hours or overnight. Drain,

discarding marinade. Grill chicken over medium-hot heat, turning once, until juices run clear, about 15-18 minutes. **Yield:** 4-6 servings.

———— 🍷 🍷 🍷 ————

## Tomato Quiche

**(Pictured below)**

*I tried this recipe at a family gathering and loved it! It's a great meatless lunch or dinner for a warm day, served hot or cold. This is my most-requested dish for parties.* —Heidi Anne Quinn
West Kingston, Rhode Island

   1 **cup chopped onion**
   2 **tablespoons butter *or* margarine**
   4 **large tomatoes, peeled, seeded, chopped**
      **and drained**
   1 **teaspoon salt**
1/4 **teaspoon pepper**
1/4 **teaspoon dried thyme**
   2 **cups (8 ounces) shredded Monterey Jack**
      **cheese**
   1 **unbaked pie pastry (10 inches)**
   4 **eggs**
1-1/2 **cups half-and-half cream**

In a skillet, saute onion in butter until tender. Add tomatoes, salt, pepper and thyme. Cook over medium-high heat until liquid is almost evaporated, about 10-15 minutes. Remove from heat. Sprinkle 1 cup cheese into bottom of pie shell. Cover with tomato mixture; sprinkle with remaining cheese. In a mixing bowl, beat eggs until foamy. Stir in cream; mix well. Pour into pie shell. Bake at 425° for 10 minutes. Reduce heat to 325°; bake 40 minutes more or until top begins to brown and a knife inserted near the center comes out clean. Let stand 10 minutes before cutting. **Yield:** 6-8 servings.

# Catfish Makes a Big Splash

MISSISSIPPI produces 75% of all catfish consumed in the nation, and good recipes abound there. The fab four shared here offer variety in flavor and cooking style.

## Catfish with Lemon/Butter Sauce

### (Pictured below)

*I created this recipe for a catfish cooking contest by modifying my recipe for shrimp and spaghetti.*
—*Rita Futral, Ocean Springs, Mississippi*

  3/4 cup butter *or* margarine
    8 ounces fresh mushrooms, sliced
    1 garlic clove, minced
  1/2 cup chicken broth *or* dry white wine
    2 tablespoons lemon juice
  1/4 to 1/3 cup chopped fresh parsley
    1 teaspoon salt
  1/2 teaspoon pepper
1-1/2 pounds catfish fillets, cut into
       bite-size pieces
   16 ounces spaghetti, cooked and drained
  1/2 cup grated Parmesan cheese
Lemon slices *or* wedges, optional
Additional parsley, optional

In a large skillet, melt butter over medium heat. Cook mushrooms and garlic, stirring occasionally, for 5 minutes. Add chicken broth, lemon juice, parsley, salt and pepper; cook 3 minutes, stirring occasionally. Add catfish; simmer, uncovered, for 6-8 minutes or until fish flakes easily with a fork. (Butter sauce will be thin.) Serve over spaghetti. Sprinkle with Parmesan cheese. Garnish with lemon and parsley if desired. **Yield:** 6-8 servings.

## Catfish Cakes

### (Pictured above)

*These cakes are crispy on the outside and moist and flavorful on the inside—a real treat! I serve them with hush puppies and coleslaw. I created the recipe at our lake cabin.* —*Jan Campbell, Purvis, Mississippi*

1-1/2 pounds catfish fillets
    2 eggs, beaten
    1 large potato, peeled, cooked and mashed
    1 large onion, finely chopped
    1 to 2 tablespoons chopped fresh parsley
    2 to 3 drops hot pepper sauce
    1 garlic clove, minced
    1 teaspoon salt
  1/2 teaspoon pepper
  1/2 teaspoon dried basil
    2 cups finely crushed butter-flavored
       crackers
Vegetable oil
Tartar sauce, optional

Poach or bake catfish fillets. Drain and refrigerate. Flake cooled fish into a large mixing bowl. Add eggs, potato, onion, parsley, hot pepper sauce, garlic, salt, pepper and basil; mix well. Shape into eight patties; coat with cracker crumbs. Heat a small amount of oil in a large skillet. Cook patties, a few at a time, until browned on both sides and heated through. Serve with tartar sauce if desired. **Yield:** 8 servings.

## Lime Broiled Catfish

### (Pictured below)

*To serve a reduced-calorie dish that is ready in about 15 minutes, I came up with this simple recipe. I think the lime juice adds a different fresh flavor to the mild taste of the fish.*
                                    —*Nick Nicholson*
                            *Clarksdale, Mississippi*

✓ Uses less fat, sugar or salt. Includes Nutritional Analysis and Diabetic Exchanges.

   1 tablespoon butter *or* margarine
   2 tablespoons lime juice
   1/2 teaspoon salt, optional
   1/4 teaspoon pepper
   1/4 teaspoon garlic powder
   2 catfish fillets (6 ounces *each*)
Lime slices *or* wedges, optional
Fresh parsley, optional

Melt butter in a saucepan. Stir in lime juice, salt if desired, pepper and garlic powder; mix well. Remove from the heat and set aside. Place fillets in a shallow baking dish. Brush each fillet generously with lime-butter sauce. Broil for 5-8 minutes or until fish flakes easily with a fork. Remove to a warm serving dish; spoon pan juices over each fillet. Garnish with lime and parsley if desired. **Yield:** 2 servings. **Nutritional Analysis:** One serving (prepared with margarine and without added salt) equals 254 calories, 156 mg sodium, 98 mg cholesterol, 2 gm carbohydrate, 31 gm protein, 14 gm fat. **Diabetic Exchanges:** 4 lean meat, 1 fat.

## Greek Grilled Catfish

### (Pictured above)

*Temperatures here on the Gulf Coast are moderate in winter, so we enjoy grilling out all year. My husband, Larry, came up with this recipe by experimenting. Our whole family likes the unique taste of this dish.*
                        —*Rita Futral, Ocean Springs, Mississippi*

✓ Uses less fat, sugar or salt. Includes Nutritional Analysis and Diabetic Exchanges.

   6 catfish fillets (8 ounces *each*)
Greek seasoning to taste
   4 ounces feta cheese, crumbled
   1 tablespoon dried mint
   2 tablespoons olive *or* vegetable oil
Fresh mint leaves *or* parsley, optional
Cherry tomatoes, optional

Sprinkle both sides of fillets with Greek seasoning. Sprinkle each fillet with 1 rounded tablespoon feta cheese and 1/2 teaspoon mint. Drizzle 1 teaspoon olive oil over each. Roll up fillets and secure with toothpicks. Grill over medium heat for 20-25 minutes or until fish flakes easily with a fork. Or, place fillets in a greased baking dish and bake at 350° for 30-35 minutes or until fish flakes easily with a fork. Garnish with mint leaves or parsley and cherry tomatoes if desired. **Yield:** 6 servings. **Nutritional Analysis:** One serving equals 288 calories, 319 mg sodium, 115 mg cholesterol, 1 gm carbohydrate, 34 gm protein, 16 gm fat. **Diabetic Exchanges:** 4-1/2 lean meat, 1 fat.

## Asparagus Ham Rolls

### (Pictured above)

*I love this delicious recipe because it includes three of my favorite locally produced foods—ham, asparagus and cheese. Prepared with leftover Easter ham and fresh asparagus, these rolls make an excellent springtime meal.* —Laurie Timm, Minneiska, Minnesota

✓ Uses less fat, sugar or salt. Includes Nutritional Analysis and Diabetic Exchanges.

- **2 tablespoons butter *or* margarine**
- **1/4 cup all-purpose flour**
- **2 cups milk**
- **1/2 cup shredded cheddar cheese**
- **1/4 teaspoon salt**
- **1/4 teaspoon white pepper**
- **24 fresh *or* frozen asparagus spears**
- **8 thin slices fully cooked ham (about 1/2 pound)**
- **1/4 cup bread crumbs**

In a saucepan, melt butter; stir in flour and cook until thick. Gradually stir in milk and cook until bubbly and thickened. Stir in cheese, salt and pepper. Remove from the heat. Place three asparagus spears on each ham slice. Roll up; secure with toothpicks if necessary. Place in a 13-in. x 9-in. x 2-in. baking pan; cover with cheese sauce. Sprinkle with crumbs. Bake at 375° for 20 minutes. **Yield:** 8 servings. **Nutritional Analysis:** One serving (prepared with margarine and fat-free milk) equals 125 calories, 492 mg sodium, 19 mg cholesterol, 11 gm carbohydrate, 11 gm protein, 7 gm fat. **Diabetic Exchanges:** 1 meat, 1 vegetable, 1/2 starch.

## Tomato Pizza

### (Pictured on page 52)

*My children like to eat pizza with a lot of toppings, so I developed this recipe. It's a delightful change from traditional meat-topped pizza.* —Lois McAtee, Oceanside, California

✓ Uses less fat, sugar or salt. Includes Nutritional Analysis and Diabetic Exchanges.

- **6 medium tomatoes, thinly sliced**
- **1 large baked pizza crust (13 to 16 inches)**
- **2 tablespoons olive *or* vegetable oil**
- **1 teaspoon salt**
- **1 teaspoon pepper**
- **1 can (2-1/4 ounces) sliced ripe olives, drained, optional**
- **1/2 cup diced green pepper**
- **1/2 cup diced onion**
- **1 tablespoon chopped fresh basil**
- **1 cup (4 ounces) shredded mozzarella cheese**
- **1 cup (4 ounces) shredded cheddar cheese**

Place tomato slices in a circle on crust, overlapping slightly until crust is completely covered. Drizzle with olive oil. Season with salt and pepper. Cover with olives if desired, green pepper and onion. Sprinkle basil over all. Cover with mozzarella and cheddar cheeses. Bake at 400° for 15 minutes or until cheese is melted. Serve immediately. **Yield:** 8 servings. **Nutritional Analysis:** One serving (prepared with low-fat mozzarella and without olives) equals 223 calories, 599 mg sodium, 22 mg cholesterol, 21 gm carbohydrate, 12 gm protein, 12 gm fat. **Diabetic Exchanges:** 1 starch, 1 meat, 1 vegetable, 1 fat.

---

## Basil Chicken Medley

*Everyone who has tried this dish has raved about it. It's a quick, colorful main course that I came up with myself.* —Susan Jansen, Smyrna, Georgia

✓ Uses less fat, sugar or salt. Includes Nutritional Analysis and Diabetic Exchanges.

- **1 tablespoon olive *or* vegetable oil**
- **3 garlic cloves, minced**
- **2 whole boneless skinless chicken breasts (about 1-1/4 pounds), cut into 1-inch chunks**
- **1 medium zucchini, cut into chunks**
- **2 medium tomatoes, cut into chunks**
- **1 tablespoon dried basil**
- **2 tablespoons vinegar**

1/4 teaspoon pepper
Cooked rice *or* pasta

Heat oil in a skillet; saute garlic. Add chicken and cook until no longer pink; remove and keep warm. Combine zucchini, tomato, basil, vinegar and pepper; toss to coat vegetables well. Add to skillet and stir-fry about 3-5 minutes. Return chicken to skillet and heat through. Serve immediately over rice or pasta. **Yield:** 4 servings. **Nutritional Analysis:** One serving equals 205 calories, 70 mg sodium, 73 mg cholesterol, 8 gm carbohydrate, 28 gm protein, 7 gm fat. **Diabetic Exchanges:** 3 lean meat, 1 vegetable.

## Garlic Pork Roast

*The garlic gives this roast its special flavor. The broth or wine boils down to make a flavorful gravy.*
—Dorothy Pritchett, Wills Point, Texas

1 boned rolled pork loin roast (4 to 5 pounds)
4 garlic cloves, peeled and cut into thin slivers
Salt and pepper to taste
1 cup broth *or* cooking wine
Horseradish, optional

Using the point of a paring knife, make slits all around the roast. Insert garlic into slits. Rub roast with salt and sprinkle with pepper. Place in a roasting pan and insert a meat thermometer. Bake at 325° for 30-40 minutes per pound or until thermometer reads 160°-170°. Remove from the pan and let stand. Meanwhile, place pan on stovetop over high heat. Skim off fat. Add broth or wine; cook until gravy is reduced by half and coats the back of a spoon. Slice meat; serve with gravy and horseradish if desired. **Yield:** 12-15 servings.

## Sugar-Glazed Ham

**(Pictured on page 52)**

*This old-fashioned sugar glaze gives your ham a pretty, golden-brown coating. The mustard and vinegar complement the brown sugar and add tangy flavor.*
—Carol Strong Battle, Heathsville, Virginia

1 fully cooked bone-in ham (5 to 7 pounds)
1 cup packed brown sugar
2 teaspoons prepared mustard
1 to 2 tablespoons cider vinegar

Score ham about 1/2 in. deep with a sharp knife. Place ham on a rack in a shallow baking pan. Bake at 325° for 2 to 2-1/2 hours (20 minutes per pound). Combine brown sugar, mustard and enough vinegar to make a thick paste. During the last hour of baking, brush glaze on ham every 15 minutes. **Yield:** 10-14 servings.

## Italian Pot Roast

**(Pictured below and on page 52)**

*I fix this pot roast when my grown children come over. I know it's one of their favorites, because all of them have asked for the recipe.* —George Seidler
Pine Grove, California

1 rump roast (4 to 5 pounds)
1 to 2 teaspoons salt
2 tablespoons vegetable oil
2 garlic cloves, minced
1/2 teaspoon dried basil
1 tablespoon dried parsley flakes
1/2 teaspoon pepper
2 medium carrots, sliced
1 medium onion, studded with 2 whole cloves
1 can (15 ounces) tomato puree
1/2 cup water *or* red wine
1/2 teaspoon beef bouillon granules
Cooked egg noodles

Rub roast with salt. In a Dutch oven, brown roast in oil. Add all remaining ingredients except noodles. Bring to a boil; reduce heat and simmer, covered, about 2-3 hours or until meat is tender. Discard onion. Remove roast; cut into slices. Serve over noodles with gravy. **Yield:** 8-10 servings.

## Baked Chicken Breasts Supreme

### (Pictured below)

*Perfect for a busy day, this main dish can be prepared a day ahead and baked before serving. My brothers don't want me to make anything else when they come to dinner! Leftovers are great for sandwiches or sliced with potato salad.*
*—Marjorie Scott*
*Sardis, British Columbia*

☑ Uses less fat, sugar or salt. Includes Nutritional Analysis and Diabetic Exchanges.

1-1/2 cups plain yogurt *or* sour cream
1/4 cup lemon juice
1/2 teaspoon Worcestershire sauce
1/2 teaspoon celery seed
1/2 teaspoon Hungarian sweet paprika
1 garlic clove, minced
1/2 teaspoon salt, optional
1/4 teaspoon pepper
8 boneless skinless chicken breast halves
2 cups fine dry bread crumbs

In a large bowl, combine first eight ingredients. Place chicken in mixture and turn to coat. Cover and marinate overnight in the refrigerator. Remove chicken from marinade; coat each piece with crumbs. Arrange on a shallow baking pan. Bake, uncovered, at 350° for 45 minutes or until juices run clear. **Yield:** 8 servings. **Nutritional Analysis:** One serving equals 271 calories, 293 mg sodium, 76 mg cholesterol, 22 gm carbohydrate, 32 gm protein, 5 gm fat. **Diabetic Exchanges:** 3-1/2 lean meat, 1 starch, 1/4 skim milk.

## Sausage-Stuffed Zucchini

*Fresh ingredients are the key to great cooking. Like most gardeners, I'm terrific at growing zucchini. It comes in handy when I reach for this recipe, which is a longtime favorite.*
*—Warren Knudtson*
*Las Vegas, Nevada*

4 medium zucchini
1/2 pound bulk mild Italian sausage
1/4 cup chopped onion
1 garlic clove, minced
1 teaspoon dried oregano
1/2 cup fresh *or* frozen corn
1 medium tomato, seeded and diced
1 cup (4 ounces) shredded cheddar cheese, *divided*

Cut each zucchini in half lengthwise. Place, cut side down, in a large skillet; add 1/2 in. of water. Bring to a boil; reduce heat and simmer until zucchini are crisp-tender, about 5 minutes. Remove zucchini and drain water. In the same skillet, cook sausage, onion and garlic until sausage is browned; drain. Add oregano, corn and tomato. Cook and stir until heated through. Remove from the heat and stir in 2/3 cup cheese; set aside. Scoop out and discard seeds from zucchini. Divide the sausage mixture among zucchini shells. Place in a greased 13-in. x 9-in. x 2-in. baking pan. Sprinkle with remaining cheese. Bake, uncovered, at 375° for 12-15 minutes or until heated through. **Yield:** 4-6 servings.

---

## Baked Ziti

*This delicious pasta dish reminds me of a cross between spaghetti and cheese pizza. I appreciate this quick-to-make meal on busy weeknights.*
*—Christopher Gordon, Springfield, Missouri*

1 medium onion, chopped
2 garlic cloves, minced
2 tablespoons olive *or* vegetable oil
1 can (28 ounces) diced tomatoes, undrained
1 teaspoon dried oregano
1 teaspoon dried basil
1/2 teaspoon salt
1/8 teaspoon pepper
8 ounces ziti, cooked and drained
2 cups (8 ounces) shredded mozzarella cheese
2 tablespoons grated Parmesan cheese

In a large skillet, saute the onion and garlic in oil until tender. Add the tomatoes, oregano, basil, salt and pepper. Cover; simmer for 20 minutes. Place the ziti in an ungreased 11-in. x 7-in. x 2-in.

baking dish. Cover with sauce. Bake, uncovered, at 350° for 20 minutes. Sprinkle with cheeses. Bake 10 minutes longer or until cheese is melted. **Yield:** 6-8 servings.

— 🍷 🍷 🍷 —

## Dilled Turkey Breast

*Dill provides a welcome change of pace in this recipe that uses leftover turkey. We like it best with mashed potatoes.* —Nancy Bohlen, Brookings, South Dakota

 1 **can (10-3/4 ounces) condensed cream of mushroom soup, undiluted**
 3/4 **cup chicken broth**
 3/4 **cup sour cream**
 1 **tablespoon dill weed**
**Sliced cooked turkey, warmed**

In a saucepan, combine the soup, chicken broth, sour cream and dill weed. Cook until heated through but do not boil. Arrange the turkey slices on a platter; pour the sauce over the turkey and serve immediately. **Yield:** 6-8 servings.

— 🍷 🍷 🍷 —

## Orange Ham Kabobs

*These citrus kabobs from the National Pork Producers Council get a kick from green and red peppers.*

✓ Uses less fat, sugar or salt. Includes Nutritional Analysis and Diabetic Exchanges.

1-1/2 **pounds fully cooked ham, cut into 24 cubes (1-inch pieces)**
 2 **medium oranges, peeled and cut into eighths**
 1 **large green pepper, cut into 16 pieces**
 1 **large sweet red pepper, cut into 16 pieces**
 1/2 **cup orange juice**
 2 **tablespoons tomato paste**
 1/4 **teaspoon ground ginger**

On eight metal skewers, alternately thread three ham cubes, two orange pieces, two green pepper pieces and two red pepper pieces. Place on a broiler pan with rack; broil 4-5 in. from the heat for 8 minutes, turning occasionally. In a small bowl, combine the orange juice, tomato paste and ginger; mix well. Brush half over kabobs; broil 2-3 minutes. Turn kabobs and brush with the remaining sauce; broil 2 minutes more or until the vegetables are tender. **Yield:** 8 servings. **Nutritional Analysis:** One serving equals 150 calories, 1,248 mg sodium, 40 mg cholesterol, 10 gm carbohydrate, 17 gm protein, 5 gm fat. **Diabetic Exchange:** 3 lean meat.

## Venison Stew

**(Pictured above)**

*I had no choice but to learn to cook some years ago while my wife recuperated from surgery. But I found I really enjoyed trying different recipes and adapting them to my own taste—that's how my now-famous venison stew recipe came to be!*
—Gene Pitts
Wilsonville, Alabama

 2 **tablespoons vegetable oil**
 2 **pounds venison stew meat**
 3 **large onions, coarsely chopped**
 2 **garlic cloves, crushed**
 1 **tablespoon Worcestershire sauce**
 1 **bay leaf**
 1 **teaspoon dried oregano**
 1 **tablespoon salt**
 1 **teaspoon pepper**
 3 **cups water**
 7 **medium potatoes, peeled and quartered**
 1 **pound carrots, cut into 1-inch pieces**
 1/4 **cup all-purpose flour**
 1/4 **cup cold water**
**Browning sauce, optional**

Heat oil in a Dutch oven. Brown meat. Add onions, garlic, Worcestershire sauce, bay leaf, oregano, salt, pepper and water. Cover and simmer 1-1/2 to 2 hours or until meat is tender. Add potatoes and carrots. Continue to cook until vegetables are tender, about 30-45 minutes. Mix flour and cold water; stir into stew. Cook and stir until thickened and bubbly. Add browning sauce if desired. Remove bay leaf. **Yield:** 8-10 servings.

## Herbed Beef Stew

**(Pictured above)**

*This stew looks as terrific as it tastes! Flavored with a variety of herbs and chock-full of vegetables, this recipe lists salt as an option, making it ideal for family members and friends who must restrict sodium.*
—Marlene Severson, Everson, Washington

> 2 **pounds beef stew meat, cut into 1-inch cubes**
> 2 **tablespoons vegetable oil**
> 3 **cups water**
> 1 **large onion, chopped**
> 2 **teaspoons pepper**
> 1 **to 2 teaspoons salt, optional**
> 1-1/2 **teaspoons garlic powder**
> 1 **teaspoon dried rosemary, crushed**
> 1 **teaspoon dried oregano**
> 1 **teaspoon dried basil**
> 1 **teaspoon ground marjoram**
> 2 **bay leaves**
> 1 **can (6 ounces) tomato paste**
> 2 **cups cubed peeled potatoes**
> 2 **cups sliced carrots**
> 1 **large green pepper, chopped**
> 1 **package (10 ounces) frozen green beans**
> 1 **package (10 ounces) frozen peas**
> 1 **package (10 ounces) frozen kernel corn**
> 1/4 **pound mushrooms, sliced**
> 3 **medium tomatoes, chopped**

Brown meat in oil in a Dutch oven. Add water, onion, seasonings and tomato paste. Cover and simmer for 1-1/2 hours or until meat is tender. Stir in potatoes, carrots and green pepper; simmer 30 minutes. Add additional water if necessary. Stir in remaining ingredients; cover and simmer 20 minutes. **Yield:** 10-12 servings.

## Louisiana Chicken

*Green peppers and mint add a surprise to this Southern-style recipe. A roasting bag keeps the chicken moist and flavorful.* —Jill Werle, Saskatoon, Saskatchewan

> 2 **tablespoons all-purpose flour**
> 1 **large plastic roasting bag with tie**
> 1 **roasting chicken (3-1/2 to 5 pounds)**
> 1 **teaspoon salt**
> 1 **teaspoon cayenne pepper**
> 3 **medium onions, quartered**
> 6 **large potatoes, peeled and quartered**
> 6 **medium carrots, peeled and cut into 2-inch pieces**
> 2 **medium green peppers, quartered**
> 2 **garlic cloves**
> 1 **tablespoon dried parsley flakes**
> 1-1/2 **teaspoons dried mint *or* 1 tablespoon chopped fresh mint**
> 2 **cups chicken broth**
> 1 **tablespoon Worcestershire sauce**

Put flour in bag and shake. Place bag into a 13-in. x 9-in. x 2-in. pan or larger roasting pan. Distribute flour evenly on bottom of bag. Sprinkle chicken with salt and cayenne pepper; place in bag. Surround chicken with onions, potatoes, carrots and green peppers. Place one garlic clove inside the chicken, and one with the vegetables. Sprinkle parsley and mint over vegetables and chicken. Combine chicken broth and Worcestershire sauce. Pour under chicken inside of bag. Fasten the bag. Puncture the top of bag five or six times with a fork. Bake at 325° for 1-1/2 to 2-1/2 hours (25 to 30 minutes per pound of chicken). **Yield:** 6-8 servings.

———— 🛒 🛒 🛒 ————

## Beef 'n' Noodle Casserole

*The recipe for this easy but rich-tasting casserole comes from the American Dairy Association.*

> 1 **package (8 ounces) medium egg noodles**
> 1/3 **cup sliced green onions**
> 1/3 **cup chopped green pepper**
> 2 **tablespoons butter *or* margarine**
> 1 **pound ground beef**
> 1 **can (6 ounces) tomato paste**
> 1/2 **cup sour cream**
> 1 **cup cottage cheese**
> 1 **can (8 ounces) tomato sauce**

Cook noodles according to package directions; drain. In a large skillet, saute onions and green pepper in butter 3 minutes or until tender. Add beef and cook until no longer pink; drain. In a medium bowl, combine tomato paste and sour cream; stir in the noodles and cottage cheese. Layer half the noodle mixture in 2-qt. casserole; top with half the beef mixture. Repeat. Pour tomato sauce evenly over the top of the casserole. Bake at 350° for 30-35 minutes or until heated through. **Yield:** 6 servings.

— 🥄 🥄 🥄 —

### Broccoli-Ham Hot Dish

**(Pictured below)**

*A friend shared this recipe with me. My family loves it because it features a favorite vegetable.*
—*Margaret Wagner Allen, Abingdon, Virginia*

    2  packages (10 ounces *each*) frozen cut
       broccoli
    2  cups cooked rice
    6  tablespoons butter *or* margarine
    2  cups soft bread crumbs (about 2-1/2
       slices)
    1  medium onion, chopped
    3  tablespoons all-purpose flour
    1  teaspoon salt
  1/4  teaspoon pepper
    3  cups milk
1-1/2  pounds fully cooked ham, cubed
Shredded cheddar *or* Swiss cheese

Cook broccoli according to package directions; drain. Spoon rice into a 13-in. x 9-in. x 2-in. baking pan. Place broccoli over rice. Melt butter in a large skillet. Sprinkle 2 tablespoons of melted butter over the bread crumbs and set aside. In remaining butter, saute onion until tender. Add flour, salt and pepper, stirring constantly until bubbly. Stir in milk and continue cooking until sauce thickens and bubbles. Cook and stir for 1 minute; add ham and heat through. Pour over rice and broccoli. Sprinkle the crumbs over all. Bake at 350° for 30 minutes or until heated through. Sprinkle with cheese; let stand 5 minutes before serving. **Yield:** 8 servings.

— 🥄 🥄 🥄 —

# 'I Wish I Had That Recipe...'

AFTER he and his wife visited Mast Farm Inn in Valle Crucis, North Carolina, Joe Noah wished he'd asked for the recipe for the fantastic rainbow trout dinner they'd eaten. He wondered if *Taste of Home* could help.

Inn owners Francis and Sibyl Pressly, who had restored the Blue Ridge Mountain inn to its circa-1900 grandeur and updated its amenities, graciously shared the recipe.

The Presslys sold Mast Farm Inn in 1996 to sisters Wanda Hinshaw and Kay Philipp. The innkeepers pride themselves on providing exquisite dinners using fresh, locally grown ingredients, including rainbow trout.

For more information about the restaurant or lodging at Mast Farm Inn, call 1-888/963-5857. To sample one version of the restaurant's famed trout in your own home, try the recipe below.

### Mountain Trout With Butter Sauce

    3  pounds mountain trout fillets, cut
       into 4-ounce portions
Salt and pepper to taste
    1  cup all-purpose flour
  1/2  cup vegetable oil
  1/2  cup butter (no substitutes)
Juice of 2 lemons
  1/2  cup chicken *or* brown gravy, optional

Season trout with salt and pepper; dredge with flour. Heat oil in a skillet. Saute trout quickly in hot oil, browning evenly on both sides. Remove trout to a shallow baking pan. Bake at 350° for 5-10 minutes or until fish flakes easily with a fork; keep warm. Meanwhile, in a saucepan, heat butter until butter begins to brown. Carefully add lemon juice (hot butter will bubble when juice is added). Blend in gravy if desired. Spoon sauce over fish or serve on the side. **Yield:** 6 servings.

— 🥄 🥄 🥄 —

## Chicken Fajitas
### (Pictured below)

*Fresh flavor with a flair describes this quick and easy recipe. Fajitas are great for hot summer evenings when you want to serve something fun and tasty, yet keep cooking to a minimum. Try topping them with sour cream, guacamole or both. My family loves them!*
*—Lindsay St. John, Plainfield, Indiana*

✓ Uses less fat, sugar or salt. Includes Nutritional Analysis and Diabetic Exchanges.

    1/4 cup lime juice
      1 garlic clove, minced
      1 teaspoon chili powder
    1/2 teaspoon ground cumin
      2 whole boneless skinless chicken breasts,
          cut into strips
      1 medium onion, cut into thin wedges
    1/2 medium sweet red pepper, cut into strips
    1/2 medium yellow pepper, cut into strips
    1/2 medium green pepper, cut into strips
    1/2 cup salsa
     12 flour tortillas (8 inches )
  1-1/2 cups (6 ounces) shredded cheddar *or*
          Monterey Jack cheese

In a small bowl, combine lime juice, garlic, chili powder and cumin. Add chicken; stir. Marinate for 15 minutes. In a nonstick skillet, cook onion, chicken and marinade for 3 minutes or until chicken is no longer pink. Add peppers; saute for 3-5 minutes or until crisp-tender. Stir in salsa. Divide mixture among tortillas; top with cheese. Roll up and serve. **Yield:** 6 servings. **Nutritional Analysis:** One serving (prepared with cheddar cheese) equals 228 calories, 353 mg sodium, 39 mg cholesterol, 19 gm carbohydrate, 17 gm protein, 12 gm fat. **Diabetic Exchanges:** 2 meat, 1 vegetable, 1 starch.

## Chicken Flowerpot Pie

*I host a "welcome spring" luncheon for friends every year. I try to do something different and creative each time.* —*Mary Anne McWhirter, Pearland, Texas*

      2 cups all-purpose flour
      1 teaspoon salt
    3/4 cup cold butter *or* margarine, cut into
          thin slices
      3 tablespoons shortening
    1/3 cup ice water
**FILLING:**
      1 broiler/fryer chicken (3 to 4 pounds),
          cut up
      2 quarts water
      1 bay leaf
      1 garlic clove, minced
  1-1/2 cups fresh *or* frozen cut green beans
  1-1/2 cups thinly sliced carrots
      1 cup diced peeled potatoes
    1/2 teaspoon dried basil
    1/2 cup sliced fresh mushrooms
      1 package (10 ounces) frozen peas
      1 can (16 ounces) whole tomatoes, drained
          and chopped
      4 tablespoons butter *or* margarine
    1/4 cup all-purpose flour
      1 cup whipping cream
      2 egg yolks
**Salt and pepper to taste**
**GLAZE:**
      1 egg yolk
      1 tablespoon cold water
**OTHER MATERIALS NEEDED:**
      6 new clay flowerpots (4-inch diameter)
**Vegetable oil**
**Aluminum foil**
**Decorative seed packets glued onto wooden
    craft sticks**

In a large mixing bowl, combine flour and salt. Using a pastry blender, cut in butter and shortening until mixture is crumbly. Sprinkle with ice water; rapidly blend together with a fork. Gather the dough into a ball, then flatten into a circle. Wrap in foil; chill at least 3 hours or overnight. For filling, place chicken, water, bay leaf and garlic in a Dutch oven. Bring to a boil; reduce heat and cook for 30-40 minutes or until chicken is tender. Remove and debone chicken; set aside. Skim fat from the stock. Add beans, carrots, potatoes and basil; cover and simmer 12-15 minutes or until the vegetables are tender. Add mushrooms, peas and tomatoes; cover and simmer for 3-5 minutes. Drain vegetables and reserve stock; set aside. Melt butter in another large kettle. Whisk in flour and cook until bubbly; stir in 1-1/2 cups of reserved stock. Discard remaining stock. In a small bowl, stir together cream and egg yolks. Whisk into the sauce; remove from heat. Season with salt and pepper. Gently fold in reserved chicken and vegetables. To assemble flowerpots, brush the outside of pots with vegetable oil. Line each pot with a 15-in. x 12-in. piece of foil; press foil down into the pot, being careful not to tear it. Fill each pot with about 1-1/2 cups of filling, leaving about 1/2-in. headroom; set aside. Roll pastry to 1/8-in. thickness; cut six 6-in. circles. Place one circle on each flowerpot, turn down the edges and flute the ends. Cut three small steam holes in the center of each pastry. In a small bowl, lightly beat glaze ingredients; brush on top of each crust. Place flowerpots on a baking sheet. Bake at 425° for 30-35 minutes or until the crust is browned and the filling is hot and bubbly. Place one stick with a seed packet in each pot before serving. **Yield:** 6 servings.

— 🌶 🌶 🌶 —

## Herbed Stuffed Green Peppers

*I like to serve garden-fresh peppers with green salad, French bread and seasonal fresh fruit.* —Bea Taus
*Fremont, California*

✓ Uses less fat, sugar or salt. Includes Nutritional Analysis and Diabetic Exchanges.

- **6 medium green peppers, tops and seeds removed**
- **1 pound ground turkey**
- **1 can (28 ounces) diced tomatoes, undrained**
- **1 medium onion, chopped**
- **2 celery ribs, chopped**
- **2 garlic cloves, minced**
- **1 teaspoon dried oregano**
- **1/2 teaspoon dried thyme**
- **1/2 teaspoon dried rosemary, crushed**
- **1/2 teaspoon dried basil**
- **1/2 teaspoon rubbed sage**
- **1/8 teaspoon pepper**
- **1-1/2 cups cooked rice**
- **1/3 cup shredded part-skim mozzarella cheese**

In a large kettle, cook peppers in boiling water 3 minutes. Drain and rinse in cold water. Set aside. In a large nonstick skillet, brown the turkey. Remove and set aside. In the same skillet, combine tomato liquid, onion, celery, garlic and herbs. Simmer until vegetables are tender and the mixture has begun to thicken. Stir in tomatoes, turkey and rice. Stuff into peppers and place in a baking pan. Bake at 350° for 30 minutes. Top each pepper with about 1 tablespoon cheese. Bake for 3 min-

utes longer or until the cheese is melted. **Yield:** 6 servings. **Nutritional Analysis:** One serving (rice prepared without salt) equals 267 calories, 483 mg sodium, 51 mg cholesterol, 29 gm carbohydrates, 21 gm protein, 10 gm fat. **Diabetic Exchanges:** 2 meat, 2 vegetable, 1 starch.

## Spicy Breaded Chicken

### (Pictured above)

*This is one of our favorite ways to make chicken. The coating really stays on, and the pan is easy to clean afterward.* —Polly Coumos, Mogadore, Ohio

✓ Uses less fat, sugar or salt. Includes Nutritional Analysis and Diabetic Exchanges.

- **1/2 cup dry bread crumbs**
- **1 tablespoon nonfat dry milk powder**
- **1-1/2 teaspoons chili powder**
- **1/4 teaspoon garlic powder**
- **1/4 teaspoon ground mustard**
- **1/4 cup fat-free milk**
- **1 broiler/fryer chicken (3 pounds), cut into pieces and skinned**

In a resealable plastic bag, mix bread crumbs, milk powder, chili powder, garlic powder and ground mustard; set aside. Place milk in a shallow pan. Dip chicken pieces into milk, then place in bag and shake to coat. Place chicken, bone side down, in a 13-in. x 9-in. x 2-in. baking pan coated with nonstickcooking spray. Bake, uncovered, at 375° for 50-55 minutes or until juices run clear. **Yield:** 6 servings. **Nutritional Analysis:** One serving equals 233 calories, 154 mg sodium, 93 mg cholesterol, 8 gm carbohydrate, 31 gm protein, 8 gm fat. **Diabetic Exchanges:** 4 lean meat, 1/2 starch.

## Barbecued Chicken

**(Pictured above)**

*My family truly loves this recipe. We don't fry foods much anymore and prefer to barbecue, so I adapted my mother's recipe for barbecue sauce to suit our tastes. Every summer, we have a neighborhood cookout. I take this chicken and watch it disappear!* —Linda Scott
Hahira, Georgia

   **2 broiler/fryer chickens (2 to 3 pounds**
      ***each*), cut up**
**SEASONING MIX:**
   **3 tablespoons salt *or* salt substitute**
   **2 tablespoons onion powder**
   **1 tablespoon paprika**
   **2 teaspoons garlic powder**
**1-1/2 teaspoons chili powder**
**1-1/2 teaspoons pepper**
  **1/4 teaspoon ground turmeric**
**Pinch ground red pepper**
**SAUCE:**
   **2 cups ketchup**
   **3 tablespoons brown sugar**
   **2 tablespoons dried minced onion**
   **2 tablespoons frozen orange juice**
      **concentrate, thawed**
   **1 tablespoon Seasoning Mix**
  **1/2 teaspoon liquid smoke, optional**

Pat chicken pieces dry so seasoning coats well; set aside. Combine seasoning mix ingredients; sprinkle generously over both sides of the chicken. Reserve 1 tablespoon mix for sauce and store leftovers in a covered container. Grill chicken, skin side down, uncovered, over medium heat for 20 minutes. Turn; grill 20-30 minutes more or until

chicken is tender and no longer pink. Meanwhile, combine all sauce ingredients in a small bowl. During the last 10 minutes of grilling, brush chicken often with sauce. **Yield:** 12 servings.

## Halloween Pizza

*Getting kids interested in cooking by making fun seasonal treats is one of my favorite pastimes. I perk up Halloween by having my grandchildren make jack-o'-lantern pizzas.* —Flo Burtnett, Gage, Oklahoma

   **1 frozen cheese pizza (12 inches)**
   **1 can (5-3/4 ounces) pitted ripe olives,**
      **drained and halved**
   **1 medium sweet red pepper**
   **1 small green pepper**

Place pizza on a baking sheet. Arrange olives in a circle around edge of pizza. Cut a nose, eyes and mouth out of red pepper. Cut a stem and eyebrows out of green pepper. Make a jack-o'-lantern face on pizza. Bake according to package directions. **Yield:** 6-8 servings.

## Sour Cream Apple Chicken

**(Pictured on page 52)**

*I've found that apples and chicken go well together because they both have subtle flavors. I developed this recipe myself. I think it's not only a great-tasting main course, it also looks nice on the table.*
—Carolyn Popwell, Lacey, Washington

   **4 boneless skinless chicken breast halves**
   **1 tablespoon vegetable oil**
   **2 medium tart apples, peeled and thinly**
      **sliced**
  **1/2 cup apple juice *or* cider**
  **1/3 cup chopped onion**
   **1 teaspoon dried basil**
  **1/2 teaspoon salt**
   **1 cup (8 ounces) sour cream**
   **1 tablespoon all-purpose flour**
**Cooked spinach noodles**
**Paprika**

In a large skillet, cook chicken in oil over medium heat until browned and no longer pink inside, about 6-8 minutes per side. Remove from skillet; keep warm. Add apples, juice, onion, basil and salt to skillet; bring to a boil. Reduce heat; cover and simmer until apples are tender. Combine sour cream and flour; add to skillet. Cook and stir until sauce is warm (do not boil). Arrange noodles on a platter. Top with chicken. Spoon apple sauce over all. Sprinkle with paprika. **Yield:** 4 servings.

---

## Mock Pasta Alfredo

*If you're on a restricted diet but still yearn for pasta in a creamy sauce, indulge yourself with this recipe. Cottage cheese is the secret ingredient.*
—*Ruby Williams, Bogalusa, Louisiana*

✓ Uses less fat, sugar or salt. Includes Nutritional Analysis and Diabetic Exchanges.

1-1/2 cups 1% cottage cheese
1/2 cup fat-free milk
2 garlic cloves, minced
2 tablespoons all-purpose flour
1 tablespoon lemon juice
1 teaspoon dried basil
1/2 teaspoon ground mustard
1/2 teaspoon pepper
1/4 teaspoon salt, optional
8 ounces corkscrew noodles, cooked and drained
1 to 2 tomatoes, seeded and chopped

In a blender or food processor, process cottage cheese, milk and garlic until smooth. Add flour, lemon juice, basil, mustard, pepper and salt if desired; process until well blended. Pour into a saucepan. Cook over medium heat until thickened. Do not boil. Serve over noodles; sprinkle with chopped tomatoes. **Yield:** 4 servings. **Nutritional Information:** One serving (prepared without added salt) equals 316 calories, 368 mg sodium, 8 mg cholesterol, 53 gm carbohydrate, 20 gm protein, 2 gm fat. **Diabetic Exchanges:** 2-1/2 starch, 2 lean meat, 1 vegetable.

---

## Octoberfest Ribs

*The name alone tells you this German main dish is a cure for chilly fall weather. The National Pork Producers Council provided the gem. Suggested accompaniments are rye bread and iced tea.*

2 jars (16 ounces *each*) sauerkraut, drained
1 tablespoon caraway seed
2 medium onions, halved
2 medium tart green apples, peeled and cut into wedges
1/4 cup packed brown sugar
2 pounds pork spareribs

In a Dutch oven, layer ingredients in order listed. Bring to a boil; reduce heat. Cover and simmer 2-3 hours or until ribs are tender. **Yield:** 6 servings.

## Chicken Tetrazzini

**(Pictured below)**

*My husband is not a casserole lover, but this creamy, cheesy dish is one of his favorites! Nutmeg gives it a wonderful, different taste. As a busy mother with three sons, I often put this easy recipe to good use.*
—*Kelly Heusmann, Cincinnati, Ohio*

2 cups sliced mushrooms
1/4 cup butter *or* margarine
1/4 cup all-purpose flour
2 cups chicken broth
1/4 cup half-and-half cream
1 tablespoon chopped fresh parsley
1 teaspoon salt
1/8 to 1/4 teaspoon ground nutmeg
1/4 teaspoon pepper
3 tablespoons dry white wine, optional
3 cups cubed cooked chicken
8 ounces spaghetti, cooked and drained
3/4 cup shredded Parmesan cheese
Additional parsley

In a skillet, cook mushrooms in butter until tender. Stir in flour; gradually add the chicken broth. Cook, stirring constantly, until sauce comes to a boil. Remove from the heat; stir in cream, parsley, salt, nutmeg, pepper and wine if desired. Fold in the chicken and spaghetti. Turn into a greased 12-in. x 8-in. x 2-in. baking dish; sprinkle with Parmesan cheese. Bake, uncovered, at 350° for 30 minutes or until heated through. Garnish with parsley. **Yield:** 8 servings.

**CHOICE CHICKEN.** Two out-of-the-ordinary dinner options, Nutty Oven-Fried Chicken (top) and Artichoke Chicken, offer extraordinary taste.

## Nutty Oven-Fried Chicken
**(Pictured at left)**

*The pecans that give this dish its unique nutty flavor are plentiful in the South. I love to make and serve this easy dish because the chicken comes out moist, tasty and crispy.* —Diane Hixon, Niceville, Florida

>     1 cup biscuit/baking mix
>   1/3 cup finely chopped pecans
>     2 teaspoons paprika
>   1/2 teaspoon salt
>   1/2 teaspoon poultry seasoning
>   1/2 teaspoon dried sage
>     1 broiler/fryer chicken (2 to 3 pounds), cut up
>   1/2 cup evaporated milk
>   1/3 cup butter *or* margarine, melted

In a shallow dish, combine the biscuit mix, pecans and seasonings; mix well. Dip the chicken pieces in milk; coat generously with pecan mixture. Place in a lightly greased 13-in. x 9-in. x 2-in. baking dish. Drizzle the melted butter over chicken. Bake, uncovered, at 350° for 1 hour or until juices run clear. **Yield:** 6-8 servings.

## Artichoke Chicken
**(Pictured at left)**

*Rosemary, mushrooms and artichokes combine to give chicken a wonderful, savory flavor. I've served this dish for a large group by doubling the recipe. It's always a hit.* —Ruth Stenson, Santa Ana, California

>     8 boneless skinless chicken breast halves
>     2 tablespoons butter *or* margarine
>     2 jars (6 ounces *each*) marinated artichoke hearts, drained
>     1 jar (4-1/2 ounces) whole mushrooms, drained
>   1/2 cup chopped onion
>   1/3 cup all-purpose flour
> 1-1/2 teaspoons dried rosemary, crushed
>     1 teaspoon salt
>   1/4 teaspoon pepper
>     2 cups chicken broth *or* 1 cup broth and 1 cup dry white wine
> **Cooked noodles**
> **Chopped fresh parsley**

In a skillet, brown chicken in butter. Remove chicken to an ungreased 13-in. x 9-in. x 2-in. baking dish; do not drain pan juices. Cut the artichokes into quarters. Arrange artichokes and mushrooms on top of chicken; set aside. Saute onion in pan juices; blend in flour, rosemary, salt and pepper.

Add chicken broth; cook until thickened and bubbly. Remove from the heat and spoon over chicken. Cover and bake at 350° for 50-60 minutes or until chicken is tender. Place noodles on serving platter; top with chicken and sauce. Sprinkle with parsley. **Yield:** 8 servings.

— 🍷 🍷 🍷 —

## Sweet-and-Sour Shrimp

### (Pictured on page 52)

*Tired of your usual shrimp recipes? Canned cherry pie filling adds convenience to this delightful dish that takes only minutes to prepare. The recipe is shared by the Cherry Marketing Institute.*

> 1 can (21 ounces) cherry pie filling
> 3 tablespoons cider vinegar
> 3 tablespoons brown sugar
> 1 teaspoon ground ginger
> 1 medium green pepper, cut into thin strips
> 1 can (8 ounces) sliced water chestnuts, drained
> 1 pound shrimp, peeled, cooked and deveined
Hot cooked rice

In a saucepan, combine pie filling, vinegar, brown sugar and ginger; mix well. Cook over medium heat until filling is hot and bubbly. Add green pepper, water chestnuts and shrimp. Cook over medium heat for 4-5 minutes or until shrimp are heated through (do not overcook). Serve over rice. **Yield:** 4 servings.

— 🍷 🍷 🍷 —

## Hearty Hitch Roasts

*Cooking these individual roasts in foil keeps the meat moist and tender. The seasonings make every mouthful especially flavorful.* —Marlene Thompson
Winchester, Ohio

> 12 pounds sirloin tip roast (about 2 inches thick)
> 1/2 cup butter *or* margarine
> 1 tablespoon browning sauce, optional
> 3 teaspoons seasoned salt
> 1-1/2 teaspoons pepper
> 1 large onion, sliced
> 3 medium green peppers, sliced into rings

Cut meat into 12 portions; place each on a piece of aluminum foil. In a saucepan, melt butter; stir in browning sauce if desired. Pour over roasts. Sprinkle with seasoned salt and pepper. Arrange onion and green pepper on roasts. Seal foil; place pouches in a roasting pan. Bake at 350° for 2 to 2-1/2 hours. **Yield:** 6-12 servings.

— 🍷 🍷 🍷 —

## Hasenpfeffer

### (Pictured below)

*My husband is an avid hunter. Almost 60 years ago, his aunt gave us this wonderful recipe. We still use it today.* —Mary Calendine, Hiddenite, North Carolina

> 1 large onion, sliced
> 3 cups vinegar
> 3 cups water
> 1 tablespoon pickling spice
> 2 teaspoons salt
> 1/2 teaspoon pepper
> 2 bay leaves
> 8 whole cloves
> 1 rabbit (2-1/2 pounds), skinned and cut into serving-size pieces
> 1/4 cup all-purpose flour
> 2 to 3 tablespoons butter *or* margarine
> 1 cup (8 ounces) sour cream

In a large non-metallic bowl, combine onion, vinegar, water and seasonings. Add rabbit pieces; cover and refrigerate for 48 hours, turning occasionally. Remove meat; strain and reserve marinade. Dry meat well; coat lightly with flour. In a skillet, melt butter; brown meat well. Gradually add 2 to 2-1/2 cups of reserved marinade. Cover and bring to a boil. Reduce heat and simmer until tender, about 30 minutes. Remove meat to a warm platter. Add sour cream to pan juices; stir just until heated through. Spoon over the meat and serve immediately. **Yield:** 6 servings.

## Cashew Chicken

### (Pictured below)

*We love eating ethnic foods, especially Oriental dishes. This chicken stir-fry is my family's favorite! The tasty sauce adds richness to carrots and broccoli.*
*—Ena Quiggle, Goodhue, Minnesota*

 1 tablespoon sesame oil
1/4 cup rice vinegar
1/4 cup sherry *or* chicken broth
 1 teaspoon garlic powder
1-1/2 pounds boneless skinless chicken breasts, cut into cubes
 3 tablespoons vegetable oil
 3 cups broccoli florets
 1 cup thinly sliced carrots
 2 teaspoons cornstarch
1/3 cup soy sauce
1/3 cup hoisin sauce
 1 tablespoon ground ginger
 1 cup roasted salted cashews
Cooked rice

In a large bowl, combine first four ingredients; add chicken and toss to coat. Cover and refrigerate for 2 hours. Remove chicken from marinade and reserve marinade. Heat oil in a wok or large skillet. Stir-fry chicken for 2-3 minutes or until it is no longer pink. With a slotted spoon, remove chicken and set aside. In the same skillet, stir-fry broccoli and carrots for 3 minutes or just until crisp-tender. Combine cornstarch, soy sauce, hoisin sauce, ginger and reserved marinade; stir into vegetables. Cook and stir until slightly thickened and heated through. Stir in cashews and chicken; heat through. Serve over rice. **Yield:** 6 servings.

## Horseradish-Glazed Ham

*This glaze is my favorite way to really spark a baked ham. We harvest horseradish (a member of the mustard family) from our fields every year. The leftovers make great sandwiches—with horseradish, of course!*
*—Cathy Seus, Tulelake, California*

 1 fully cooked bone-in *or* boneless ham (5 to 6 pounds)
Whole cloves
 1 cup packed brown sugar
1/3 cup prepared horseradish
1/4 cup lemon juice

Score ham and stud with cloves. Bake according to package directions. Meanwhile, combine brown sugar, horseradish and lemon juice. Baste ham during the last 30 minutes of baking. **Yield:** about 20-24 servings.

---

## Phyllo Chicken

### (Pictured on page 52)

*Some years ago I found this recipe and streamlined it to fit our family. The broccoli adds a lot to the rich flavor. Phyllo is fun to work with, and its flakiness turns standard ingredients into a special, satisfying entree.*
*—Joyce Mummau, Mt. Airy, Maryland*

1/2 cup butter *or* margarine, melted, *divided*
 12 sheets phyllo pastry dough
 3 cups diced cooked chicken
1/2 pound bacon, cooked and crumbled
 1 package (10 ounces) frozen chopped broccoli, thawed and drained
 2 cups (8 ounces) shredded cheddar *or* Swiss cheese
 6 eggs
 1 cup half-and-half cream *or* evaporated milk
1/2 cup milk
 1 teaspoon salt
1/2 teaspoon pepper

Brush sides and bottom of a 13-in. x 9-in. x 2-in. baking dish with some of the melted butter. Place one sheet of phyllo in bottom of dish; brush with butter. Repeat with five more sheets of phyllo. (Keep remaining phyllo dough covered with waxed paper to avoid drying out.) In a bowl, combine chicken, bacon, broccoli and cheese; spread evenly over phyllo in baking dish. In another bowl, whisk together eggs, cream, milk, salt and pepper; pour over chicken mixture. Cover filling with one sheet of phyllo; brush with butter. Repeat with remaining phyllo dough. Brush top with remaining butter. Bake, uncovered, at 375° for 35-40 minutes or until a knife inserted near the center comes out clean. **Yield:** 10-12 servings.

— 🍳 🍳 🍳 —

## Popeye Special

*This recipe is a family favorite that I created and named myself. The spinach packs it with a real "Popeye punch".* —*Marcy Cella, L'Anse, Michigan*

- 1 pound ground beef
- 1/2 pound fresh mushrooms, sliced
- 1/2 pound fresh spinach, torn
- 6 green onions, sliced
- 1/4 cup chopped celery
- 1/4 cup chopped sweet red pepper
- 1 teaspoon garlic salt
- 1/2 teaspoon pepper
- 6 eggs, beaten

In a large skillet, brown beef and mushrooms; drain. Add spinach, onions, celery, red pepper, garlic salt and pepper. Cook and stir for 1 minute. Add eggs; cook and stir just until the eggs are set. Serve immediately. **Yield:** 4-6 servings.

— 🍳 🍳 🍳 —

## Lemon-Garlic Grilled Chicken

*When you want something hot without heating up the kitchen, this chicken recipe comes to the rescue.* —*Donna Leuw, Calgary, Alberta*

☑ Uses less fat, sugar or salt. Includes Nutritional Analysis and Diabetic Exchanges.

- 4 boneless skinless chicken breast halves (1 pound)
- 2 tablespoons lemon juice
- 2 teaspoons olive *or* vegetable oil
- 1 garlic clove, minced
- 1/2 teaspoon dried oregano
- 1/8 teaspoon cayenne pepper

Place chicken in a resealable plastic bag or shallow glass container. Combine remaining ingredients; pour over chicken. Seal bag or cover container. Refrigerate for at least 20 minutes, turning once. Drain and discard marinade. Grill chicken, uncovered, over medium-hot heat for 12-15 minutes or until the juices run clear, turning once. **Yield:** 4 servings. **Nutritional Analysis:** One serving equals 153 calories, 64 mg sodium, 73 mg cholesterol, trace carbohydrate, 27 gm protein, 4 gm fat. **Diabetic Exchange:** 4 lean meat.

## Pheasant and Wild Rice

### (Pictured above)

*Everyone in my family hunts, so we have an abundance of game. This recipe also works well with wild turkey or grouse and even with chicken if you prefer. I love to make this dish on special occasions and for guests.* —*Debbie McCoic, Hillsboro, Wisconsin*

- 1 can (10-3/4 ounces) condensed cream of mushroom soup, undiluted
- 2 soup cans water
- 3/4 cup chopped onion
- 2-1/2 teaspoons dried parsley flakes
- 2 teaspoons dried oregano
- 2 teaspoons garlic powder
- 1-1/2 teaspoons paprika
- 2 teaspoons salt
- 1 teaspoon pepper
- 6 bacon strips, cut up
- 1 oven cooking bag
- 2 cups uncooked wild rice
- 1/2 pound fresh mushrooms, sliced
- 1 large pheasant, halved *or* 2 small pheasants (about 4 pounds)

In a saucepan, combine first nine ingredients; bring to a boil. Meanwhile, place bacon in an oven cooking bag. Sprinkle rice and mushrooms over bacon. Add pheasant. Pour soup mixture into bag. Seal and slit according to package directions. Bake at 325° for 2 to 2-1/2 hours. **Yield:** 6-8 servings.

# Cabbage for Modern Times

EUROPEAN immigrants brought their favorite stuffed cabbage recipes to the New World in the late 19th century. These two modern ones are from Katherine Stefanovich of Desert Hot Springs, California.

— ▼ ▼ ▼ —

## Hungarian Stuffed Cabbage

1 medium head cabbage
1 can (28 ounces) sauerkraut, *divided*
1/2 pound ground beef
1/2 pound ground pork
1/2 cup long grain rice, cooked
1 teaspoon salt
1/2 teaspoon pepper
1 egg
3 bacon strips, diced
1 cup chopped onion
2 garlic cloves, minced
1 tablespoon Hungarian paprika
1/4 teaspoon cayenne pepper
1 can (16 ounces) diced tomatoes, undrained
1 tablespoon caraway seeds
2 cups water
2 tablespoons all-purpose flour
1 cup (8 ounces) sour cream

Prepare the cabbage leaves as directed below right. Spoon half of sauerkraut into the bottom of a Dutch oven; set aside. In a bowl, combine the beef, pork, rice, salt, pepper and egg. In a saucepan, cook bacon until crisp. Drain on paper towels. In drippings, saute onion and garlic until tender. Add bacon and half of onion mixture to meat mixture; mix well. Place about 3 tablespoons on each cabbage leaf. Roll up, tucking in sides. Place rolls, seam side down, on sauerkraut in Dutch oven. Coarsely chop remaining cabbage leaves; place over rolls. To remaining onion mixture, add paprika, cayenne pepper, tomatoes, caraway seeds, water and remaining sauerkraut. Cook until heated through. Pour over rolls. Cover and bake at 325° for 1 hour and 45 minutes. In a small bowl, gradually stir flour into sour cream. Stir in 1-2 tablespoons hot cooking liquid; mix well. Spoon over rolls. Bake, uncovered, 15-20 minutes longer or until sauce is thickened. **Yield:** 4-6 servings.

## New-World Stuffed Cabbage

1 medium head cabbage
1 can (16 ounces) sauerkraut, *divided*
3 bacon strips, diced
1 cup finely chopped onion
2 garlic cloves, minced
1/4 cup all-purpose flour
1 tablespoon Hungarian paprika
1/4 teaspoon cayenne pepper
1 can (16 ounces) crushed tomatoes
2 cups beef broth
1/2 cup long grain rice, cooked
1 pound ground turkey
2 tablespoons chopped fresh parsley
1 teaspoon salt
1/2 teaspoon pepper
1 egg, beaten

Prepare the cabbage leaves as directed below. Spoon half of sauerkraut into a Dutch oven; set aside. In a heavy saucepan, fry bacon until crisp. Remove to paper towels. In drippings, saute onion and garlic until tender. Remove half to a bowl to cool. To remaining mixture, add flour, paprika and cayenne pepper. Cook and stir for 1-2 minutes. Stir in tomatoes and broth; bring to a boil. Remove from heat; set aside. To cooled onion mixture, add rice, turkey, parsley, salt, pepper, egg and bacon; mix well. Place about 3-4 tablespoons on each leaf. Roll up, tucking in sides. Place rolls, seam side down, on sauerkraut in Dutch oven. Cover with remaining sauerkraut. Chop remaining leaves; place over sauerkraut. Pour tomato mixture over all, adding water to cover if necessary. Cover and bake at 325° for about 2 hours. **Yield:** 4-6 servings.

### Preparing Cabbage Leaves

Remove the core from the head of the cabbage. Place cabbage in a saucepan and cover with water. Bring to a boil; boil until outer leaves loosen from the head. Lift out cabbage; remove softened leaves. Return to boiling water to soften more leaves. Repeat until all leaves are removed. Remove tough center stalk from each leaf. Set aside 12 large leaves for rolls. The remaining leaves will be chopped and added to the filling.

## Chicken Cheese Lasagna

**(Pictured above)**

*This creamy pasta dish gives an old favorite a new twist! Three cheeses and chicken blended with the fresh taste of spinach make it a real crowd pleaser.*
*—Mary Ann Kosmas, Minneapolis, Minnesota*

- 1 medium onion, chopped
- 1 garlic clove, minced
- 1/2 cup butter *or* margarine
- 1/2 cup all-purpose flour
- 1 teaspoon salt
- 2 cups chicken broth
- 1-1/2 cups milk
- 4 cups (16 ounces) shredded mozzarella cheese, *divided*
- 1 cup grated Parmesan cheese, *divided*
- 1 teaspoon dried basil
- 1 teaspoon dried oregano
- 1/2 teaspoon white pepper
- 1 carton (15 ounces) ricotta cheese
- 1 tablespoon minced fresh parsley
- 9 lasagna noodles (8 ounces), cooked and drained
- 2 packages (10 ounces *each*) frozen spinach, thawed and well drained
- 2 cups cubed cooked chicken

In a saucepan, saute onion and garlic in butter until tender. Stir in flour and salt; cook until bubbly. Gradually stir in broth and milk. Bring to a boil, stirring constantly. Boil 1 minute. Stir in 2 cups mozzarella, 1/2 cup Parmesan cheese, basil, oregano and pepper; set aside. In a bowl, combine ricotta cheese, parsley and remaining mozzarella; set aside. Spread one-quarter of the cheese sauce into a greased 13-in. x 9-in. x 2-in. baking dish; cover with one-third of the noodles. Top with half of ricotta mixture, half of spinach and half of chicken. Cover with one-quarter of cheese sauce and one-third of noodles. Repeat layers of ricotta mixture, spinach, chicken and one-quarter cheese sauce. Cover with remaining noodles and cheese sauce. Sprinkle remaining Parmesan cheese over all. Bake at 350°, uncovered, for 35-40 minutes. Let stand 15 minutes. **Yield:** 12 servings.

---

## Lemon Herbed Salmon

**(Pictured below and on front cover)**

*We sometimes send our delicious Washington salmon all the way to Michigan for my sister to use in this family-favorite dish. The tasty topping can be used on other fish, too. Fresh thyme really sparks the flavor.*
*—Perlene Hoekema, Lynden, Washington*

- 2-1/2 cups soft bread crumbs
- 4 garlic cloves, minced
- 1/2 cup chopped fresh parsley
- 6 tablespoons grated Parmesan cheese
- 1/4 cup chopped fresh thyme *or* 1 tablespoon dried thyme
- 2 teaspoons grated lemon peel
- 1/2 teaspoon salt
- 6 tablespoons butter *or* margarine, melted, *divided*
- 1 salmon fillet (3 to 4 pounds)

In a bowl, combine bread crumbs, garlic, parsley, Parmesan cheese, thyme, lemon peel and salt; mix well. Add 4 tablespoons butter and toss lightly to coat; set aside. Pat salmon dry. Place skin side down in a greased baking dish. Brush with remaining butter; cover with crumb mixture. Bake at 350° for 20-25 minutes or until salmon flakes easily with a fork. **Yield:** 8 servings.

## Spicy Tomato Steak

### (Pictured below)

*I came up with this recipe about 30 years ago, after eating a similar dish on vacation in New Mexico. I came home and tried to duplicate it from memory, with delicious results!* —Anne Landers, Louisville, Kentucky

✓ Uses less fat, sugar or salt. Includes Nutritional Analysis and Diabetic Exchanges.

    2 tablespoons vinegar
    1 teaspoon salt
    1 teaspoon pepper
    1 pound round steak, trimmed and cut into 1/4-inch strips
  1/4 cup all-purpose flour
    2 tablespoons olive *or* vegetable oil
    3 medium tomatoes, peeled, cut into wedges and seeded
    2 medium potatoes, peeled and thinly sliced
    2 cans (4 ounces *each*) chopped green chilies
    1 garlic clove, minced
    1 teaspoon dried basil

In a bowl, combine vinegar, salt and pepper; toss with beef. Cover and marinate for 30 minutes; drain. Place flour in a bowl; add beef and toss to coat. In a skillet, cook beef in oil over medium heat for 15-20 minutes or until tender. Add remaining ingredients. Cover and simmer for 20-30 minutes or until the potatoes are tender, stirring occasionally. **Yield:** 6 servings. **Nutritional Analysis:** One serving equals 195 calories, 757 mg sodium, 24 mg cholesterol, 16 gm carbohydrate, 16 gm protein, 8 gm fat. **Diabetic Exchanges:** 2 lean meat, 1 starch, 1/2 fat.

## Liver with Peppers and Onions

*I found the secret to getting my children to eat liver was to start early, before other kids let them know that liver is supposed to be "yucky". This tasty stir-fry has good flavor.* —Naomi Giddis, Grawn, Michigan

  1/2 cup all-purpose flour
    1 teaspoon salt
  1/4 teaspoon pepper
    1 pound liver, cut into bite-size pieces
    4 tablespoons vegetable oil, *divided*
    1 large onion, thinly sliced into rings
    1 medium green pepper, cut into 1-inch pieces
    1 medium sweet red pepper, cut into 1-inch pieces
    1 cup beef broth
    2 tablespoons soy sauce
    1 tablespoon cornstarch
Cooked rice *or* noodles

In a bowl, combine flour, salt and pepper. Add liver; toss to coat. Heat 2 tablespoons oil in a large skillet. Add onion and peppers; cook until crisp-tender. Remove from pan; set aside. Add remaining oil to the skillet. Cook and stir liver for 5-7 minutes or until no pink remains. In a small bowl, combine beef broth, soy sauce and cornstarch; stir into liver. Cook and stir constantly until sauce thickens. Return vegetables to the skillet and cook until heated through. Serve over rice or noodles. **Yield:** 4-6 servings.

---

## Beef Vegetable Stir-Fry

*My family enjoys stir-fries because of their crunch and variety of vegetables. This is a recipe I turn to often— and still get complimented on!* —Cathy Stelbrink, Kampsville, Illinois

✓ Uses less fat, sugar or salt. Includes Nutritional Analysis and Diabetic Exchanges.

    1 pound ground round
    1 medium onion, sliced
    2 garlic cloves, minced
    1 medium green pepper, julienned
    4 ounces fresh mushrooms, sliced
    1 package (16 ounces) frozen stir-fry vegetables, thawed
    1 can (14 ounces) bean sprouts, drained
    1 can (8 ounces) sliced water chestnuts, drained
    1 cup reduced-sodium beef broth
    2 tablespoons cornstarch
  1/4 cup reduced-sodium soy sauce
  3/4 teaspoon ground ginger

In a large skillet, stir-fry the meat until browned; drain. Add onion and garlic; stir-fry 2 minutes. Add green pepper, mushrooms, vegetables, sprouts and water chestnuts. Stir-fry 3-4 minutes or until crisp-tender. Combine broth, cornstarch, soy sauce and ginger; stir into skillet. Bring to a boil; cook for 1 minute. **Yield:** 8 servings. **Nutritional Analysis:** One serving (1 cup) equals 202 calories, 346 mg sodium, 38 mg cholesterol, 11 gm carbohydrate, 16 gm protein, 8 gm fat. **Diabetic Exchanges:** 2 lean meat, 2 vegetable.

## Ham Roll-Ups

*My children came up with the name of this recipe more than 30 years ago. It's my favorite way to use ham. The roll-ups are made like cinnamon buns, only they use baking powder biscuit dough. With their colorful swirls, they look special, too.* —Thelma Jean Young
Nanaimo, British Columbia

2-1/2 cups all-purpose flour
   4 teaspoons baking powder
  1/2 teaspoon salt
  1/3 cup shortening
   1 cup milk
   3 cups cubed fully cooked ham (1/4-inch pieces)
  1/2 cup minced onion
   2 teaspoons ground mustard
**CHEESE SAUCE:**
   2 teaspoons butter *or* margarine
   2 teaspoons all-purpose flour
  1/2 cup milk
   1 teaspoon steak sauce
   1 teaspoon ground mustard
  1/2 teaspoon salt
  1/8 teaspoon pepper
   2 cups (8 ounces) shredded cheddar cheese

In a bowl, combine flour, baking powder and salt. Cut in the shortening until mixture is crumbly. Add milk all at once and stir just until moistened. Turn onto a well-floured surface and knead gently 8-10 times. Roll into a 12-in. x 11-in. rectangle. In a bowl, combine ham, onion and mustard; sprinkle over dough. Starting on the long end, roll up jelly-roll style. Cut into 1-in. slices and place, cut side down, 2 in. apart on a greased baking sheet. Bake at 400° for 12-15 minutes or until golden brown. For sauce, melt butter in a saucepan over medium heat. Stir in flour; gradually add milk. Cook and stir until thickened. Add steak sauce, mustard, salt, pepper and cheese. Stir until melted. Serve with roll-ups. **Yield:** 10 servings.

## Swiss Elk Steak

**(Pictured above)**

*Growing up in Montana, I enjoyed eating elk on a regular basis. You'll find the elk cooks up nice and tender. Plus, it's elegant enough to serve company.*
—Carma Ochse, Bremerton, Washington

   2 pounds elk steak
**All-purpose flour**
   2 tablespoons butter *or* margarine
   1 can (15 ounces) tomato sauce
  1/2 cup beef broth *or* red wine
   2 tablespoons Worcestershire sauce
  1/2 cup diced onion
  1/2 cup diced green pepper
   1 can (2-1/4 ounces) sliced ripe olives, drained
   1 cup sliced fresh mushrooms
  1/2 teaspoon salt
  1/2 teaspoon pepper
   4 slices Swiss cheese, optional
**Cooked noodles**

Dredge the elk steak lightly in flour; shake off any excess. Melt the butter in a large skillet; brown the steak on both sides. Place in a shallow baking pan. Combine the next nine ingredients; pour over the steak. Cover and bake at 350° for 1-1/2 hours or until cooked to desired tenderness. If desired, place cheese over steak before serving. Serve over noodles. **Yield:** 4 servings.

Mix remaining Parmesan cheese with reserved flour mixture; sprinkle over zucchini. Sprinkle paprika on top. Cover and simmer for 25 minutes or until pork chops are tender. **Yield:** 6 servings. **Nutritional Analysis:** One serving equals 279 calories, 638 mg sodium, 78 mg cholesterol, 9 gm carbohydrate, 27 gm protein, 15 gm fat. **Diabetic Exchanges:** 3 meat, 1-1/2 vegetable.

— 🛒 🛒 🛒 —

## Deluxe Potato Ham Bake

*A longtime favorite for potluck dinners is transformed from a side dish to a main dish with the addition of flavorful cubed ham. This one is always one of the first to go. People at the end of the line are disappointed if the pan is empty.* —Diane Wilson Wing
Salt Lake City, Utah

>  2 cans (10-3/4 ounces *each*) condensed
>  cream of chicken soup, undiluted
>  4 tablespoons butter *or* margarine
>  1 cup (8 ounces) sour cream
>  1-1/2 cups (6 ounces) shredded cheddar cheese
>  1 medium onion, chopped
>  2 cups cubed fully cooked ham
>  1 package (32 ounces) frozen Southern-
>  style hash brown potatoes, thawed
>  **TOPPING:**
>  4 tablespoons butter *or* margarine
>  3/4 cup crushed cornflakes

In a large bowl, combine first five ingredients; mix well. Stir in ham and potatoes. Spread into a greased 13-in. x 9-in. x 2-in. baking dish. Combine topping ingredients; sprinkle over casserole. Bake, uncovered, at 350° for 1 hour or until potatoes are tender. **Yield:** 10-12 servings.

— 🛒 🛒 🛒 —

## Stuffed Chicken Breasts

*The blend of fresh vegetables and rice tucked inside the chicken is fabulous. It's hard to believe this dish is low in fat.* —Jamie Harris, Bodega, California

✓ Uses less fat, sugar or salt. Includes Nutritional Analysis and Diabetic Exchanges.

>  4 boneless skinless chicken breast halves
>  1/2 cup diced fresh mushrooms
>  1/2 cup diced green pepper
>  1/4 cup diced onion
>  3 garlic cloves, minced
>  1/4 cup reduced-sodium vegetable *or* chicken
>  broth

## Skillet Pork Chops with Zucchini

**(Pictured above)**

*My husband and I live on a small farm with our two sons. We're always blessed with plenty of zucchini from our garden in summer, so I try lots of different zucchini recipes. This is one of my family's favorites.*
—Diane Banaszak, West Bend, Wisconsin

✓ Uses less fat, sugar or salt. Includes Nutritional Analysis and Diabetic Exchanges.

>  3 tablespoons all-purpose flour
>  5 tablespoons grated Parmesan cheese,
>  *divided*
>  1-1/2 teaspoons salt
>  1/2 teaspoon dill weed
>  1/4 teaspoon pepper
>  6 pork chops (about 3/4 inch thick)
>  1 tablespoon vegetable oil
>  2 medium onions, sliced
>  1/3 cup water
>  3 medium zucchini (about 1 pound), sliced
>  1/2 teaspoon paprika

In a large resealable plastic bag, combine flour, 2 tablespoons Parmesan cheese, salt, dill weed and pepper. Place pork chops in bag and shake to coat; shake off excess flour and reserve. Heat oil in a large skillet over medium-high; brown pork chops on both sides. Reduce heat. Place onion slices on chops. Add water to skillet; cover and simmer for 15 minutes. Place zucchini slices over the onion.

1 cup cooked rice
2 cups crushed cornflakes
1/2 teaspoon garlic powder
1/8 teaspoon cayenne pepper
1 cup fat-free milk

Pound chicken breasts to 1/4-in. thickness and set aside. In a saucepan, combine mushrooms, green pepper, onion, garlic and broth; bring to a boil. Reduce heat and simmer 3 minutes. Remove from the heat; add rice. Mix well and set aside. Combine cornflakes, garlic powder and cayenne pepper; mix well. Set aside. Spoon a fourth of the rice mixture onto the center of each chicken breast. Fold chicken around rice mixture; seal with toothpicks. Dip chicken in milk. Coat all sides with cornflake mixture. Place chicken in a shallow baking dish that has been coated with nonstick cooking spray. Spray tops of chicken with cooking spray. Bake at 375° for 55-60 minutes or until juices run clear. **Yield:** 4 servings. **Nutritional Analysis:** One serving equals 399 calories, 572 mg sodium, 74 mg cholesterol, 55 gm carbohydrate, 34 gm protein, 4 gm fat. **Diabetic Exchanges:** 3 starch, 3 lean meat, 1 vegetable.

---

## Meat Loaf-Stuffed Peppers

*With my husband, who won't eat the same thing twice, I've had to learn to be creative with leftovers. When leftover meat loaf is dressed with homegrown peppers he doesn't know he is really getting yesterday's main course!* —Kim Barker, Richmond, Texas

6 large green peppers
1 jar (27 to 32 ounces) spaghetti sauce *or* 3 cups leftover spaghetti sauce, *divided*
2 cups cubed leftover meat loaf
1 to 1-1/2 cups cooked rice
1/4 cup chopped onion
1/4 cup chopped green pepper
3/4 cup shredded cheddar cheese

Remove the tops and seeds from the green peppers. Immerse peppers in boiling water for 3 minutes; drain. Pour 1 cup of spaghetti sauce into the bottom of a shallow baking dish; set dish aside. In a saucepan, combine the meat loaf, rice, onion, chopped green pepper and remaining spaghetti sauce. Cook and stir over medium-high heat for 5-10 minutes or until heated through. Stuff each pepper with meat loaf mixture; place on sauce in baking dish. Bake, uncovered, at 375° for 15-20 minutes or until heated through. Sprinkle with the cheese and let stand until melted. **Yield:** 6 servings.

## Cranberry Chicken

**(Pictured below)**

*My husband loves chicken when it's nice and moist, like it is in this autumn recipe. I serve it over hot fluffy rice with a salad and warm rolls on the side.* —Dorothy Bateman, Carver, Massachusetts

1/2 cup all-purpose flour
1/2 teaspoon salt
1/4 teaspoon pepper
6 boneless skinless chicken breast halves
1/4 cup butter *or* margarine
1 cup fresh *or* frozen cranberries
1 cup water
1/2 cup packed brown sugar
Dash ground nutmeg
1 tablespoon cider vinegar *or* red wine, optional
Cooked rice

In a shallow dish, combine flour, salt and pepper; dredge chicken. In a skillet, melt butter over medium heat. Brown the chicken on both sides. Remove and keep warm. In the same skillet, add cranberries, water, brown sugar, nutmeg and vinegar if desired. Cook and stir until the cranberries burst, about 5 minutes. Return chicken to skillet. Cover and simmer for 20-30 minutes or until chicken is tender, basting occasionally with the sauce. Serve over rice. **Yield:** 4-6 servings.

# Breakfast & Brunch

***These down-home breakfast main dishes are sure to satisfy even the heartiest of appetites.***

**RISE-AND-SHINE ENTREES.** Clockwise from upper left: Sausage Gravy (p. 82), Morning Mix-Up (p. 83), Baked Peach Pancake (p. 83), Stuffed Apricot French Toast (p. 81), Apple Pecan Pancakes (p. 81), Egg and Sausage Strata (p. 83), Bacon and Cheese Breakfast Pizza (p. 82) and Breakfast Burritos (p. 84).

## Quiche Lorraine

**(Pictured below)**

*Ideal for a brunch or luncheon, this classic recipe highlights a delicious meal. Try serving a wedge with fresh fruit of the season and homemade muffins for a plate that will look as good as the food tastes!*
—Marcy Cella, L'Anse, Michigan

**CRUST:**
- 2 cups sifted unbleached *or* bleached all-purpose flour
- 1/2 teaspoon salt
- 3/4 cup butter-flavored shortening
- 3 to 4 tablespoons cold water

**FILLING:**
- 12 bacon strips, cooked and crumbled
- 4 eggs
- 2 cups half-and-half cream
- 1/4 teaspoon salt
- 1/8 teaspoon ground nutmeg
- 1-1/4 cups shredded Swiss cheese

In a mixing bowl, combine the flour and salt. Cut in the shortening with a pastry blender until the mixture resembles peas. Add water, a little at a time, until the dough comes away from the bowl. Shape the dough into a ball. Divide in half. On a lightly floured surface, roll half of the dough to fit a 9-in. pie plate; transfer to pie plate. Trim and flute the edges. Chill. Wrap the remaining dough; chill or freeze for another use. For the filling, sprinkle the crumbled bacon in the chilled pie crust. In a bowl, beat the eggs, cream, salt and nutmeg. Stir in the cheese. Pour into the crust. Bake at 425° for 15 minutes. Reduce the temperature to 325°; continue to bake for 30-40 minutes or until a knife inserted near the center comes out clean. Let stand 10 minutes before cutting. **Yield:** 6 servings.

## Peanut Butter and Jelly French Toast

*I've always tried to make cooking fun—for myself, my daughters and my grandchildren. If people see you're having a good time, they'll want to join and have fun themselves. Cooking also teaches children the importance of following directions and being organized. This recipe is easy to make and kids really like it.*
—Flo Burtnett, Gage, Oklahoma

- 12 slices bread
- 3/4 cup peanut butter
- 6 tablespoons jelly *or* jam (flavor of your choice)
- 3 eggs
- 3/4 cup milk
- 1/4 teaspoon salt
- 2 tablespoons butter *or* margarine

Spread peanut butter on six slices of bread; spread jelly on other six slices of bread. Put one slice of each together to form sandwiches. In mixing bowl, lightly beat eggs; add milk and salt and mix together. Melt butter in a large skillet over medium heat. Dip sandwiches in egg mixture, coating well. Place in skillet and brown both sides. Serve immediately. **Yield:** 6 servings.

---

## Country Breakfast Cereal

*With this hearty eye-opener, the USA Rice Federation confirms that rice is nice in any meal of the day! It's a delicious alternative to oatmeal. Top it with fresh strawberries, raspberries or blueberries.*

✓ Uses less fat, sugar or salt. Includes Nutritional Analysis and Diabetic Exchanges.

- 3 cups cooked brown rice
- 2 cups milk
- 1/2 cup raisins
- 1 tablespoon butter *or* margarine
- 1 teaspoon ground cinnamon
- 1/8 teaspoon salt

Honey, brown sugar *or* fresh fruit, optional

In a large saucepan, combine rice, milk, raisins, butter, cinnamon and salt. Bring to a boil, stirring occasionally. Reduce heat; cover and simmer for 8-10 minutes or until thickened. If desired, top with honey, brown sugar or fruit. **Yield:** 6 servings. **Nutritional Analysis:** One serving (prepared with fat-free milk and margarine and served plain) equals 197 calories, 110 mg sodium, 1 mg cholesterol, 39 gm carbohydrate, 6 gm protein, 3 gm fat. **Diabetic Exchanges:** 1 starch, 1 fruit, 1/2 skim milk, 1/2 fat.

## Apple Pecan Pancakes

### (Pictured on page 79)

*Apples and pecans add a light crunch to these fluffy pancakes. Because they're easy to prepare and have a nice cinnamon flavor, they make a perfect breakfast, especially on a crisp fall morning.*
—*Renae Moncur, Burley, Idaho*

  1 cup all-purpose flour
  2 tablespoons brown sugar
  2 teaspoons baking powder
1/2 teaspoon salt
1/2 teaspoon ground cinnamon
3/4 cup plus 2 tablespoons milk
  2 eggs, *separated*
  1 teaspoon vanilla extract
1/2 cup finely chopped peeled apple
1/2 cup finely chopped pecans

In a bowl, combine flour, brown sugar, baking powder, salt and cinnamon. Stir in milk, egg yolks and vanilla. Add apple and pecans. Beat egg whites until stiff peaks form; fold into batter. Pour batter by 1/4 cupfuls onto a hot greased griddle or skillet. Turn when bubbles begin to form and the edges are golden. Cook until the second side is golden. **Yield:** 12 pancakes.

—————— 🍴 🍴 🍴 ——————

## Stuffed Apricot French Toast

### (Pictured on page 79)

*In our family, this special recipe is often served for our Christmas Day brunch. I'm always looking for something unique to serve, and this rich, colorful dish certainly fills the bill. It tastes so good!* —*Deb Leland Three Rivers, Michigan*

  1 package (8 ounces) cream cheese, softened
1-1/2 teaspoons vanilla extract, *divided*
1/2 cup finely chopped walnuts
  1 loaf (1-1/2 pounds) French bread
  4 eggs
  1 cup whipping cream
1/2 teaspoon ground nutmeg
  1 jar (12 ounces) apricot preserves
1/2 cup orange juice

In a mixing bowl, beat cream cheese and 1 teaspoon vanilla until fluffy. Stir in nuts; set aside. Cut bread into 1-1/2-in. slices; cut a pocket in the top of each slice. Fill each pocket with about 2 tablespoons of cream cheese mixture. In another bowl, beat eggs, cream, nutmeg and remaining vanilla. Dip both sides of bread into egg mixture, being careful not to squeeze out the filling. Cook on a lightly greased griddle until golden brown on both sides. Place on an ungreased baking sheet; bake at 300° for 20 minutes. Meanwhile, combine preserves and orange juice in a small saucepan; heat through. Drizzle over hot French toast. **Yield:** about 8 servings.

## Oatmeal Waffles

### (Pictured above)

*This recipe can be used to make pancakes as well as waffles. Both are delicious because of their hearty, whole-grain flavor. For a special treat, serve them topped with fruit or a flavored syrup.*
—*Mrs. Francis Stoops, Stoneboro, Pennsylvania*

  2 eggs, beaten
  2 cups buttermilk
  1 cup quick-cooking oats
  1 tablespoon molasses
  1 tablespoon vegetable oil
  1 cup whole wheat flour
1/2 teaspoon salt
  1 teaspoon baking soda
  1 teaspoon baking powder
Milk, optional

In a large bowl, mix eggs and buttermilk. Add oats and mix well. Stir in molasses and oil. Combine flour, salt, baking soda and baking powder; stir into the egg mixture. If batter becomes too thick, thin with a little milk. Pour about 3/4 cup batter onto a greased preheated waffle maker. Bake according to manufacturer's directions. **To make pancakes:** Drop batter by 1/4 cupfuls onto a hot greased griddle. Turn when bubbles begin to form on top of pancake. **Yield:** 5 waffles (7 inches) or about 15 standard-size pancakes.

### Sausage Gravy

**(Pictured above and on page 78)**

*This savory sausage gravy is a specialty among country folks in our area. It's best served over fresh, hot biscuits. It makes a real stick-to-the-ribs dish that we always enjoy and carries a traditional flavor that can showcase locally produced sausage.*
—*Mrs. J. N. Stine, Roanoke, Virginia*

  1 pound sage-flavored bulk pork sausage
  2 tablespoons finely chopped onion
  6 tablespoons all-purpose flour
  1 cup milk
  1/2 teaspoon poultry seasoning
  1/2 teaspoon ground nutmeg
  1/4 teaspoon salt
Dash  Worcestershire sauce
Dash hot pepper sauce
  12 biscuits

Crumble the sausage into a large saucepan; cook over medium-low heat. Add the onion; cook and stir until transparent. Drain, discarding all but 2 tablespoons of drippings. Stir in the flour; cook over medium-low heat about 6 minutes or until mixture bubbles and turns golden. Stir in the milk. Add the seasonings; cook, stirring, until thickened. To serve, slice biscuits and spoon gravy over halves. **Yield:** 4-6 servings.

### Easy Light Pancakes

*Our house is often filled with our kids' friends, and they always seem to be hungry. There are seldom any leftovers when I make these pancakes.*
—*Ernest Foster, Climax, New York*

  1 cup all-purpose flour
  2 tablespoons sugar
  2 tablespoons baking powder
  1/2 teaspoon salt
  1 cup milk
  2 tablespoons vegetable oil
  1 teaspoon vanilla extract

In a large bowl, combine flour, sugar, baking powder and salt. In another bowl, combine milk, oil and vanilla; add to dry ingredients and stir just until moistened. Preheat a lightly greased griddle or skillet. Pour batter by 1/4 cupfuls onto griddle; cook until light brown. Turn and cook other side. Serve immediately with syrup or topping of your choice. **Yield:** 8 pancakes.

### Triple Berry Wake-Up Breakfast

*This scrumptious stuffed French-toast earned "most outstanding" honors in a local berry festival contest. It sure perks up a Sunday morning!*
—*Leandra Holland, Westlake, California*

  1 carton (8 ounces) spreadable strawberry cream cheese
  4 pieces white bread, crusts removed
  1/2 pint fresh strawberries, sliced
  1 egg
  2 tablespoons milk
  1 tablespoon butter *or* vegetable oil
Strawberry syrup *or* confectioners' sugar

Spread some cream cheese on two pieces of bread. Top with sliced berries, making a complete blanket over the cheese. Top each with the remaining bread. In a bowl, beat egg and milk. In a frying pan or griddle, melt butter or heat oil over medium-high. Dip the sandwich in the egg mixture and fry until golden on both sides. Top with strawberry syrup or confectioners' sugar and serve immediately. **Yield:** 2 servings.

### Bacon and Cheese Breakfast Pizza

**(Pictured on page 78)**

*A firefighter shared this recipe with me. It's good for breakfast and even a simple dinner.* —*Dina Davis Madison, Florida*

Pastry for single-crust pie (9 inches)
  1/2 pound bacon, cooked and crumbled
  2 cups (8 ounces) shredded Swiss cheese
  4 eggs

1-1/2 cups (12 ounces) sour cream
2 tablespoons chopped fresh parsley

Roll pastry to fit into a 12-in. pizza pan. Bake at 425° for 5 minutes. Sprinkle bacon and cheese over crust. In a bowl, beat eggs, sour cream and parsley until smooth; pour over pizza. Bake for 20-25 minutes or until pizza is puffy and lightly browned. **Yield**: 6 main-dish or 18 appetizer servings.

---

## Morning Mix-Up

**(Pictured on page 78)**

*This filling dish is super for breakfast or supper. Eggs, cheese, hash browns and ham go well together.*
—Kim Scholting, Springfield, Nebraska

2 cups frozen hash browns
1 cup chopped fully cooked ham
1/2 cup chopped onion
2 tablespoons vegetable oil
6 eggs
Salt and pepper to taste
1 cup (4 ounces) shredded cheddar cheese
Minced fresh chives

In a large skillet, saute potatoes, ham and onion in oil for 10 minutes or until potatoes are tender. In a small bowl, beat eggs, salt and pepper. Add to the skillet; cook, stirring occasionally, until eggs are set. Remove from the heat and gently stir in cheese. Spoon onto a serving platter; sprinkle with chives. **Yield:** 4 servings.

---

## Baked Peach Pancake

**(Pictured on page 79)**

*This pancake makes for a dramatic presentation. I usually take it right from the oven to the table, fill it with peaches and sour cream and serve with bacon or ham. Whenever I go home, my mom (the best cook I know) asks me to make this.*   —Nancy Wilkinson
*Princeton, New Jersey*

2 cups fresh *or* frozen sliced peeled peaches
4 teaspoons sugar
1 teaspoon lemon juice
3 eggs
1/2 cup all-purpose flour
1/2 cup milk
1/2 teaspoon salt
2 tablespoons butter *or* margarine
Ground nutmeg
Sour cream, optional

In a bowl, combine peaches, sugar and lemon juice; set aside. In a mixing bowl, beat eggs until fluffy. Add flour, milk and salt; beat until smooth. Place butter in a 10-in. skillet; bake at 400° for 3-5 minutes or until melted. Immediately pour batter into hot skillet. Bake for 20-25 minutes or until pancake has risen and is puffed all over. Fill with peach slices; sprinkle with nutmeg. Serve immediately with sour cream if desired. **Yield:** 4-6 servings.

---

## Egg and Sausage Strata

**(Pictured below and on page 78)**

*I especially like to make this breakfast dish when we have weekend guests. I fix it the night before, and the next morning I can sit, eat and enjoy our company.*
—Gail Carney, Arlington, Texas

12 slices white bread, crusts removed, cubed
1-1/2 pounds bulk pork sausage
1/3 cup chopped onion
1/4 cup chopped green pepper
1 jar (2 ounces) chopped pimientos, drained
6 eggs
3 cups milk
2 teaspoons Worcestershire sauce
1 teaspoon ground mustard
1/2 teaspoon salt
1/4 teaspoon pepper
1/4 teaspoon dried oregano

Line a greased 13-in. x 9-in. x 2-in. pan with bread cubes; set aside. In a skillet, brown sausage with the onion and green pepper; drain. Stir in pimientos; sprinkle over bread. In a bowl, beat eggs, milk, Worcestershire sauce, mustard, salt, pepper and oregano. Pour over sausage mixture. Cover and refrigerate overnight. Remove from refrigerator 30 minutes before baking. Bake, covered, at 325° for 1 hour and 20 minutes. Uncover and bake 10 minutes longer or until a knife inserted near the center comes out clean. Let stand 10 minutes before serving. **Yield:** 12-15 servings.

## Buttermilk Pecan Waffles

### (Pictured below)

*I like cooking with buttermilk. These nutty, golden waffles are my husband's favorite breakfast, so we enjoy them often. They're as easy to prepare as regular waffles, but their unique taste makes them exceptional.*

*—Edna Hoffman, Hebron, Indiana*

- 2 cups all-purpose flour
- 1 tablespoon baking powder
- 1 teaspoon baking soda
- 1/2 teaspoon salt
- 4 eggs
- 2 cups buttermilk
- 1/2 cup butter *or* margarine, melted
- 3 tablespoons chopped pecans

Combine the flour, baking powder, baking soda and salt; set aside. In a mixing bowl, beat eggs until light. Add buttermilk; mix well. Add dry ingredients and beat until batter is smooth. Stir in butter. Pour about 3/4 cup batter onto a lightly greased preheated waffle iron. Sprinkle with a few pecans. Bake according to manufacturer's directions until golden brown. Repeat until batter and pecans are gone. **Yield:** 7 waffles (about 8 inches each).

## Sausage Quiche

*I started cooking years ago when a back injury kept me home from work for several months. This quiche is a family favorite among young and old alike.*

*—Ernest Foster, Climax, New York*

- 1 package (8 ounces) breakfast sausage links
- 1 unbaked pie pastry (9 inches)
- 1 cup (4 ounces) shredded cheddar cheese
- 4 eggs
- 1 pint whipping cream
- 1/8 to 1/4 teaspoon ground nutmeg

In a skillet, brown sausages until done. Drain and cut into small pieces; place in the bottom of pie shell. Sprinkle with cheese. In a mixing bowl, beat eggs; add cream and nutmeg. Pour over cheese. Bake at 350° for 55-60 minutes or until a knife inserted near the center comes out clean. **Yield:** 6-8 servings.

— 🏆 🏆 🏆 —

## Breakfast Burritos

### (Pictured on page 78)

*I discovered this different recipe at a workshop on holiday breakfasts offered at our church. It was a big hit! It works really well when you're cooking for a crowd. I like to serve salsa or hot sauce with the burritos.*

*—Catherine Allan, Twin Falls, Idaho*

- 1 bag (16 ounces) frozen Southern-style hash browns
- 12 eggs
- 1 large onion, chopped
- 1 green pepper, chopped
- 1/2 pound bulk pork sausage, browned and drained
- 12 flour tortillas (10 inches), warmed
- 3 cups (12 ounces) shredded cheddar cheese

Salsa, optional

In a large skillet, fry hash browns according to package directions; remove and set aside. In a large bowl, beat eggs; add onions and green pepper. Pour into the same skillet; cook and stir until eggs are set. Remove from heat. Add hash browns and sausage; mix gently. Place about 3/4 cup of filling on each tortilla and top with about 1/4 cup cheese. Roll up and place on a greased baking sheet. Bake at 350° for 15-20 minutes or until heated through. Serve with salsa if desired. **Yield:** 12 servings.

### Waffle Iron Maintenance

If you haven't used your waffle iron for a while, use a pastry brush to lightly coat the grids with vegetable oil. Wipe off excess with paper towel. Or spray the grids with nonstick vegetable spray.

## Oat Pancakes

### (Pictured below)

*My daughter brought this recipe home from school one day, and we loved it. Since then, these pancakes have been a regular part of Sunday morning breakfast. We serve them with maple syrup, flavored syrup or applesauce and a big helping of grits.* —Linda Hicks
Pinconning, Michigan

✓ Uses less fat, sugar or salt. Includes Nutritional Analysis and Diabetic Exchanges.

> 1 cup quick-cooking oats
> 1 cup all-purpose flour
> 2 tablespoons sugar
> 2 teaspoons baking powder
> 1 teaspoon salt
> 2 eggs, lightly beaten
> 1-1/2 cups milk
> 1/4 cup vegetable oil
> 1 teaspoon lemon juice

In a mixing bowl, combine oats, flour, sugar, baking powder and salt. Make a well in the center. Combine egg, milk, oil and lemon juice; pour into well and stir just until moistened. Pour batter by 1/4 cupfuls onto a lightly greased hot griddle; turn when bubbles form on top of pancakes. Cook until second side is golden brown. **Yield:** 6 servings. **Nutritional Analysis:** One serving (2 pancakes, prepared with fat-free milk) equals 241 calories, 581 mg sodium, 71 mg cholesterol, 25 gm carbohydrate, 8 gm protein, 12 gm fat. **Diabetic Exchanges:** 1-1/2 starch, 1/2 skim milk, 1 fat.

## Hash Brown Quiche

### (Pictured above)

*We love to have guests stay with us, and this is a great dish to serve for breakfast. To save time in the morning, I sometimes make the hash brown crust and chop the ham, cheese and peppers the night before. As a teacher and farm wife, I'm always looking for easy recipes like this one.*
—Jan Peters
Chandler, Minnesota

> 3 cups frozen loose-pack shredded hash browns, thawed
> 1/3 cup butter *or* margarine, melted
> 1 cup diced fully cooked ham
> 1 cup (4 ounces) shredded cheddar cheese
> 1/4 cup diced green pepper
> 2 eggs
> 1/2 cup milk
> 1/2 teaspoon salt
> 1/4 teaspoon pepper

Press hash browns between paper towel to remove excess moisture. Press into the bottom and up the sides of an ungreased 9-in. pie plate. Drizzle with butter. Bake at 425° for 25 minutes. Combine the ham, cheese and green pepper; spoon over crust. In a small bowl, beat eggs, milk, salt and pepper. Pour over all. Reduce heat to 350°; bake for 25-30 minutes or until a knife inserted near the center comes out clean. Allow to stand for 10 minutes before cutting. **Yield:** 6 servings.

# Breads, Rolls & Muffins

*The wonderful aroma will call
your family to the table
when you serve a basketful
of these tempting baked goods.*

**OVEN-FRESH FAVORITES.** Clockwise from upper left: Angel Biscuits (p. 92), Cinnamon Coffee Cake (p. 91), Feather-Light Muffins (p. 90), Lemon Cheese Braid (p. 94), Apple Raisin Bread (p. 97), Spinach Garlic Bread (p. 93), Chili Relleno Squares (p. 86) and Savory Almond-Buttermilk Biscuits (p. 94).

## Raspberry Lemon Muffins

### (Pictured above)

*These are my all-time favorite muffins, and I have a hard time eating just one!* —Sharon Shine
*Bradford, Pennsylvania*

   2 **cups all-purpose flour**
   1 **cup sugar**
   1 **tablespoon baking powder**
1/2 **teaspoon salt**
   2 **eggs, lightly beaten**
   1 **cup half-and-half cream**
1/2 **cup vegetable oil**
   1 **teaspoon lemon extract**
1-1/2 **cups fresh *or* frozen raspberries**

In a large bowl, combine flour, sugar, baking powder and salt. Combine the eggs, cream, oil and lemon extract; stir into dry ingredients just until moistened. Fold in raspberries. Spoon into 18 greased or paper-lined muffin cups. Bake at 400° for 18-20 minutes or until golden brown. **Yield:** 1-1/2 dozen.

## Finnish Easter Bread

*My friends nicknamed me "The Happy Norwegian of Bear Gulch" because they say I'm always smiling and offering them fresh bread. This is a favorite of my three kids and my grandchildren.* —Ben Middleton
*Walla Walla, Washington*

   3 **packages (1/4 ounce *each*) active dry yeast**
1/2 **cup water (110° to 115°)**
1-1/2 **cups warm half-and-half cream (110° to 115°)**

  6 **to 7 cups all-purpose flour, *divided***
  5 **egg yolks**
  1 **cup sugar**
  1 **cup milk**
  1 **cup butter *or* margarine, melted**
1-1/2 **teaspoons salt**
  2 **teaspoons ground cardamom**
  2 **tablespoons grated orange peel**
  2 **teaspoons grated lemon peel**
  2 **cups rye flour**
  1 **cup golden raisins**
  1 **cup chopped blanched almonds**
**Additional melted butter *or* margarine**

In a mixing bowl, dissolve yeast in water. Stir in cream and 2 cups all-purpose flour; beat until smooth. Cover and let rise in a warm place until doubled, about 1-1/2 hours. Dough will be very soft and spongy in texture. Punch dough down. Stir in egg yolks, sugar, milk, butter, salt, cardamon and orange and lemon peel. Beat until thoroughly combined. Stir in rye flour until well blended. Stir in raisins and almonds; mix well. By hand, add enough remaining all-purpose flour to form a stiff dough. Turn out onto a lightly floured surface; knead until smooth and elastic, about 6-8 minutes. Place in a greased bowl, turning once to grease top. Cover and let rise in a warm place until doubled, about 1 to 1-1/2 hours. Punch dough down; shape into a smooth ball. Divide into two pieces. Place each piece into a greased 9-in. x 5-in. x 3-in. loaf pan. Cover and let rise in a warm place, about 45 minutes. Do not let breads rise over top of pans. Bake at 350° for 55-60 minutes or until breads sound hollow when tapped. Cover breads loosely with foil during last 15 minutes if tops are browning too fast. Remove from oven; brush tops with melted butter. Let cool in pans about 20 minutes; remove to cool on wire racks. **Yield:** 2 loaves.

## Winter Squash Bread

*One year, my son asked me to bake this bread for his birthday rather than a cake, saying he liked it better! Nowadays, our grandchildren relish each slice.*
—Audrey Thibodeau, Gilbert, Arizona

  2 **packages (1/4 ounce *each*) active dry yeast**
  1 **cup warm milk (110° to 115°)**
  4 **to 5 cups all-purpose flour**
  2 **cups whole wheat flour**
  2 **cups mashed winter squash**
1/4 **cup sugar**
  2 **tablespoons butter *or* margarine, softened**
  2 **teaspoons salt**

# Muffins Are Quick to Please

MAKING muffins from scratch used to be too much bother for Katrina Shaner of Stronghorst, Illinois. Then her sister passed along the recipe for Quick Muffin Mix. "These are as fast and easy as a box mix, but better," Katrina says. "The Blueberry Muffins are so fruity, my family adores them."

## Quick Muffin Mix

2-1/2 cups all-purpose flour
2-1/2 cups whole wheat flour
   1 cup wheat bran cereal
   1 cup quick-cooking oats
1-1/2 cups sugar
   2 tablespoons baking powder
   2 teaspoons salt

Combine all ingredients in a large airtight container. Store at room temperature until ready to use. Stir well before measuring for the muffin recipe at right. **Yield:** about 6 cups.

## Blueberry Muffins

   3 cups Quick Muffin Mix (recipe at left)
   2 tablespoons brown sugar
   1 teaspoon ground cinnamon
1-1/4 cups fresh *or* frozen blueberries
   1 cup milk
   2 eggs
  1/4 cup applesauce
   1 teaspoon vanilla extract

In a mixing bowl, combine first three ingredients. Stir in blueberries. In another bowl, beat milk, eggs, applesauce and vanilla. Stir into blueberry mixture just until moistened. Fill greased or paper-lined muffin cups two-thirds full. Bake at 425° for 15-18 minutes or until muffins test done. Cool in pan 10 minutes before removing to a wire rack. **Yield:** about 1 dozen.

---

In a large mixing bowl, dissolve yeast in warm milk. Add 2 cups all-purpose flour, whole wheat flour, squash, sugar, butter and salt; beat until smooth. Add enough remaining all-purpose flour to form a soft dough. Turn out onto a floured surface; knead until smooth and elastic, about 6-8 minutes. Place in a greased bowl, turning once to grease top. Cover and let rise in a warm place until doubled, about 1 hour. Punch the dough down. Divide into two pieces. Place each into a greased 9-in. x 5-in. x 3-in. loaf pan. Cover and let rise until doubled, about 1 hour. Bake at 375° for 30-35 minutes. Remove from pans to cool on wire racks. **Yield:** 2 loaves.

🥤 🥤 🥤

## Chili Corn Muffins

### (Pictured at right)

*Hot corn bread was one of my childhood favorites. This muffin version has a Southwest flavor that I devised.* —Sarah Hovley, Santa Cruz, California

2-1/2 cups all-purpose flour
   1 cup yellow cornmeal
  1/4 cup sugar
   5 teaspoons baking powder
1-1/2 teaspoons salt
   1 teaspoon chili powder
   2 eggs

1-1/2 cups milk
  2/3 cup vegetable oil
  1/2 cup finely chopped onion
   1 can (4 ounces) chopped green chilies, drained

In a large bowl, combine flour, cornmeal, sugar, baking powder, salt and chili powder. In a small bowl, beat the eggs; add milk, oil, onion and chilies. Stir into dry ingredients just until moistened. Fill greased or paper-lined muffin cups two-thirds full. Bake at 400° for 20-25 minutes or until muffins test done. **Yield:** about 1-1/2 dozen.

## Feather-Light Muffins

**(Pictured below and on page 87)**

*Your family will likely gobble up these airy muffins, which won me a blue ribbon at our county fair! Pretty as well as tasty, their hint of spice will brighten breakfast, brunch or lunch for family or company.*
*—Sonja Blow, Groveland, California*

>     1/3  cup shortening
>     1/2  cup sugar
>       1  egg
>   1-1/2  cups cake flour
>   1-1/2  teaspoons baking powder
>     1/2  teaspoon salt
>     1/4  teaspoon ground nutmeg
>     1/2  cup milk
> TOPPING:
>     1/2  cup sugar
>       1  teaspoon ground cinnamon
>     1/2  cup butter *or* margarine, melted

In a mixing bowl, cream shortening, sugar and egg. Combine dry ingredients; add to creamed mixture alternately with milk. Fill greased muffin cups two-thirds full. Bake at 325° for 20-25 minutes or until golden. Let cool for 3-4 minutes. Meanwhile, combine sugar and cinnamon in a small bowl. Roll warm muffins in melted butter, then in sugar mixture. Serve warm. **Yield:** 8-10 muffins.

## Cinnamon Rolls

*My wife likes to tell people that after I retired, I went from being the breadwinner to the bread baker! It all started with a bread-making class at a nearby community college. Now my breads and rolls are favorites of friends and family.*
*—Ben Middleton*
*Walla Walla, Washington*

>       2  packages (1/4 ounce *each*) active dry
>          yeast
>     1/2  cup sugar, *divided*
>       1  cup water (110° to 115°)
>       1  cup milk
>       6  tablespoons butter *or* margarine
>       7  to 7-1/2 cups all-purpose flour
>       3  eggs, beaten
>       1  teaspoon salt
> FILLING:
>     1/4  cup butter *or* margarine, softened
>       5  teaspoons ground cinnamon
>     3/4  cup packed brown sugar
>     3/4  cup raisins *or* currants
> Confectioners' sugar icing, optional

In a large mixing bowl, dissolve yeast and 1 tablespoon sugar in water. In a saucepan, heat milk and butter to 110°-115°; add to yeast mixture. Stir in 3 cups flour, eggs, salt and remaining sugar. Stir in enough remaining flour to form a soft dough. Turn out onto a lightly floured surface; knead until smooth and elastic, about 6-8 minutes. Place in a greased bowl, turning once to grease top. Cover and let rise in a warm place until doubled, about 1 hour. Punch dough down and divide in half. Roll each half into a 15-in. x 12-in. rectangle. Brush with softened butter. Combine cinnamon, sugar and raisins or currants; sprinkle evenly over each rectangle. Roll up tightly, jelly-roll style, starting with the long side. Slice each roll into 12 pieces. Place in two greased 13-in. x 9-in. x 2-in. baking pans. Cover and let rise until doubled, about 30 minutes. Bake at 350° for 25-30 minutes or until golden brown. Cool in pans for 5 minutes; invert onto a wire rack. Frost with icing if desired. Serve warm. **Yield:** 2 dozen.

## Rosemary Raisin Bread

*On a whim, I decided to add rosemary to my favorite raisin bread recipe. My family and I were really happy with the result. This bread is very tasty toasted.*
*—Clarice Schweitzer, Sun City, Arizona*

>       1  package (1/4 ounce) active dry yeast
>     1/4  cup warm water (110° to 115°)
>       3  cups all-purpose flour

1/2 cup warm milk (110° to 115°)
1/4 cup olive _or_ vegetable oil
  3 tablespoons sugar
  1 teaspoon dried rosemary, crushed
  1 teaspoon salt
  1 egg plus 1 egg white
1/2 cup raisins
GLAZE:
Olive _or_ vegetable oil
  1 egg yolk
  1 tablespoon water

In a large mixing bowl, dissolve the yeast in warm water. Let stand for 5 minutes. Add 1 cup of the flour, milk, oil, sugar, rosemary, salt, egg and egg white. Beat on low for about 30 seconds. Increase speed to medium and continue beating for 2 minutes. Stir in the raisins and remaining flour. Turn out onto a floured surface; knead until smooth and elastic, about 6-8 minutes. Place in a greased bowl, turning once to grease top. Cover and let rise in a warm place until doubled, about 1 hour. Punch down and shape into a flat 8-1/2-in. round. Place on a greased baking sheet; brush with olive oil. Cover and let rise until doubled, about 30 minutes. With a sharp knife, cut a cross in the top of the loaf. Combine the egg yolk with water and brush over loaf. Bake at 350° for 35 minutes or until golden brown. **Yield:** 1 loaf.

## Honey Muffins

_These basic muffins from the National Honey Board become extraordinary with the addition of honey and orange juice. The moist morsels are terrific for breakfast or snacking._

  2 cups all-purpose flour
1/4 cup sugar
  2 teaspoons baking powder
  1 teaspoon baking soda
1/2 teaspoon salt
  2 eggs
1/2 cup honey
1/2 cup orange juice
1/3 cup butter _or_ margarine, melted
  1 teaspoon vanilla extract

In a large bowl, combine flour, sugar, baking powder, baking soda and salt; set aside. In a mixing bowl, beat eggs. Add honey, orange juice, butter and vanilla; mix well. Stir into dry ingredients just until moistened. Fill 12 greased muffin cups two-thirds full. Bake at 375° for 15-20 minutes or until golden. **Yield:** 1 dozen.

## Cinnamon Coffee Cake

**(Pictured above and on page 86)**

_I love the texture of this old-fashioned, streusel-topped coffee cake. Always a crowd pleaser, its sweet vanilla flavor enriched by sour cream may remind you of breakfast at Grandma's!_     —Eleanor Harris
Cape Coral, Florida

    1 cup butter _or_ margarine, softened
2-3/4 cups sugar, _divided_
    2 teaspoons vanilla extract
    4 eggs
    3 cups all-purpose flour
    2 teaspoons baking powder
    1 teaspoon baking soda
    1 teaspoon salt
    2 cups (16 ounces) sour cream
    2 tablespoons ground cinnamon
  1/2 cup chopped walnuts

In a large mixing bowl, cream the butter and 2 cups sugar until fluffy. Add the vanilla. Add the eggs, one at a time, beating well after each addition. Combine the flour, baking powder, baking soda and salt; add alternately with sour cream, beating just enough after each addition to keep batter smooth. Spoon one-third of the batter into a greased 10-in. tube pan. Combine the cinnamon, nuts and remaining sugar; sprinkle one-third over batter in pan. Repeat layers two more times. Bake at 350° for 70 minutes or until cake tests done. Cool for 10 minutes. Remove from pan to a wire rack to cool completely. **Yield:** 16-20 servings.

ter. Place on a lightly greased baking sheet. Cover; let rise in a warm place about 1-1/2 hours. Bake at 450° for 8-10 minutes. Brush tops with melted butter. **Yield:** about 2-1/2 dozen.

---

## Garlic-Parmesan Rolls

*Frozen bread dough gives a head start to these yummy, fresh-from-the-oven dinner rolls. My family adores them.* —Loretta Ruda, Kennesaw, Georgia

> 1 loaf (1 pound) frozen bread dough, thawed
> 6 tablespoons grated Parmesan cheese
> 1 teaspoon garlic powder
> 1/2 cup butter *or* margarine, melted

Cut bread dough into 16 pieces; shape into balls. Place pieces on a floured surface; cover and let rise in a warm place for 10 minutes. In a bowl, stir Parmesan cheese and garlic powder into butter. Using a spoon, roll balls in butter mixture; arrange loosely in a 9-in. round baking pan. Cover and let rise in a warm place until doubled. Bake at 375° for 10-15 minutes or until golden brown. Warm leftover butter mixture; when rolls are baked, pull them apart and dip them again. Serve warm. **Yield:** 16 rolls.

---

## Kiwifruit Danish

*Kiwi has a distinct sweet-tart taste that's like no other fruit. My husband and I grow it on vines that look like giant grapevines. Not only is it delicious, it's high in Vitamin C and potassium. Kiwifruit Danish are an easy, attractive treat.* —Debbie Shick, McFarland, California

> 1 package (3 ounces) refrigerated crescent rolls
> 1 package (3 ounces) cream cheese, softened
> 1 egg yolk
> 2 tablespoons sugar
> 1/2 teaspoon almond extract
> 1/2 cup apricot jam
> 2 to 3 kiwifruit, pared and sliced

Unroll crescent roll dough and shape into eight triangles with equal sides. Combine cream cheese, egg yolk, sugar and almond extract; blend well. Place 1 tablespoon cream cheese mixture in center of each triangle; top with kiwifruit slice. Pull points of triangle to center and pinch to seal. Bake on

## Angel Biscuits

**(Pictured above and on page 86)**

*I first received a sample of these light, wonderful biscuits, along with the recipe, from an elderly gentleman friend. I now bake them often as a Saturday-morning treat, served with butter and honey. They're perfect with sausage gravy, too.* —Faye Hintz, Springfield, Missouri

> 2 packages (1/4 ounce *each*) active dry yeast
> 1/4 cup warm water (110° to 115°)
> 2 cups warm buttermilk (110° to 115°)
> 5 cups all-purpose flour
> 1/3 cup sugar
> 2 teaspoons baking powder
> 1 teaspoon baking soda
> 2 teaspoons salt
> 1 cup shortening
> Melted butter *or* margarine

Dissolve yeast in warm water. Let stand 5 minutes. Stir in the buttermilk; set aside. In a large mixing bowl, combine flour, sugar, baking powder, baking soda and salt. Cut in shortening with a pastry blender until crumbly. Stir in yeast/buttermilk mixture; mix well. Turn out onto a lightly floured surface; knead lightly 3-4 times. Roll to a 1/2-in. thickness. Cut with a 2-1/2-in. biscuit cut-

greased baking sheet at 375° for 12-15 minutes or until golden brown. Cool on rack. Heat jam. Top each Danish with another kiwifruit slice; brush with jam. **Yield:** 8 servings.

— 🍴 🍴 🍴 —

## Potato Herb Bread

_Everyone agrees my garden-fresh chives add fabulous flavor to this moist and tasty bread. Plus, the green flecks are quite pretty._ —Carol Mead
_Los Alamos, New Mexico_

   2 packages (1/4 ounce _each_) active dry
        yeast
   2 tablespoons plus 1 teaspoon sugar,
        _divided_
 1/2 cup warm water (110° to 115°)
   1 can (10-3/4 ounces) condensed cream
        of potato soup, undiluted
   1 cup hot water
 1/2 cup nonfat dry milk powder
 1/2 cup sour cream
 1/2 cup snipped fresh chives
   2 tablespoons butter _or_ margarine, melted
   2 teaspoons salt
   1 teaspoon dried tarragon
   6 to 6-1/2 cups all-purpose flour

In a small bowl, dissolve yeast and 1 teaspoon sugar in warm water. Let stand for 5 minutes. In a large mixing bowl, combine soup and hot water. Stir in yeast mixture, milk powder, sour cream, chives, butter, salt, tarragon and remaining sugar. Mix well. Add enough flour to form a stiff dough. Turn dough onto a floured surface; knead until smooth and elastic, about 6-8 minutes. Place in a greased bowl, turning once to grease top. Cover and let rise in a warm place until doubled, about 1 hour. Punch dough down. Divide in half. Shape into two loaves and place in greased 9-1/4-in. x 5-1/4-in. x 2-3/4-in. loaf pans. Cover and let rise until doubled, about 30 minutes. Bake at 400° for 30 minutes or until golden. **Yield:** 2 loaves.

— 🍴 🍴 🍴 —

## Spinach Garlic Bread

### (Pictured at right and on page 86)

_I don't do as much cooking now as I did when my six children were growing up. I've found that this bread makes a nice appetizer and goes great with any Italian meal. Try it with a soup and salad, too._
  —Ruby Williams, Bogalusa, Louisiana

   1 loaf French _or_ Italian bread (about
        1 pound)
   1 medium onion, chopped
   2 garlic cloves, minced
   3 tablespoons olive _or_ vegetable oil
   1 package (10 ounces) frozen chopped
        spinach, thawed and well drained
   1 tablespoon grated Parmesan cheese
   1 teaspoon Italian seasoning
 1/2 teaspoon fennel seed, crushed
   1 large tomato, chopped and seeded
 1-1/2 cups (6 ounces) shredded mozzarella
        cheese
   1 tablespoon dried basil
**Chopped fresh parsley, optional**

Cut bread in half lengthwise. Place with cut side up on a baking sheet; set aside. In a skillet, saute onion and garlic in oil until tender. Add spinach and stir until heated through, about 1 minute. Remove from the heat. Stir in Parmesan cheese, Italian seasoning and fennel seed; mix well. Spread evenly over bread halves. Sprinkle with tomato, mozzarella and basil. Bake at 400° for 8-10 minutes or until cheese is melted. Garnish with parsley if desired. Cut into slices and serve immediately. **Yield:** 8-10 servings.

eggs, salt and 2 cups flour; beat on low speed for 3 minutes. Stir in enough of the remaining flour to form a soft dough. Turn out onto a floured surface; knead until smooth and elastic, about 6-8 minutes. Place in a greased bowl, turning once to grease top. Cover and let rise in a warm place until doubled, about 1 hour. Meanwhile, beat filling ingredients in a mixing bowl until fluffy; set aside. Punch dough down. On a floured surface, roll into a 14-in. x 12-in. rectangle. Place on a greased baking sheet. Spread filling down center third of rectangle. On each long side, cut 1-in.-wide strips, 3 in. into center. Starting at one end, fold alternating strips at an angle across filling. Seal end. Cover and let rise for 30 minutes. Bake at 375° for 25-30 minutes or until golden brown. Cool. Combine icing ingredients; drizzle over bread. **Yield:** 12-14 servings.

---

## Lemon Cheese Braid

**(Pictured above and on page 87)**

*This recipe came from my mom, who is an excellent cook. It always gets rave reviews. Although fairly simple to make, when you finish you'll feel a sense of accomplishment because it tastes delicious and looks so impressive.* —Grace Dickey, Vernonia, Oregon

> 1 package (1/4 ounce) active dry yeast
> 3 tablespoons warm water (110° to 115°)
> 1/4 cup sugar
> 1/3 cup milk
> 1/4 cup butter *or* margarine, melted
> 2 eggs
> 1/2 teaspoon salt
> 3 to 3-1/2 cups all-purpose flour
> FILLING:
> 2 packages (one 8 ounces, one 3 ounces) cream cheese, softened
> 1/2 cup sugar
> 1 egg
> 1 teaspoon grated lemon peel
> ICING:
> 1/2 cup confectioners' sugar
> 2 to 3 teaspoons milk
> 1/4 teaspoon vanilla extract

In a mixing bowl, dissolve yeast in warm water; let stand for 5 minutes. Add sugar, milk, butter,

## Savory Almond-Buttermilk Biscuits

**(Pictured on page 86)**

*Chock-full of almonds, these biscuits are an updated version of a Southern classic. With their crunchy character, they always garnered praise from patrons at Dairy Hollow House, the inn I ran with my husband, Ned. The inn is now a non-profit retreat for writers. It provides them with the solitude they need to create.* —Crescent Dragonwagon, Eureka Springs, Arkansas

> 3 tablespoons butter *or* margarine, ***divided***
> 1 small onion, finely chopped
> 2 garlic cloves, minced
> 2 cups all-purpose flour
> 1 tablespoon baking powder
> 1 teaspoon salt
> 1/2 teaspoon baking soda
> 1/3 cup shortening
> 1 cup buttermilk
> 1/2 cup coarsely chopped almonds, toasted
> 2 tablespoons minced fresh parsley
> 1-1/2 teaspoons minced fresh sage *or* 1/2 teaspoon dried sage
> 1-1/2 teaspoons minced fresh rosemary *or* 1/2 teaspoon dried rosemary, crushed
> 1-1/2 teaspoons minced fresh thyme *or* 1/2 teaspoon dried thyme

In a skillet, melt 1 tablespoon butter; saute the onion and garlic until tender, about 5 minutes. Cool completely. Combine the flour, baking powder, salt and baking soda. Cut in shortening until crumbly. Add the buttermilk, almonds, parsley, sage, rosemary, thyme and onion mixture; stir just until mixed. Turn out onto a floured surface; knead lightly for 1 minute. On a floured surface, roll the dough to 1/2-in. thickness. Cut with a 2-in. round biscuit cutter. Place on an ungreased baking sheet. Bake at 450° for 10-15 minutes or until golden brown. Melt the remaining butter and brush on warm biscuits. **Yield:** 1 dozen.

— ▼ ▼ ▼ —

## Blueberry Oat Muffins

*Everyone gets "the blues" now and then. To bring back smiles, I always prescribe delicious blueberries. My husband, Dave, and I grow the berries, and I often share our favorite recipes, such as this one, with customers at our roadside market.* —Connie Sanders
*Belle River, Prince Edward Island*

    1 cup quick-cooking oats
    1 cup sour milk*
    1 cup all-purpose flour
  3/4 cup packed brown sugar
    1 teaspoon baking powder
  1/2 teaspoon baking soda
  1/2 teaspoon salt
    1 egg, beaten
  1/4 cup butter *or* margarine, melted
    1 cup fresh blueberries

In a bowl, combine oats and milk; let stand a few minutes. In another bowl, combine flour, brown sugar, baking powder, baking soda and salt; mix well. Stir egg and butter into oat mixture. Add oat mixture all at once to dry ingredients. Stir just until moistened. Gently fold in blueberries. Fill well-greased muffin tins 3/4 full. Bake at 400° for 15-20 minutes. **Yield:** 12 muffins. **\*Editor's Note:** To sour milk, place 1 tablespoon white vinegar in a measuring cup; add enough milk to equal 1 cup.

— ▼ ▼ ▼ —

## Grandma Russell's Bread

### (Pictured at right)

*I remember as a child always smelling fresh homemade bread and rolls whenever I walked into Grandma's house. The warm slices were delicious and melted in my mouth!* —Janet Polito, Nampa, Idaho

    1 package (1/4 ounce) active dry yeast
  1/3 cup warm water (110° to 115°)
  1/2 cup sugar, *divided*
    1 cup milk
  1/2 cup butter *or* margarine
    1 tablespoon salt

    1 cup mashed potatoes
    2 eggs, beaten
  5 to 6 cups all-purpose flour
**CINNAMON FILLING:**
  1/4 cup butter *or* margarine, melted
  3/4 cup sugar
    1 tablespoon ground cinnamon

In a large bowl, combine yeast, warm water and 1 teaspoon sugar; set aside. In a saucepan, heat milk, butter, salt and remaining sugar until butter melts. Remove from the heat; stir in potatoes until smooth. Cool to lukewarm; add eggs and mix well. To yeast mixture add the potato mixture and 5 cups flour. Stir in enough remaining flour to form a soft dough. Turn out onto a floured surface; knead until smooth and elastic, about 6-8 minutes. Place in a greased bowl, turning once to grease top. Cover and let rise in a warm place until doubled, about 1-1/2 hours. Punch down and divide in half. **For white bread:** Shape two loaves and place in greased 8-1/2-in. x 4-1/2-in. x 2-1/2-in. loaf pans. **For cinnamon bread:** Roll each half into a 16-in. x 8-in. rectangle. Brush with melted butter; combine sugar and cinnamon and sprinkle over butter. Starting at the narrow end, roll up into a loaf, sealing the edges and ends. Place in greased 8-1/2-in. x 4-1/2-in. x 2-1/2-in. loaf pans. **For cinnamon rolls:** Roll each half into an 18-in. x 12-in. rectangle. Brush with melted butter; sprinkle with cinnamon-sugar. Starting at the narrow end, roll up and seal edges and ends. Cut each into 12 pieces of 1-1/2 in. Place in greased 9-in. round baking pans. **To bake:** Cover and let rise until doubled. Bake loaves at 375° for 20 minutes; bake rolls at 375° for 25-30 minutes. Cover with foil if they brown too quickly. **Yield:** 2 loaves or 2 dozen rolls.

## Corny Onion Shortcake

*Corn cakes are a family tradition that dates back to my grandmother. I serve this onion shortcake instead of a vegetable side dish. Everyone loves it.* —Carol Mead
Los Alamos, New Mexico

- 1/4 cup butter *or* margarine
- 1 large sweet onion, finely chopped
- 1-1/2 cups corn muffin mix
- 1 egg
- 1/3 cup milk
- 1 cup cream-style corn
- 1 cup (8 ounces) sour cream
- 1/2 teaspoon salt
- 1 cup (4 ounces) shredded cheddar cheese, *divided*

In a skillet, melt butter over medium heat. Saute onion until tender. Remove from heat; set aside. In a bowl, combine muffin mix, egg, milk and corn. Spread into a greased 9-in. baking pan. Combine sour cream, sauteed onion, salt and half the cheddar cheese; spread over batter. Sprinkle with remaining cheese. Bake at 425° for 30 minutes. Cut into squares; serve warm. **Yield:** 9 servings.

---

## Chili Relleno Squares

**(Pictured below and on page 86)**

*My family requests these squares regularly. They're easy to prepare and make a nice complement to a Mexican or Spanish meal. They're like an extra-cheesy version of corn bread.* —Fran Carll
Long Beach, California

- 3 cups (12 ounces) shredded Monterey Jack cheese
- 1-1/2 cups (6 ounces) shredded cheddar cheese
- 2 cans (4 ounces *each*) chopped green chilies, drained
- 2 eggs
- 2 tablespoons milk
- 1 tablespoon all-purpose flour

Layer both cheeses and the chilies in a greased 8-in. square baking dish, starting and ending with cheese. In a bowl, beat the eggs. Add the milk and flour; pour over cheese. Bake at 375° for 30 minutes or until set. Cut into small squares. Serve warm. **Yield:** 16 servings.

---

## Parmesan Herb Bread

*This zesty bread was an experiment that ended up winning grand prize in a local baking contest. The herbs really add a savory filling.* —Audrey Thibodeau
Gilbert, Arizona

- 2-1/4 cups water
- 3/4 cup butter *or* margarine, *divided*
- 6 to 7 cups all-purpose flour
- 2 packages (1/4 ounce *each*) active dry yeast
- 2 tablespoons sugar
- 1 teaspoon salt

**FILLING:**
- 1/2 cup grated Parmesan cheese
- 2 tablespoons dried chives
- 2 tablespoons dried parsley flakes
- 1 teaspoon garlic powder
- 1/2 teaspoon dried savory
- 1/2 teaspoon dried thyme

Cornmeal

In a saucepan, heat water and 1/4 cup butter to 120°-130°. In a large bowl, combine 3 cups flour, yeast, sugar and salt. Add water mixture and beat until smooth. Add enough remaining flour to form a soft dough. Turn out onto a floured surface; knead until smooth and elastic, about 6-8 minutes. Place in a greased bowl, turning once to grease top. Cover and let rise in a warm place until doubled, about 1 hour. Punch dough down and divide in half; roll each half into an 18-in. x 15-in. rectangle. Soften remaining butter; spread on rectangles. In a small bowl, combine first six filling ingredients; sprinkle over butter. Starting at the wide end, roll up each rectangle into a loaf, sealing edges and ends. Sprinkle two ungreased baking sheets with cornmeal; place the loaves with seam side down on cornmeal. Use a knife to cut five slashes in the top of each loaf; sprinkle with cornmeal. Cover and let rise until doubled, about 1 hour. Bake at 375° for 15 minutes. Reduce heat to 350°; bake 20-25 minutes longer. Serve warm or cold. **Yield:** 2 loaves.

— 🎺 🎺 🎺 —

## Cinnamon Mini Muffins

*These mini muffins are wonderful with a bowl of fresh fruit for breakfast or as an anytime snack.*
—*Bonni Larson, New Berlin, Wisconsin*

✓ Uses less fat, sugar or salt. Includes Nutritional Analysis and Diabetic Exchanges.

1-1/2 cups all-purpose flour
  1/2 cup sugar
    2 teaspoons baking powder
  1/2 teaspoon salt
  1/2 teaspoon ground nutmeg
  1/2 teaspoon ground allspice
    1 egg, lightly beaten
  1/2 cup fat-free milk
  1/3 cup margarine, melted
**TOPPING:**
    2 tablespoons sugar
  1/2 teaspoon ground cinnamon
  1/4 cup margarine, melted

In a large bowl, combine flour, sugar, baking powder, salt, nutmeg and allspice. Combine the egg, milk and margarine; mix well. Stir into dry ingredients just until moistened. Spoon into greased or paper-lined mini muffin cups. Bake at 400° for 12-14 minutes or until muffins test done. For topping, combine sugar and cinnamon. Brush the tops of warm muffins with margarine; sprinkle with cinnamon-sugar. **Yield:** 2 dozen. **Nutritional Analysis:** One serving (one muffin) equals 96 calories, 128 mg sodium, 9 mg cholesterol, 12 gm carbohydrate, 1 gm protein, 5 gm fat.

— 🎺 🎺 🎺 —

## Apple Raisin Bread

**(Pictured above right and on page 86)**

*I've been making this bread for many years. It smells so good in the oven and tastes even better. I make bread almost every Saturday, and it doesn't stay around long with our sons home from college in the summer.*
—*Perlene Hoekema, Lynden, Washington*

    2 packages (1/4 ounce *each*) active dry yeast
1-1/2 cups warm water (110° to 115°), *divided*

    1 teaspoon sugar
    3 eggs, beaten
    1 cup applesauce
  1/2 cup honey
  1/2 cup vegetable oil
    2 teaspoons salt
    8 to 9 cups all-purpose flour
1-1/2 cups diced peeled tart apples
    2 tablespoons lemon juice
1-1/2 cups raisins
    2 tablespoons cornmeal
**GLAZE:**
    1 egg, beaten
**Sugar**

In a small bowl, combine yeast, 1/2 cup water and sugar; set aside. In a large bowl, combine eggs, applesauce, honey, oil, salt and remaining water; mix well. Stir in yeast mixture. Gradually add enough flour to form a soft dough. Turn out onto a floured surface; knead until smooth and elastic, about 10 minutes. Place dough in a greased bowl, turning once to grease top. Cover and let rise in a warm place until doubled, about 1 hour. Punch down and turn over in bowl. Cover and let rise 30 minutes. In a small bowl, combine apples, lemon juice and raisins. Divide dough into three parts; knead one-third of the apple mixture into each part. Shape each into round flat balls. Place each in a greased 8-in. round baking pan that has been sprinkled with cornmeal. Cover and let rise until doubled, about 1 hour. For glaze, brush each loaf with egg and sprinkle with sugar. Bake at 350° for 30-35 minutes or until bread sounds hollow when tapped. **Yield:** 3 loaves.

# Cakes, Cookies & Candies

**Home-baked goodies fill the house with rich aromas and cheerful smiles. If your cookie jar or cake pan is empty, fill it up with one of these tempting treats.**

—— 🍰 🍰 🍰 ——

**BAKER'S BONANZA.** Clockwise from upper left: Pecan Squares (p. 103), Crisp Sugar Cookies (p. 112), Idaho Potato Cake (p. 100), Moist Chocolate Cake (p. 111), Apple Walnut Cake (p. 106) and Lemon Custard Pudding Cake (p. 104).

## Wyoming Whopper Cookies

### (Pictured above)

*These big country cookies fill up a hungry cowboy after a long ride rounding up cattle. They're not just for wranglers, though. They pack well for work, picnics and other occasions.*
—*Jamie Hirsch*
*Powell, Wyoming*

        2/3  cup butter *or* margarine
    1-1/4  cups packed brown sugar
        3/4  cup sugar
            3  eggs, beaten
    1-1/2  cups chunky-style peanut butter*
            6  cups old-fashioned oats (not quick-cooking)
            2  teaspoons baking soda
    1-1/2  cups raisins
            2  cups (12 ounces) semisweet chocolate chips

In a large saucepan, melt butter over low heat. Blend in sugars, eggs and peanut butter; mix until smooth. Add oats, baking soda, raisins and chocolate chips (dough will be sticky). Drop on a greased baking sheet with an ice cream scoop or large spoon. Flatten slightly. Bake at 350° for about 15 minutes. Remove cookies to a wire rack to cool. **Yield:** 2 dozen. **\*Editor's Note:** Jamie uses Jif brand peanut butter. If unavailable, use another brand, but add several tablespoons of water to the mixture.

## Cinnamon Stars

*These cookies are such a hit with my family that a few always seem to disappear before I can even finish them! I spread jam on half of the spicy stars, then top them with the other half of the batch of cookies, which have been glazed for an extra dose of sweetness. People always comment on how attractive they are.*
—*Flo Burtnett, Gage, Oklahoma*

        2  cups all-purpose flour
        1  cup sugar
        1  teaspoon ground cinnamon
    3/4  teaspoon baking powder
    1/4  teaspoon salt
    1/2  cup cold butter *or* margarine
        1  egg, lightly beaten
    1/4  cup milk
**GLAZE/FILLING:**
        2  cups confectioners' sugar
    1/2  teaspoon vanilla extract
        2  to 3 tablespoons milk
**Colored sugar, optional**
    2/3  cup raspberry, strawberry *or* cherry jam

In a medium bowl, combine the flour, sugar, cinnamon, baking powder and salt. Cut in butter until crumbly. Combine the egg and milk; add to flour mixture and stir just until moistened. Cover and chill at least 1 hour. On a lightly floured surface, roll the dough to 1/8-in. thickness. Cut with a 3-in. cookie cutter dipped in flour. Place on ungreased baking sheets. Bake at 375° for 7-9 minutes or until edges are lightly browned. Remove to a wire rack; cool completely. For the glaze, combine sugar, vanilla and enough milk to achieve a spreading consistency. Spread on half of the cookies; sprinkle with colored sugar if desired. Let stand until set. Place 1/2 teaspoon of jam on each unglazed cookie and top with a glazed cookie. **Yield:** 2-1/2 dozen sandwich cookies.

———  🥄 🥄 🥄  ———

## Flowerpot Dirt Cake

*Every year I host a luncheon to welcome spring. I like to surprise my friends and leave them with a special memory. This delicious cake does the trick. Sometimes people are a little hesitant because they don't think you can really eat out of a clay flowerpot, but once I explain that the pot is new, clean and lined with foil, they like the idea and dig right in!*
—*Mary Anne McWhirter, Pearland, Texas*

    1  package cream-filled chocolate cookies
    1  package (8 ounces) cream cheese, softened

4 tablespoons butter *or* margarine, softened
1 cup confectioners' sugar
3-1/2 cups cold milk
2 packages (3.4 ounces *each*) instant vanilla
   pudding mix
1 carton (12 ounces) frozen whipped
   topping, thawed
1 new flowerpot (8 x 10 inches)
**Silk flowers**
**Candy gummy worms**

In a food processor or blender, crush the cookies until fine. Set aside. In a mixing bowl, beat the cream cheese, butter and sugar until smooth. In another bowl, mix the milk and pudding mix until well blended. Fold into cream cheese mixture. Fold in the whipped topping. In the flowerpot, alternate layers of cookie crumbs and pudding mixture, ending with crumbs. Chill several hours or overnight. Decorate with silk flowers and gummy worms. **Yield:** 12 servings.

———— 🍸 🍸 🍸 ————

## Raspberry Crunch Brownies

*You wouldn't even know this raspberry dessert is low-fat. It's moist, with a rich, dark-chocolate flavor and a nut-like crunch.* —Rita Winterberger
Huson, Montana

✓ Uses less fat, sugar or salt. Includes Nutritional Analysis and Diabetic Exchanges.

1/4 cup vegetable oil
1-1/4 cups sugar
4 egg whites
1 cup all-purpose flour
1/2 teaspoon baking powder
1/4 teaspoon salt
2/3 cup baking cocoa
1-1/2 teaspoons vanilla extract
1/4 cup raspberry jam
2 tablespoons Grape-Nuts cereal, optional

In a mixing bowl, beat oil and sugar. Add egg whites and continue beating until well mixed. Combine flour, baking powder, salt and cocoa; add to mixing bowl and beat until moistened. Stir in vanilla (batter will be thick). Coat a 9-in. square pan with nonstick cooking spray. Spread batter into pan. Bake at 350° for 20-25 minutes or until a toothpick inserted in the center comes out clean. Cool 10 minutes on a wire rack. Spread with jam and sprinkle with Grape-Nuts if desired. Cool completely. **Yield:** 2 dozen. **Nutritional Analysis:** One serving equals 105 calories, 47 mg sodium, 0 mg cholesterol, 19 gm carbohydrates, 2 gm protein, 3 gm fat. **Diabetic Exchanges:** 1 starch, 1/2 fat.

## Pecan Squares

**(Pictured below and on page 98)**

*These bars are good for snacking when you're on the road or for taking to gatherings. They're different from ordinary dessert bars...if you love pecan pie, you'll likely find them irresistible!* —Sylvia Ford
Kennett, Missouri

**CRUST:**
2 cups all-purpose flour
1/3 cup sugar
3/4 cup butter *or* margarine, softened
1/4 teaspoon salt
**FILLING:**
4 eggs, lightly beaten
1-1/2 cups corn syrup
1-1/2 cups sugar
3 tablespoons butter *or* magarine, melted
1-1/2 teaspoons vanilla extract
2-1/2 cups chopped pecans

In a large mixing bowl, blend together the flour, sugar, butter and salt until the mixture resembles coarse crumbs. Press firmly and evenly into a greased 15-in. x 10-in. x 1-in. baking pan. Bake at 350° for 20 minutes. Meanwhile, in another bowl, combine the first five filling ingredients. Stir in the pecans. Spread evenly over hot crust. Bake at 350° for 25-30 minutes or until set. Cool on a wire rack. **Yield:** 4 dozen.

## Old-Fashioned Oatmeal Cookies

*These are my favorite cookies to take on a trip because they stay moist and aren't too sweet. My mother passed the recipe on to me, and I've made it too many times since then to count!*
—Michelle Wise
*Spring Mills, Pennsylvania*

    1 **cup raisins**
    1 **cup water**
  3/4 **cup shortening**
1-1/2 **cups sugar**
    2 **eggs**
    1 **teaspoon vanilla extract**
2-1/2 **cups all-purpose flour**
    1 **teaspoon baking soda**
    1 **teaspoon salt**
    1 **teaspoon ground cinnamon**
  1/2 **teaspoon baking powder**
  1/4 **teaspoon ground cloves**
    2 **cups quick-cooking oats**
  1/2 **cup chopped walnuts, optional**

In a saucepan, cook the raisins in water over medium heat until plump, about 15 minutes. Drain, reserving liquid. Add enough water to liquid to measure 1/2 cup. In a mixing bowl, cream the shortening, sugar, eggs and vanilla. Stir in the raisin liquid. Blend in the dry ingredients. Stir in the raisins and oats. Add nuts if desired. Drop by teaspoonfuls about 2 in. apart onto ungreased baking sheets. Bake at 375° for 10-12 minutes or until lightly browned. **Yield:** 5 dozen.

---

## Salted Peanut Chews

*I took these great treats to an evening reunion years ago. They disappeared fast, and soon people were asking for the recipe.* —Irene Yoder, Millersburg, Ohio

1-1/2 **cups all-purpose flour**
  1/2 **cup packed brown sugar**
  3/4 **cup butter *or* margarine, softened, *divided***
    3 **cups miniature marshmallows**
    2 **cups (12 ounces) peanut butter chips**
  2/3 **cup corn syrup**
    2 **teaspoons vanilla extract**
    2 **cups crisp rice cereal**
    2 **cups salted peanuts**

In a mixing bowl, combine flour, brown sugar and 1/2 cup butter; mix well. Press into an ungreased 13-in. x 9-in. x 2-in. baking pan. Bake at 350° for 12-15 minutes or until lightly browned. Sprinkle marshmallows over top and bake 3-5 minutes longer or until marshmallows begin to melt; set

## Lemon Custard Pudding Cake

### (Pictured above and on page 98)

*With its creamy lemon bottom layer topped by a light white cake, this recipe makes an excellent company dessert. It's a perfect light finale to a big meal for family and guests, and it's not hard to make.*
—Alberta McKay, Bartlesville, Oklahoma

    4 **eggs, *separated***
  1/3 **cup lemon juice**
    1 **teaspoon grated lemon peel**
    1 **tablespoon butter *or* margarine, melted**
1-1/2 **cups sugar**
  1/2 **cup all-purpose flour**
  1/2 **teaspoon salt**
1-1/2 **cups milk**
**Whipped cream**

In a mixing bowl, beat egg yolks until thick and lemon colored, about 5-8 minutes. Blend in lemon juice, peel and butter. Combine sugar, flour and salt; add alternately with milk, beating well after each addition. Beat egg whites until stiff; fold into batter. Pour into a 1-1/2-qt. baking dish; set in a pan of hot water. Bake at 350° about 50 minutes or until lightly browned. Serve warm topped with whipped cream. **Yield:** 8 servings.

aside. In a large saucepan, cook and stir peanut butter chips, corn syrup, vanilla and remaining butter until chips are melted and smooth. Remove from the heat; stir in cereal and peanuts. Pour over prepared crust, spreading to cover. Cool before cutting into bars. **Yield:** about 2 dozen.

— 🛒 🛒 🛒 —

## Peppermint Candy

*Pairing peppermint and chocolate is a natural. Family and friends gobble up these sweet confections.*
*—Kandy Clarke, Columbia Falls, Montana*

- 1 cup (6 ounces) semisweet chocolate chips
- 1 can (14 ounces) sweetened condensed milk, *divided*
- 1 cup (6 ounces) vanilla chips
- 1 tablespoon peppermint extract
- 2 to 3 drops green food coloring

In a saucepan, melt chocolate chips and 3/4 cup condensed milk over low heat, stirring occasionally. Line an 8-in. square baking pan with waxed paper; butter the paper. Spread half of melted chocolate mixture into pan; chill for 5-10 minutes (keep remaining melted chocolate at room temperature). In another saucepan, melt vanilla chips. Stir in remaining condensed milk and mix well. Remove from the heat; add extract and food coloring. Chill. Spread over chocolate layer; spread reserved melted chocolate on top. Chill. Cut into 1-in. pieces. **Yield:** 5 dozen.

— 🛒 🛒 🛒 —

## Toffee Squares

*Like many country cooks, I enjoy heating up my oven for the holidays with a variety of cookie recipes. I make 16 kinds and fill tins as Christmas gifts.*
*—Judy Scholovich, Waukesha, Wisconsin*

- 1 cup butter *or* margarine, softened
- 1 cup packed brown sugar
- 1 egg yolk
- 1 teaspoon vanilla extract
- 2 cups all-purpose flour
- 1/4 teaspoon salt
- 2 packages (4 ounces *each*) German sweet chocolate
- 1/2 cup chopped nuts

In a mixing bowl, cream butter and sugar. Add egg yolk, vanilla, flour and salt; mix well. Spread into a greased 13-in. x 9-in. x 2-in. baking pan. Bake at 350° for 20-25 minutes or until golden brown. Melt chocolate in a heavy saucepan over low heat, stirring constantly. Spread over hot bars. Sprinkle immediately with nuts. Cool; cut into 1-1/4-in. squares. **Yield:** 4-1/2 dozen.

— 🛒 🛒 🛒 —

## Chocolate-Covered Cherry Cookies

**(Pictured below)**

*I always make these cookies for family holiday gatherings, and there's never even one cookie to bring back home.* *—Marie Kinyon, Mason, Michigan*

- 1/2 cup butter *or* margarine
- 1 cup sugar
- 1 egg
- 1-1/2 teaspoons vanilla extract
- 1-1/2 cups all-purpose flour
- 1/2 cup baking cocoa
- 1/4 teaspoon salt
- 1/4 teaspoon baking powder
- 1/4 teaspoon baking soda
- 48 maraschino cherries, blotted dry

**FROSTING:**
- 1 cup (6 ounces) semisweet chocolate chips
- 1/2 cup sweetened condensed milk
- 1 to 3 teaspoons maraschino cherry juice

In a mixing bowl, cream butter and sugar until fluffy; beat in egg and vanilla. Combine dry ingredients; gradually add to creamed mixture (batter will be very firm). Shape into 48 balls, about 1 in. round; place on ungreased baking sheets. Push one cherry halfway into each ball. For frosting, melt chocolate chips in condensed milk in a small saucepan over low heat, stirring constantly. Remove from heat; add cherry juice and stir until smooth. Spoon 1 teaspoon of frosting over each cherry (the frosting will spread over cookie during baking). Bake at 350° for 10-12 minutes. Cool on wire racks. **Yield:** 4 dozen.

## Apple Walnut Cake

**(Pictured below and on page 98)**

*This moist cake is perfect for brunch. It gets its appeal from big chunks of sweet apples, nutty flavor and creamy frosting. The recipe, originally my mom's, is a unique harvest treat.*

—*Renae Moncur*
*Burley, Idaho*

    1-2/3 cups sugar
        2 eggs
      1/2 cup vegetable oil
        2 teaspoons vanilla extract
        2 cups all-purpose flour
        2 teaspoons baking soda
    1-1/2 teaspoons ground cinnamon
        1 teaspoon salt
      1/2 teaspoon ground nutmeg
        4 cups chopped unpeeled apples
        1 cup chopped walnuts
**FROSTING:**
        2 packages (3 ounces *each*) cream cheese,
          softened
        3 tablespoons butter *or* margarine, softened
        1 teaspoon vanilla extract
    1-1/2 cups confectioners' sugar

In a mixing bowl, beat sugar and eggs. Add oil and vanilla; mix well. Combine flour, baking soda, cinnamon, salt and nutmeg; gradually add to sugar mixture, mixing well. Stir in apples and walnuts. Pour into a greased and floured 13-in. x 9-in. x 2-in. baking pan. Bake at 350° for 50-55 minutes or until cake tests done. Cool on a wire rack. For frosting, beat cream cheese, butter and vanilla in a mixing bowl. Gradually add confectioners' sugar until the frosting has reached desired spreading consistency. Frost cooled cake. **Yield:** 16-20 servings.

---

## Carol's Springerle Cookies

*Springerle cookies are a European holiday tradition brought to America by German settlers. A design is pressed into each anise-flavored cookie before baking.*
—*Carol Dillon, Camp Hill, Pennsylvania*

        4 eggs
        2 cups sugar
        1 teaspoon anise extract *or* 4 tablespoons
          anise seed
        4 cups cake flour (no substitutes)
        1 teaspoon baking powder

In a mixing bowl, beat eggs at high speed until thick and light colored. Gradually add sugar, beating until dissolved, about 10 minutes. Add anise. Sift flour and baking powder; fold into egg mixture. Cover and let rest for 15 minutes. Divide dough into thirds. On a well-floured surface or pastry cloth, roll one piece of dough with a floured rolling pin to 1/4-in. thickness. Flour Springerle mold and quickly press design. Cut around design and place on a greased baking sheet. Repeat with remaining dough. Cover lightly with a towel. Allow cookies to dry for 12 hours or overnight. Dust off excess flour with a pastry brush. Bake at 300° for 15-18 minutes or until light brown on bottom only. Cookies will "spring" or rise during baking. Cool. Store in an airtight container. **Yield:** 15 cookies. **Editor's Notes:** Lemon or almond extract can be substituted for the anise extract or seed. After cookies have cooled, the design can be "painted" with food coloring. If cookies become hard, place a cut apple in the storage container to soften.

---

## Chocolate-Covered Cherries

*These yummy cherries are my family's favorite festive dessert—plus, they make great gifts. Youngsters love helping to dip the cherries in chocolate. Best of all, you can prepare them ahead. The candy just gets better as it's stored, with the centers becoming even juicier.*
—*Linda Hammerich, Bonanza, Oregon*

2-1/2 cups confectioners' sugar
1/4 cup butter *or* margarine, softened
1 tablespoon milk
1/2 teaspoon almond extract
2 jars (8 ounces *each*) maraschino cherries with stems, well drained
2 cups (12 ounces) semisweet chocolate chips
2 tablespoons shortening

In a mixing bowl, combine sugar, butter, milk and extract; mix well. Knead into a large ball. Roll into 1-in. balls and flatten each into a 2-in. circle. Wrap around cherries and lightly roll in hands. Place with stems up on waxed paper-lined baking sheet. Cover loosely and refrigerate 4 hours or overnight. Melt the chocolate chips and shortening in a double boiler or microwave-safe bowl. Holding on to stem, dip cherries into chocolate; set on waxed paper to harden. Store in a covered container. Refrigerate 1-2 weeks before serving. **Yield:** about 3 dozen.

— 🍵 🍵 🍵 —

## Chocolate Monster Cookies

*My four grandsons started attending "Grandma's Cooking School" when they were as young as 4. This recipe from my hand-written cookbook is a favorite of the youngest, Brandon. He has fun making them and is always delighted with the results—as is the rest of the family.* —Helen Hilbert, Liverpool, New York

2 cups butter *or* margarine
2 cups sugar
2 cups packed brown sugar
4 eggs
2 teaspoons vanilla extract
4 cups all-purpose flour
1 tablespoon baking powder
2 teaspoons baking soda
1 teaspoon salt
2 cups cornflakes
2 cups rolled oats
1 package (8 ounces) flaked coconut
1 package (12 ounces) semisweet chocolate chips
1 cup chopped walnuts

In a large mixing bowl, cream butter and sugars. Add eggs and vanilla; mix well. In a small bowl, combine flour, baking powder, baking soda and salt; gradually add to creamed mixture, mixing well after each addition. Stir in cornflakes, oats and coconut. (It may be necessary to transfer to a larger bowl to stir in the cornflakes, oats and coconut.) Stir in chocolate chips and nuts. Divide

dough into six sections. On a piece of waxed paper, shape each section into a 7-in. x 1-1/2-in. roll. Refrigerate several hours or overnight. Cut into 1/2-in. slices. Place 3 in. apart on ungreased cookie sheets. Bake at 350° for 13-15 minutes. **Yield:** 7-1/2 dozen.

— 🍵 🍵 🍵 —

## Blarney Stones

*To top off our dinner on St. Patrick's Day, I bake these appropriately Irish cookies, but they taste good anytime. You can even change the food coloring to fit other holidays.* —Connie Lou Blommers, Pella, Iowa

1 cup butter *or* margarine, softened
3/4 cup packed brown sugar
1/4 cup sugar
1/2 teaspoon vanilla extract
1/2 teaspoon almond extract
1 package (3.4 ounces) instant pistachio pudding mix
2 eggs
Green food coloring, optional
2-1/2 cups all-purpose flour
1 teaspoon baking soda
2 cups (12 ounces) butterscotch chips
1 cup chopped walnuts

In a mixing bowl, cream butter, sugars, extracts and pudding mix. Add eggs, one at a time, beating well after each addition. Add a few drops of green food coloring if desired. Combine flour and baking soda; gradually add to creamed mixture. Stir in chips and nuts (batter will be stiff). Cover and chill for several hours. Shape into 1/2-in. balls; place 2 in. apart on ungreased baking sheets. Bake at 350° for 8 minutes. Remove from baking sheets to wire racks; cool. **Yield:** 25 dozen.

---

### *Helpful Hints for Cookies*

- Once the flour has been added, take care not to overmix the dough. Too much handling develops the gluten and can produce tough cookies.
- Shiny heavy-gauge aluminum baking sheets conduct heat well and will produce the most evenly baked and browned cookies.
- Dark sheets absorb more oven heat and can cause cookies to overbrown. To alleviate the problem, line dark sheets with heavy-duty aluminum foil.
- If you have only thin, lightweight baking sheets, place one directly on top of the other to prevent cookies from overbrowning.

## Mom's Soft Raisin Cookies

### (Pictured above)

*With four sons in the service during World War II, my mother sent these favorite cookies as a taste from home to "her boys" in different parts of the world. These days, my grandchildren are enjoying them as we did, along with my stories of long ago.*
*—Pearl Cochenour, Williamsport, Ohio*

    1 cup water
    2 cups raisins
    1 cup shortening
1-3/4 cups sugar
    2 eggs, lightly beaten
    1 teaspoon vanilla extract
3-1/2 cups all-purpose flour
    1 teaspoon baking powder
    1 teaspoon baking soda
    1 teaspoon salt
  1/2 teaspoon ground cinnamon
  1/2 teaspoon ground nutmeg
  1/2 cup chopped walnuts

Combine raisins and water in a small saucepan; bring to a boil. Cook for 3 minutes; remove from the heat and let cool (do not drain). In a mixing bowl, cream shortening; gradually add sugar. Add eggs and vanilla. Combine dry ingredients; gradually add to creamed mixture and blend thoroughly. Stir in nuts and raisins. Drop by teaspoonfuls 2 in. apart on greased baking sheets. Bake at 350° for 12-14 minutes. **Yield:** about 6 dozen.

## Pumpkin Spice Cake

*We sometimes call this Thanksgiving Cake because it's a tasty alternative to pumpkin pie, but we don't relegate it to just that holiday. I think you'll agree it's delicious any time of the year.*
*—Kathy Rhoads*
*Circleville, Ohio*

    1 package (18-1/4 ounces) spice cake mix
    3 eggs
    1 cup cooked *or* canned pumpkin
  1/2 cup water
  1/2 cup vegetable oil
    1 package (3.4 ounces) instant vanilla pudding mix
    1 teaspoon ground cinnamon
  1/2 cup chopped pecans
Cream cheese frosting of your choice *or* whipped cream

In a mixing bowl, combine cake mix, eggs, pumpkin, water, oil, pudding mix and cinnamon. Beat at medium speed for 5 minutes. Stir in pecans. Pour into a greased and floured 10-in. fluted tube pan. Bake at 350° for 45-55 minutes or until cake tests done. Let cool in pan 10 minutes before removing to a wire rack. Frost cake or serve with whipped cream. **Yield:** 16-20 servings.

— ▼ ▼ ▼ —

## Whole Wheat Snickerdoodles

*These soft, chewy cookies make a super snack. They're sweet but not overly so. Their light cardamom taste goes great with a tall glass of cold milk.*
*—Jana Horsfall, Garden City, Kansas*

    1 cup butter *or* margarine, softened
1-1/2 cups sugar
    1 egg plus 1 egg white
1-1/2 cups whole wheat flour
1-1/4 cups all-purpose flour
    1 teaspoon baking soda
  1/4 teaspoon salt
TOPPING:
    2 tablespoons sugar
    2 teaspoons ground cinnamon

In a mixing bowl, cream butter and sugar until fluffy. Add egg and egg white; beat well. Combine the dry ingredients; add to creamed mixture and beat well. In a small bowl, combine topping ingredients. Shape dough into walnut-sized balls; roll in cinnamon-sugar. Place 2 in. apart on ungreased baking sheets. Bake at 400° for 8-10 minutes. (Cookies will puff up and flatten as they bake.) **Yield:** about 5 dozen.

## Moist Chocolate Cake

**(Pictured below and on page 98)**

*This cake reminds me of my grandmother, because it was one of her specialties. I bake it often for family parties, and it always brings back fond memories. The cake is light and airy with a delicious chocolate taste. This recipe is a keeper!* —*Patricia Kreitz Richland, Pennsylvania*

   2 cups all-purpose flour
   1 teaspoon salt
   1 teaspoon baking powder
   2 teaspoons baking soda
3/4 cup baking cocoa
   2 cups sugar
   1 cup vegetable oil
   1 cup hot brewed coffee
   1 cup milk
   2 eggs
   1 teaspoon vanilla extract

**ICING:**
   1 cup milk
   5 tablespoons all-purpose flour
1/2 cup butter, softened
1/2 cup shortening
   1 cup sugar
   1 teaspoon vanilla extract

Sift together all dry ingredients in a large mixing bowl. Add oil, coffee and milk; mix at medium speed for 2 minutes. Add eggs and vanilla; beat 2 more minutes. Pour into two greased and floured 9-in. cake pans (or two 8-in. cake pans and six muffin cups). Bake at 325° for 25-30 minutes. Meanwhile, for icing, combine the milk and flour in a saucepan; cook until thick. Cover and refrigerate. In a medium mixing bowl, beat butter, shortening, sugar and vanilla until creamy. Add chilled milk/flour mixture and beat for 10 minutes. Frost cooled cake. **Yield:** 12 servings.

## Crisp Sugar Cookies

**(Pictured below and on page 98)**

*My grandmother always had sugar cookies in her pantry. We grandchildren would empty that big jar quickly because those cookies were the best. Now I regularly bake these wonderful treats to share with friends.* —Evelyn Poteet, Hancock, Maryland

- 1 cup butter *or* margarine, softened
- 2 cups sugar
- 2 eggs
- 1 teaspoon vanilla extract
- 5 cups all-purpose flour
- 1-1/2 teaspoons baking powder
- 1 teaspoon baking soda
- 1/2 teaspoon salt
- 1/4 cup milk

In a mixing bowl, cream the butter and sugar. Add the eggs and vanilla. Combine the flour, baking powder, baking soda and salt; add to the creamed mixture alternately with the milk. Cover and refrigerate for 15-30 minutes. On a floured surface, roll out the dough to 1/8-in. thickness. Cut out cookies into desired shapes and place 2 in. apart on a greased baking sheet. Bake at 350° for 10 minutes or until edges are lightly browned. **Yield:** 8 dozen (2-1/2-inch cookies).

## Chocolate Chip Date Cake

*This bar-like cake travels well because there's no messy frosting to melt. It also stays nice and moist—if there's any left over, that is.* —Pam Jennings, Prairie City, Iowa

- 1 cup water
- 1 cup chopped dates
- 1 cup shortening
- 1 cup sugar
- 2 eggs, lightly beaten
- 1 teaspoon vanilla extract
- 1-3/4 cups all-purpose flour
- 1 tablespoon baking cocoa
- 1/2 teaspoon salt
- 1/2 cup semisweet chocolate chips
- 1/2 cup chopped walnuts

In a small saucepan, bring water and dates to a boil. Remove from heat; cool. In a mixing bowl, cream together shortening and sugar. Add eggs and vanilla; mix well. Combine flour, cocoa and salt; add to creamed mixture. Add dates and cooking liquid; mix well. Place in a greased 13-in. x 9-in. x 2-in. baking pan. Sprinkle with chocolate chips and walnuts. Bake at 350° for 30-35 minutes. Remove to a wire rack to cool. **Yield:** 32 servings.

------ 🥄 🥄 🥄 ------

## Fudge-Nut Oatmeal Bars

*When I make these bars for lunches and snacks, they're gone in a jiffy!* —Kim Stoller, Smithville, Ohio

- 1 cup butter *or* margarine, softened
- 2 cups packed brown sugar
- 2 eggs
- 2 teaspoons vanilla extract
- 3 cups quick-cooking oats
- 2-1/2 cups all-purpose flour
- 1 teaspoon baking soda
- 1 teaspoon salt

**FUDGE FILLING:**

- 1 can (14 ounces) sweetened condensed milk
- 2 cups (12 ounces) semisweet chocolate chips
- 2 tablespoons butter *or* margarine
- 1/2 teaspoon salt
- 2 teaspoons vanilla extract
- 1 cup chopped walnuts

In a mixing bowl, cream the butter and brown sugar. Add the eggs and vanilla; mix well. Combine the oats, flour, baking soda and salt; add to the creamed mixture. Spread two-thirds in the bottom of an ungreased 15-in. x 10-in. x 1-in. baking pan; set aside. For the filling, heat the milk, chocolate chips, butter and salt in a saucepan or microwave-safe bowl until melted. Remove from the heat; stir in the vanilla and walnuts. Spread over the oat mixture in pan. Drop remaining oat mixture by tablespoonfuls over chocolate. Bake at 350° for 20-25 minutes. **Yield:** 2-1/2 to 3 dozen.

## Sugarless Applesauce Cake

*My mother-in-law is diabetic, so I made this cake for her birthday. Everyone commented how moist and spicy it was. The cake also won a first-place ribbon at our county fair!* —Kay Hale, Doniphan, Missouri

✓ Uses less fat, sugar or salt. Includes Nutritional Analysis and Diabetic Exchanges.

- **1 cup raisins**
- **1 cup diced dried fruit**
- **2 cups water**
- **2 cups all-purpose flour**
- **1 teaspoon baking soda**
- **1/2 teaspoon salt**
- **1/2 teaspoon ground nutmeg**
- **1-1/2 teaspoons ground cinnamon**
- **2 eggs, beaten *or* egg substitute equivalent**
- **1 cup unsweetened applesauce**
- **2 tablespoons liquid sweetener**
- **3/4 cup vegetable oil**
- **1 teaspoon vanilla extract**
- **1/2 cup chopped nuts**

Combine raisins, fruit and water in a saucepan; cook, uncovered, until water is evaporated and fruit is soft. Set aside to cool. Meanwhile, in a large mixing bowl, combine flour, baking soda, salt, nutmeg and cinnamon. In another bowl, combine eggs, applesauce, sweetener, oil and vanilla. Add nuts and fruit mixture. Stir into dry ingredients; blend thoroughly. Pour into a greased 10-in. fluted tube pan. Bake at 350° for 35-40 minutes or until the cake tests done. **Yield:** 32 servings. **Nutritional Analysis:** One serving (prepared with egg substitute) equals 125 calories, 60 mg sodium, 0 mg cholesterol, 15 gm carbohydrate, 2 gm protein, 7 gm fat. **Diabetic Exchanges:** 1 fat, 1/2 starch, 1/2 fruit.

## Rhubarb Upside-Down Cake

**(Pictured above right)**

*I've baked this cake every spring for many years, and my family loves it! At potluck dinners it disappears quickly, drawing compliments even from those who normally don't care for rhubarb. Use your own fresh rhubarb or find a neighbor who will trade stalks for the recipe.* —Helen Breman, Mattydale, New York

**TOPPING:**
- **3 cups fresh rhubarb, cut into 1/2-inch slices**
- **1 cup sugar**
- **2 tablespoons all-purpose flour**
- **1/4 teaspoon ground nutmeg**
- **1/4 cup butter *or* margarine, melted**

**BATTER:**
- **1-1/2 cups all-purpose flour**
- **3/4 cup sugar**
- **2 teaspoons baking powder**
- **1/4 teaspoon salt**
- **1/2 teaspoon ground nutmeg**
- **1/4 cup butter *or* margarine, melted**
- **2/3 cup milk**
- **1 egg**

**Sweetened whipped cream, optional**

Sprinkle rhubarb in a greased 10-in. ovenproof skillet. Combine sugar, flour and nutmeg; sprinkle over rhubarb. Drizzle with butter. For batter, combine flour, sugar, baking powder, salt and nutmeg in a mixing bowl. Add butter, milk and egg; beat until smooth. Spread over rhubarb mixture. Bake at 350° for 35 minutes or until the cake tests done. Loosen edges immediately and invert onto serving dish. Serve warm, topped with whipped cream if desired. **Yield:** 8-10 servings.

# Pies & Desserts

***When you're contemplating
what to make for dessert,
turn to this chapter
for a tempting selection of
pies, puddings, trifles and crisps.***

**SWEET CREATIONS.** Clockwise from upper left: Golden Apple Bundles (p. 119), Raspberry Trifle (p. 120), Citrus Cheesecake (p. 124) Strawberry Shortbread Shortcake (p. 121), Creamy Raspberry Dessert (p. 122), Berry Creme Parfaits (p. 125) and Washington State Apple Pie (p. 125).

utes or until center is set. Cool. For topping, combine flour and sugar in a saucepan. Drain pineapple, reserving juice. Stir in 1 cup of reserved pineapple juice. Bring to a boil, stirring constantly. Boil and stir 1 minute. Remove from heat; fold in pineapple. Cool. Whip cream until stiff peaks form; fold into topping. Spread carefully over dessert. Refrigerate 6 hours or overnight. Garnish with strawberries if desired. **Yield:** 12-16 servings.

### Pineapple Cheese Torte

**(Pictured above)**

*This light and yummy pineapple dessert looks prettiest when it's garnished with fresh strawberries. I serve this cool dessert at summer picnics or family get-togethers. It's always popular!*
—Diane Bradley
Sparta, Michigan

**CRUST:**
  1 cup all-purpose flour
  1/4 cup confectioners' sugar
  1/4 cup finely chopped almonds
  1/3 cup butter *or* margarine, softened
**FILLING:**
  2 packages (8 ounces *each*) cream cheese, softened
  1/2 cup sugar
  2 eggs
  2/3 cup unsweetened pineapple juice
**PINEAPPLE TOPPING:**
  1/4 cup all-purpose flour
  1/4 cup sugar
  1 can (20 ounces) crushed pineapple
  1/2 cup whipping cream
**Fresh strawberries, optional**

Combine crust ingredients; pat into the bottom of an 11-in. x 7-in. x 2-in. baking dish. Bake at 350° for 20 minutes. Beat cream cheese in a mixing bowl until fluffy; beat in sugar and eggs. Stir in juice. Pour filling over hot crust. Bake at 350° for 25 min-

### Old-Fashioned Oatmeal Pie

**(Pictured below)**

*Honey adds just the right amount of sweetness to this pie from the National Honey Board. The combination of honey, brown sugar, oats and coconut is delicious.*

  2 eggs
  3/4 cup honey
  3/4 cup quick-cooking oats
  3/4 cup flaked coconut
  3/4 cup packed brown sugar
  1/2 cup butter *or* margarine, softened
  1/2 cup currants
  1/2 cup chopped walnuts
  1 unbaked pie pastry (9 inches)
**Whipped cream, optional**

In a mixing bowl, beat the eggs. Add the honey, oats, coconut, brown sugar, butter, currants and walnuts; mix well. Pour into the pie shell. Bake at 350° for 40-45 minutes or until browned and a knife inserted near the center comes out clean. Cool. Serve with a dollop of whipped cream if desired. **Yield:** 8 servings.

## Raspberry Delight

*When I was a young man, I taught in a one-room schoolhouse and lived in the bachelor's quarters. At lunchtime, I'd often trade my store-bought cookies for the students' homemade goodies. Of course, nothing tastes as good as homemade, and that inspired me to do more cooking for myself. Pretzels are the surprising "secret ingredient" in this tasty dessert.*
*—Warren Knudtson, Las Vegas, Nevada*

> 2 cups crushed pretzels
> 2 tablespoons sugar
> 1/3 cup chopped pecans
> 3/4 cup butter *or* margarine, softened

**FILLING:**

> 1 package (8 ounces) cream cheese, softened
> 3/4 cup sugar
> 1 carton (8 ounces) frozen whipped topping, thawed
> 1 package (6 ounces) raspberry gelatin
> 2 cups boiling water
> 2 packages (10 ounces *each*) unsweetened frozen raspberries (do not thaw)

In a bowl, combine the crushed pretzels, sugar, chopped pecans and butter. Press into the bottom of an ungreased 13-in. x 9-in. x 2-in. baking pan. Bake at 350° for 10 minutes or until lightly browned; cool completely. In a medium mixing bowl, beat the cream cheese and sugar until smooth. Fold in the whipped topping; spread over cooled crust. In another bowl, dissolve the gelatin in boiling water. Stir in the frozen raspberries until the gelatin is almost set. Spread berry mixture over filling. Chill several hours or overnight. **Yield:** 12-16 servings.

— 🍴 🍴 🍴 —

## Fluffy Cranberry Cheese Pie

### (Pictured above right)

*This pie has a light texture and zippy flavor that matches its vibrant color. It's festive for the holidays or anytime, and easy because you make it ahead. Folks tell me it's like getting two desserts at once—cheesecake and fruit pie!*
*—Mary Parkonen*
*West Wareham, Massachusetts*

**CRANBERRY TOPPING:**

> 1 package (3 ounces) raspberry gelatin
> 1/3 cup sugar
> 1-1/4 cups cranberry juice
> 1 can (8 ounces) jellied cranberry sauce

**FILLING:**

> 1 package (3 ounces) cream cheese, softened

> 1/4 cup sugar
> 1 tablespoon milk
> 1 teaspoon vanilla extract
> 1/2 cup whipped topping
> 1 pastry shell (9 inches), baked

In a mixing bowl, combine gelatin and sugar; set aside. In a saucepan, bring cranberry juice to a boil. Remove from the heat and pour over gelatin mixture, stirring to dissolve. Stir in the cranberry sauce. Chill until slightly thickened. Meanwhile, in another mixing bowl, beat cream cheese, sugar, milk and vanilla until fluffy. Fold in the whipped topping. Spread evenly into pie shell. Beat cranberry topping until frothy; pour over filling. Chill overnight. **Yield:** 6-8 servings.

---

### Cranberry Care

- When you see a cranberry recipe, you probably think of fall, since that's when fresh berries are in season. Berries stored in an airtight plastic bag will keep in the refrigerator for at least a month. They can be frozen for up to a year.
- Discard any soft, discolored or shriveled berries.
- There's no need to defrost cranberries before using them in a recipe.
- Cook whole cranberries only until they pop—or they'll turn to mush and start to taste bitter.

of fudge topping. Freeze 1 hour. Spread remaining ice cream on top. Drizzle with remaining fudge topping. Freeze several hours or overnight. Garnish with fresh raspberries if desired. Let pie stand at room temperature about 15 minutes before cutting. **Yield:** 8 servings.

## Caramel Apple Crisp

*This typical New England dessert is one of my most requested recipes. Although it makes a fairly big batch, it doesn't take long for it to get gobbled up.*
—Janet Siciak, Bernardston, Massachusetts

  1/2  **cup all-purpose flour**
  1/2  **cup sugar**
  1/2  **teaspoon ground cinnamon**
  1/4  **teaspoon ground nutmeg**
   40  **caramels, quartered**
    9  **cups sliced peeled tart apples**
  1/4  **cup orange juice**
**TOPPING:**
  1/2  **cup sugar**
  1/3  **cup all-purpose flour**
    3  **tablespoons cold butter *or* margarine**
  2/3  **cup quick-cooking oats**
  1/2  **cup chopped walnuts**

In a bowl, combine flour, sugar, cinnamon and nutmeg; add caramels and stir to coat. In another bowl, toss apples with orange juice. Add caramel mixture and mix. Spread into a greased 13-in. x 9-in. x 2-in. baking pan. For topping, combine sugar and flour in a small bowl; cut in butter until crumbly. Add oats and walnuts; sprinkle over apples. Bake at 350° for 45 minutes or until apples are tender. **Yield:** 16-20 servings.

## Cookie Ice Cream Pie

**(Pictured above)**

*Searching for a summer dessert that's fast, easy and doesn't require baking? Just "chill out" and enjoy this chocolate-topped ice cream pie courtesy of the United Dairy Industry Association and the Wisconsin Milk Marketing Board.*

   10  **cream-filled chocolate sandwich cookies, finely crushed**
    3  **tablespoons butter *or* margarine, melted**
   14  **whole cream-filled chocolate sandwich cookies**
**FILLING:**
  1/2  **gallon raspberry ripple ice cream, softened, *divided***
  1/2  **cup prepared fudge topping, *divided***
**Fresh raspberries, optional**

Combine crushed cookies and butter; mix well. Press onto bottom only of a 9-in. pie plate. Stand whole cookies up around edges, pressing lightly into crust. Freeze 1 hour. For filling, spread half of ice cream over crushed cookies. Drizzle with 1/4 cup

## Butterscotch Pumpkin Pie

*Although pumpkin pie is a fall favorite, this quick and cool recipe is great even in the heat of summer. What a nice change of pace!*
—Elizabeth Fehr
Cecil Lake, British Columbia

✓ Uses less fat, sugar or salt. Includes Nutritional Analysis and Diabetic Exchanges.

    1  **cup graham cracker crumbs**
  1/4  **cup margarine, melted**
**FILLING:**
    1  **cup fat-free milk**
    1  **package (.9 ounce) sugar-free instant butterscotch pudding mix**

1 cup cooked *or* canned pumpkin
1 teaspoon ground cinnamon
1/2 teaspoon ground nutmeg
TOPPING:
 1 cup reduced-fat whipped topping
 1 teaspoon vanilla extract

Combine crumbs and margarine; mix well. Press into a 9-in. pie plate. Bake at 350° for 10 minutes; cool. For filling, combine milk and pudding mix in a mixing bowl; beat well. Add pumpkin, cinnamon and nutmeg; mix well. Pour into crust. Chill for at least 2 hours. Combine topping ingredients; dollop on individual slices. **Yield:** 8 servings. **Nutritional Analysis:** One serving (with 2 tablespoons topping) equals 148 calories, 203 mg sodium, 1 mg cholesterol, 17 gm carbohydrate, 3 gm protein, 9 gm fat. **Diabetic Exchanges:** 2-1/2 fat, 1 starch.

— ♟ ♟ ♟ —

# 'I Wish I Had That Recipe...'

LOCALS SAID the Louisburg Cafe in Louisburg, Minnesota served up the best bread pudding ever. Cafe owner Emily Hansen graciously shared her recipe with *Taste of Home* readers.

Operating a business in a 40-person town is a struggle, Emily learned. Visitor traffic wasn't consistent enough to keep her restaurant open.

Emily's great food and positive attitude can now be found at the nearby Madison Lutheran Home, where she's the cook.

## Louisburg Cafe Bread Pudding

 6 eggs, beaten
 6 cups milk
3/4 cup sugar
 1 cup raisins
10 to 12 cups broken bread *or* rolls *or* doughnuts

Combine first four ingredients in a large bowl. Blend in pieces of bread, rolls or doughnuts. Pour mixture into a 13-in. x 9-in. x 2-in baking pan. Bake at 350° for 45 minutes or until set. **Yield:** 24 servings.

— ♟ ♟ ♟ —

## Golden Apple Bundles
### (Pictured below and on page 114)

*This recipe is an interesting way to use apples. I usually make the bundles on Fridays, so when family and friends drop in on the weekend, I have a nice dessert to serve. They bake up flaky and golden brown outside and moist inside. —Lila Eller, Everett, Washington*

 2 cups chopped peeled tart apples
1/3 cup chopped walnuts
1/4 cup packed brown sugar
1/4 cup raisins
 1 tablespoon all-purpose flour
1/2 teaspoon lemon peel
1/2 teaspoon ground cinnamon
Pastry for double-crust pie
Milk
Sugar

In a bowl, combine the apples, walnuts, brown sugar, raisins, flour, lemon peel and cinnamon; set aside. Roll pastry to 1/8-in. thickness. Cut into 5-in. circles. Spoon about 1/4 cup apple mixture into center of each circle. Moisten edges of pastry with water. Fold over and seal edges with a fork. Cut two small slits in each bundle. Place on a greased baking sheet. Bake at 450° for 10 minutes. Reduce heat to 400°; bake 10 minutes longer. Brush each with milk and sprinkle with sugar; bake 5 minutes longer. **Yield:** 10-12 servings.

## Raspberry Trifle

**(Pictured below and on page 114)**

*Beautiful and luscious, this trifle is an impressive way to use fresh raspberries. Plus, people will never know how nice and easy it is to prepare if you use purchased pound cake or lady fingers.*
—Marcy Cella, L'Anse, Michigan

1 package (16 ounces) pound cake, cut into 18 slices *or* 2 packages (3 ounces *each*) ladyfingers
2 packages (3.4 ounces *each*) instant vanilla pudding mix
1 jar (18 ounces) raspberry jam
1-1/2 pints fresh raspberries
Whipped cream and fresh raspberries for garnish

Arrange one-third of sliced cake on the bottom of a trifle dish or large decorative bowl. Prepare pudding according to package directions. Place one-third more cake pieces around inside of bowl, using half of pudding to hold them in place. Gently stir together jam and raspberries; spoon half over pudding. Cover with remaining cake pieces. Layer remaining pudding and raspberry mixture. Chill. Garnish with whipped cream and fresh raspberries. **Yield:** 8-10 servings.

## Persimmon Rice Pudding

*As a girl, I always helped with canning and preserving fruit, including persimmons. Now I buy large quantities at the grocery store. I love to serve this unique dessert for fall and winter gatherings.*
—Opal Amidon, Garden Grove, California

4 cups cooked long grain rice
2 cups ripe persimmon pulp
1-1/4 cups sugar
1-1/4 cups milk
1/3 cup all-purpose flour
1 egg, beaten
1 teaspoon vanilla extract
1/4 cup chopped walnuts
1/4 cup raisins

In a large bowl, combine rice and persimmon pulp; set side. Combine sugar, milk, flour, egg and vanilla; add to rice mixture and mix well. Stir in walnuts and raisins. Pour into a greased 3-qt. baking dish. Bake, uncovered, at 350° for 45 minutes or until pudding is set. Serve warm or cold. **Yield:** 10-12 servings.

———— 🍷 🍷 🍷 ————

## Dairy Hollow House Almond Pie

*At the Dairy Hollow House, a popular country inn and restaurant I ran with my husband, Ned, we enjoyed serving food that went beyond one region or nationality. California almonds add a delicious twist to this Southern recipe. We've since turned Dairy Hollow House into a non-profit writers' colony.*
—Crescent Dragonwagon, Eureka Springs, Arkansas

1/2 cup butter (no substitutes)
3 eggs
1 cup sugar
3/4 cup light corn syrup
1/4 cup honey
1 teaspoon vanilla extract
1/4 teaspoon almond extract
1/8 teaspoon salt
1 cup chopped almonds, toasted
1 unbaked pastry shell (9 inches)
Lightly sweetened whipped cream, optional

In a saucepan, melt butter over low heat until golden brown. Cool. In a mixing bowl, beat eggs. Add sugar, corn syrup, honey, extracts, salt and melted butter. Stir in almonds; pour into pastry shell. Bake at 425° for 10 minutes. Reduce heat to 325°; bake 35-40 minutes longer or until a knife inserted near center comes out clean. Cool. Garnish with whipped cream if desired. **Yield:** 8 servings.

## Watermelon Bombe

### (Pictured above)

*This sherbet dessert looks like actual watermelon slices—complete with "seeds"—when cut. It is fun to eat and refreshing, too.* —Renae Moncur
Burley, Idaho

**About 1 pint lime sherbet**
**About 1 pint pineapple sherbet**
**About 1-1/2 pints raspberry sherbet**
  **1/4 cup miniature semisweet chocolate chips**

Line a 1-1/2-qt. metal mixing bowl with plastic wrap. Press slightly softened lime sherbet against the bottom and sides of bowl. Freeze, uncovered, until firm. Spread pineapple sherbet evenly over lime sherbet layer. Freeze, uncovered, until firm. (Lime and pineapple sherbet layers should be thin.) Pack raspberry sherbet in center of sherbet-lined bowl. Smooth the top to resemble a cut watermelon. Cover and freeze until firm, about 8 hours. Just before serving, uncover bowl of molded sherbet. Place a serving plate on the bowl and invert. Remove bowl and peel off plastic wrap. Cut the bombe into wedges; press a few chocolate chips into the raspberry section of each wedge to resemble watermelon seeds. **Yield:** 8 servings.

### *Berry Fine Eating*

Always wash fresh strawberries before hulling. One pint of strawberries will yield 1-1/2 to 2 cups of sliced or chopped berries.

## Strawberry Shortbread Shortcake

### (Pictured below and on page 115)

*Crisp chocolate shortbread makes a delectable base for this dazzling shortcake recipe shared by the California Strawberry Commission.*

  **1 cup butter *or* margarine, softened**
  **1 cup confectioners' sugar**
  **2 cups all-purpose flour**
  **1 ounce semisweet chocolate, grated**
  **1 cup whipping cream, whipped and sweetened**
  **2 pints fresh strawberries, sliced**

In mixing bowl, cream butter and sugar. Mix in flour and chocolate. Form dough into two balls (one slightly larger than the other). On a floured surface, roll balls into 7-in. circles (one thicker than the other). Transfer to greased baking sheets. Prick all over with fork. Bake at 350° for 25-30 minutes or just until golden. Allow to cool 5 minutes; cut thinner circle into eight equal wedges. Cool on racks. To assemble, place circle on a serving plate. Top with whipped cream and strawberries. Set wedges into the cream at an angle, points toward center. Cut into wedges. **Yield:** 8 servings.

## Creamy Raspberry Dessert

**(Pictured below and on page 114)**

*Do-ahead and delicious, this dessert is a favorite because of its pretty color, creamy texture and terrific flavor. A light, no-bake filling makes it easy. Try garnishing with fresh berries for a pretty look.*
—Julianne Johnson, Grove City, Minnesota

    1 cup graham cracker crumbs
    3 tablespoons sugar
 1/4 cup butter *or* margarine, melted
**FILLING:**
    1 package (10 ounces) frozen raspberries,
      thawed
 1/4 cup cold water
    1 envelope unflavored gelatin
    1 package (8 ounces) cream cheese,
      softened
 1/2 cup sugar
    1 cup whipping cream, whipped
**Whipped cream and fresh raspberries for garnish**

Combine crumbs, sugar and butter. Press onto the bottom of an 8-in. or 9-in. springform pan. Bake at 350° for 10 minutes. Cool. Meanwhile, for filling, drain raspberries and reserve juice. Set berries aside. In a small saucepan, combine juice, cold water and gelatin. Let stand for 5 minutes. Cook and stir over low heat until gelatin dissolves. Remove from the heat; cool for 10 minutes. In a mixing bowl, beat cream cheese and sugar until blended. Add berries and gelatin mixture; beat on low until thoroughly blended. Chill until partially set. Watch carefully, as mixture will set quickly. By hand, gently fold in whipped cream. Spoon into the crust. Chill for 6 hours or overnight. Just before serving, run knife around edge of pan to loosen. Remove sides of pan. Top with whipped cream and fresh raspberries. **Yield:** 10 servings.

## County Fair Pie

**(Pictured above)**

*I'm glad my family loves this pie, because it's so quick and easy to make that I never have to say no to requests. At potlucks, someone always asks for the recipe.*
—Judy Acuff, Lathrop, Missouri

 1/2 cup butter *or* margarine, melted
    1 cup sugar
 1/2 cup all-purpose flour
    2 eggs
    1 teaspoon vanilla extract
    1 cup coarsely chopped walnuts
    1 cup (6 ounces) semisweet chocolate chips
 1/2 cup butterscotch chips
    1 unbaked pastry shell (9 inches)

In a mixing bowl, beat the butter, sugar, flour, eggs and vanilla until well blended. Stir in nuts and chips. Pour into pie shell. Bake at 325° for 1 hour or until golden brown. Cool on a wire rack. **Yield:** 6-8 servings.

---

### *Pleasing Pie Crusts*

Pie crust ingredients (even the flour) should be cold to produce the very best results. All-purpose or pastry flour makes a tasty, flaky crust. Cake flour is too soft, and bread flour has too much gluten to make a tender pie crust.

---

### ▼ ▼ ▼

# '*I Wish I Had That Recipe...*'

IT'S LIKELY you've tasted a special dish at a favorite restaurant and wanted to try making it at home. Such was the case for Renie Smith of Rapid City, South Dakota. "The Lemon Cream Cheese Pie at Al's Oasis in Chamberlain, South Dakota is wonderful—I'd love to be able to make it," she told us.

"But the owners and staff are always bustling to serve hungry customers, and I've never asked about it. Do you think they'd share that recipe with *Taste of Home* readers?"

When we phoned Al's Oasis with Renie's request, Dee Geddes, a member of the family who owns Al's, said, "We'll be happy to share!"

Dee told us her family's restaurant is known for home-baked pies, buffalo burgers and delicious prime rib.

And why was she so willing to share such a popular recipe? "When I got my first issue of *Taste of Home*," Dee said, "I saw several recipes in it that I thought I could use in the restaurant!"

Spacious Al's Oasis seats 450 people and is located along Interstate 90 between Chamberlain and Oacoma, South Dakota. The phone number is 1-605/734-6051.

## Lemon Cream Cheese Pie

> 1 cup sugar
> 1/2 cup cornstarch

2-1/2 cups cold water
   3 egg yolks, beaten
2/3 cup lemon juice, *divided*
1/8 teaspoon salt
   3 tablespoons butter *or* margarine
   1 can (14 ounces) sweetened condensed milk
   1 package (8 ounces) cream cheese, softened
   1 package (3.4 ounces) instant lemon pudding mix
   2 pie shells (9 inches), baked
**Whipped cream**
**Lemon slices**

In a saucepan, combine sugar and cornstarch. Gradually stir in water, mixing until smooth. Cook and stir over medium-high heat until thickened and clear. Quickly stir in egg yolks. Bring to a boil; boil for 1 minute, stirring constantly. Remove from the heat; stir in 1/3 cup lemon juice, salt and butter. Cool for several hours or overnight. In a mixing bowl, blend condensed milk and cream cheese until smooth. Stir in pudding mix and remaining lemon juice. Fold into chilled lemon filling. Divide and spoon into baked pie shells. Refrigerate for several hours. Garnish with whipped cream and lemon slices. **Yield:** 2 pies (12-16 servings).

### ▼ ▼ ▼

---

## Crustless French Apple Pie

*This is a delicious apple pie. The fact that there's no crust means it's low in fat and can fit into restricted diets. The streusel topping makes it special.*
—*Nichole Tucker, Liberty, Missouri*

✓ Uses less fat, sugar or salt. Includes Nutritional Analysis and Diabetic Exchanges.

   6 cups sliced peeled tart apples
1-1/4 teaspoons ground cinnamon
  1/4 teaspoon ground nutmeg
   1 cup sugar
  3/4 cup fat-free milk
  3/4 cup reduced-fat biscuit/baking mix
   4 egg whites
**STREUSEL:**

3/4 cup reduced-fat biscuit/baking mix
1/2 cup Grape-Nuts
1/3 cup packed brown sugar
  2 tablespoons reduced-fat margarine, softened

Coat a 10-in. pie plate with nonstick cooking spray. In a bowl, combine apples, cinnamon and nutmeg; place in pie plate. In a mixing bowl, beat sugar, milk, biscuit mix and egg whites until smooth. Pour over apples. Combine all streusel ingredients in a bowl; mix until crumbly. Sprinkle over pie. Bake at 325° for 70-75 minutes or until knife inserted near center comes out clean. Cool. **Yield:** 8 servings. **Nutritional Analysis:** One serving equals 305 calories, 375 mg sodium, 0 cholesterol, 67 gm carbohydrate, 5 gm protein, 3 gm fat.

## Citrus Cheesecake

**(Pictured below and on page 115)**

*Here's the perfect cheesecake for spring or for a special gathering any time of year. The rich, cookie-like crust and creamy filling make the zesty, citrus taste a wonderful surprise. This dessert takes time to prepare, but one bite will tell you it's worth it!*
—*Marcy Cella, L'Anse, Michigan*

    1 **cup sifted all-purpose flour**
1/4 **cup sugar**
    1 **teaspoon grated lemon peel**
1/2 **teaspoon vanilla extract**
    1 **egg yolk**
1/4 **cup butter *or* margarine, softened**
**FILLING:**
    5 **packages (8 ounces *each*) cream cheese, softened**
1-3/4 **cups sugar**
    3 **tablespoons all-purpose flour**
1-1/2 **teaspoons grated lemon peel**
1-1/2 **teaspoons grated orange peel**
1/4 **teaspoon vanilla extract**
    5 **eggs**
    2 **egg yolks**
1/4 **cup whipping cream**

**TOPPING:**
1-1/2 **cups (12 ounces) sour cream**
    3 **tablespoons sugar**
    1 **teaspoon vanilla extract**

In a bowl, combine flour, sugar, peel and vanilla. Make a well; add yolk and butter. Mix with hands until ball is formed. Wrap with plastic wrap; chill at least 1 hour. Grease bottom and sides of a 9-in. springform pan. Remove sides. Divide dough in half. Between waxed paper, roll half of dough to fit bottom of pan. Peel off top paper; invert dough onto bottom of pan. Remove paper; trim dough to fit pan. Bake at 400° for 6-8 minutes or until lightly browned. Cool. Divide remaining dough into thirds. Fold a piece of waxed paper in half; place one-third inside folded paper. Roll dough into 9-1/2- x 2-1/2-in. strip. Trim and patch as needed. Repeat with remaining dough to make two more strips. Tear away top layer of paper from strips. Put together pan with crust on bottom. Fit dough strips to side of pan, overlapping ends. Press ends of dough together; press sides of dough to bottom crust to seal. Chill. Beat cream cheese, sugar, flour, peels and vanilla until mixed. Beat in eggs and yolks. Add cream; beat just until mixed. Pour into crust. Bake at 500° for 10 minutes. Reduce heat to 250°; bake 1 hour. Cool slightly. Combine topping ingredients; spread over cake. Chill overnight. **Yield:** 12-16 servings.

---

## Homemade Pudding Mix

*Whole milk and butter give this delicious chocolate pudding its rich, creamy flavor. For a fat-free version, leave out the butter and substitute water for the 2 cups of milk in the pudding. Since the mix already includes nonfat dry milk, it will still be creamy and calcium rich.* —*Gayle Becker, Mt. Clemens, Michigan*

**DRY MIX:**
    4 **cups nonfat dry milk powder**
2-2/3 **cups sugar**
1-1/3 **cups cornstarch**
    1 **to 1-1/3 cups baking cocoa**
1/2 **teaspoon salt**
**PUDDING:**
    2 **cups milk**
    1 **tablespoon butter *or* margarine**
1/2 **teaspoon vanilla extract**

For mix, sift together all ingredients. Store in an airtight container or resealable plastic bag. For pudding, combine 1 cup mix with milk in a saucepan. Bring to a boil, stirring constantly. Stir in butter and vanilla. Pour into individual serving dishes. Serve warm. **Yield:** 9 batches (4 servings per batch).

## Berry Creme Parfaits

**(Pictured below and on page 114)**

*Two "dairy" fine ingredients—cold milk and smooth sour cream—combine with fresh summer berries in this pretty dessert from the United Dairy Industry Association and the Wisconsin Milk Marketing Board.*

    1/2 cup sugar
      1 envelope unflavored gelatin
  1-3/4 cups milk
      2 cups (16 ounces) sour cream
      1 teaspoon vanilla extract
      2 cups fresh *or* frozen blueberries *or*
        raspberries, thawed

In a medium saucepan, combine sugar and gelatin. Stir in milk. Cook and stir over medium heat until gelatin is dissolved. Remove from the heat; stir in sour cream and vanilla. Cover and chill for about 2 hours or until the mixture mounds when dropped from a spoon. Spoon 1/8 cup of berries into parfait glasses or glass bowls. Top each with about 1/8 cup of creme mixture. Repeat layers. Serve immediately. **Yield:** 8 servings.

## Washington State Apple Pie

**(Pictured above and on page 114)**

*This pie won Grand Champion in the Apple Pie category at the 1992 Okanogan County Fair. The pie looks traditional, but making your own filling gives it a different flair and great taste.*          —Dolores Scholz
*Tonasket, Washington*

      6 cups sliced peeled tart apples (5 to 6
        medium)
      2 tablespoons water
      1 tablespoon lemon juice
    1/2 cup sugar
    1/2 cup packed brown sugar
      3 tablespoons all-purpose flour
      1 teaspoon ground cinnamon
    1/4 teaspoon ground nutmeg
    1/8 teaspoon ground ginger
    1/8 teaspoon salt
**Pastry for double-crust pie (9 inches)**

In a saucepan, combine apples, water and lemon juice; cook over medium-low heat just until the apples are tender. Remove from the heat and cool (do not drain). In a large bowl, combine sugars, flour, cinnamon, nutmeg, ginger and salt; add apples and toss to coat. Place bottom pastry in pie plate; add apple mixture. Cover with top pastry; seal and flute edges. Cut slits in top crust. Bake at 450° for 10 minutes. Reduce heat to 350°; bake 35-45 minutes longer or until golden brown. **Yield:** 6-8 servings.

# Country-Style Condiments

**These sauces, marinades and jams will give your home-cooked meals a special touch and flavor.**

**EXCEPTIONAL EXTRAS.** Clockwise from upper left: Cranberry Vinegar (p. 132), No-Salt Seasoning (p. 130), Tomato Chutney (p. 131) and Chocolate Sauce (p. 132).

# Spice Up Summer Grilling

RUTHIE and Charlie Knote of Cape Girardeau, Missouri wrote the book on great grilling. *Barbecuing and Sausage-Making Secrets* is packed with 250 recipes for rubs, marinades and sauces.

Try a few of their recipes below, or contact the Culinary Institute of Smoke-Cooking, 1342 Columbine St., Denver, CO 80206-2304 for cookbook and course information. The phone number is 1-303/321-7424.

## All-Purpose Marinade

  1 cup vegetable oil
1/4 cup soy sauce
1/2 cup vinegar
1/3 cup lemon juice
1/2 cup Worcestershire sauce
  2 tablespoons ground mustard
  1 teaspoon salt
  1 tablespoon pepper
  2 teaspoons chopped fresh parsley
1/2 teaspoon garlic powder
1/2 to 1 teaspoon hot pepper sauce, optional

Combine all ingredients in a blender container or food processor. Puree until parsley is finely minced. Can be used as a marinade or baste for beef or game. **Yield:** 2-1/2 cups.

— 🌶 🌶 🌶 —

## Teriyaki Marinade

1/2 cup soy sauce
  3 tablespoons sugar
  2 tablespoons sherry *or* beef broth
1/2 teaspoon garlic powder
1/2 teaspoon ground ginger

Combine all ingredients in a bowl; mix well. Pour over beef; cover and refrigerate for 2 to 24 hours. **Yield:** 1/2 cup.

— 🌶 🌶 🌶 —

## Barbecue Sauce with Mustard

1/2 cup sugar
1/4 teaspoon ground oregano
1/2 teaspoon ground thyme
  1 teaspoon salt
1/2 teaspoon pepper

1/8 teaspoon cayenne pepper
1/2 teaspoon cornstarch
1/2 cup vinegar
  1 cup molasses
  1 cup ketchup
  1 cup prepared mustard
  2 tablespoons vegetable oil

Combine first seven ingredients in a saucepan. Stir in enough vinegar to make a paste. Combine molasses, ketchup, mustard, oil and rest of vinegar; add to paste. Bring to a boil, stirring constantly. Reduce heat; simmer 10 minutes. Remove from heat; cool completely. Pour into a glass jar; cover tightly. Store refrigerated for up to 3 months. Baste smoked chicken, turkey, ham or hot dogs. **Yield:** about 4 cups.

— 🌶 🌶 🌶 —

## Seafood Butter Sauce and Baste

1/2 cup butter *or* margarine
1/2 teaspoon dried rosemary, crushed
1/2 teaspoon dried tarragon
3/4 teaspoon salt
  1 tablespoon lemon juice

Melt butter in a small saucepan over medium heat. Add all of the remaining ingredients. Brush on seafood; baste occasionally during grilling. May also be served warm as a dipping sauce with shrimp, crawfish, crab and lobster. **Yield:** 1/2 cup.

— 🌶 🌶 🌶 —

## Lemon Pepper Thyme Rub

  6 tablespoons lemon-pepper seasoning
  2 tablespoons ground thyme
  2 tablespoons paprika
  2 teaspoons dried minced garlic
  1 teaspoon sugar
1/2 teaspoon salt
1/4 teaspoon ground coriander
1/8 teaspoon ground cumin
1/8 teaspoon cayenne pepper

Combine all ingredients in a bowl; mix well. Apply generously to steaks or hamburgers. Store unused portion in a covered glass container. **Yield:** 1/2 cup.

## Honey Fruit Dressing

### (Pictured above)

*I love to use this dressing for a salad of colorful fresh fruits. Mix the dressing with a medley of watermelon, cantaloupe, peaches, grapes, strawberries or whatever you have on hand for a flavorful brunch dish.*
—*Dorothy Anderson, Ottawa, Kansas*

2/3 cup sugar
1 teaspoon ground mustard
1 teaspoon paprika
1 teaspoon celery seed
1/4 teaspoon salt
1/3 cup honey
1/3 cup vinegar
1 tablespoon lemon juice
1 teaspoon grated onion
1 cup vegetable oil

In a mixing bowl, combine sugar, mustard, paprika, celery seed and salt. Add honey, vinegar, lemon juice and onion. Pour oil into mixture very slowly, beating constantly. Serve with fresh fruit. Store in the refrigerator. **Yield:** 2 cups.

— 🝯 🝯 🝯 —

## Strawberry Vinegar

*Rosy-colored and unexpected, this flavored vinegar won a prize at a "berry-off" cooking contest. The vinegar makes a delightful vinaigrette for salads or other vegetables, such as broccoli and asparagus.*
—*Marilyn Nash, Orange City, Florida*

**Fresh whole strawberries, rinsed**
**Vinegar**
**Sugar**

Fill a large jar with rinsed strawberries (do not hull). Cover with vinegar and seal. Refrigerate for 10 days. Strain and measure vinegar; discard berries. For each pint of vinegar, add 3 cups of sugar. Bring mixture to a boil; boil 2 minutes. Cool. Pour into sterile bottles or jars; seal.

— 🝯 🝯 🝯 —

## Lo-Cal Blueberry Jam

*Fresh blueberry jam is tasty, plus it's rich in vitamin C, vitamin A and iron. This is a favorite on our farm, where we grow 24 acres of blueberries.*
—*Connie Sanders, Belle River, Prince Edward Island*

5 cups fresh blueberries *or* 2 packages
  (12 ounces *each*) unsweetened frozen
  blueberries, thawed
1 package (1-3/4 ounces) fruit pectin
  powder
2 tablespoons lemon juice
3-1/2 teaspoons liquid artificial sweetener

In a saucepan, mash blueberries. Stir in pectin and lemon juice. Bring to a boil; boil 1 minute. Remove from the heat; stir in the sweetener. Stir for 2 minutes. Spoon into jars. Cool. Cover, seal and refrigerate. **Yield:** 1-1/2 pints.

— 🝯 🝯 🝯 —

## Maple Cherry Syrup

*This fruity warm syrup will add flair and flavor to pancakes, waffles or French toast at your breakfast table. Orange juice, lemon juice and tart cherries mix with traditional maple syrup in this recipe provided by the Cherry Marketing Institute.*

3/4 cup maple syrup
1/2 cup packed brown sugar
1/4 cup honey
Juice of 1 orange plus 1 teaspoon grated peel
Juice of 1/2 lemon plus 1/2 teaspoon grated peel
1 tablespoon butter *or* margarine
1/2 teaspoon ground cinnamon
1/2 cup dried tart cherries, chopped

In a medium saucepan, combine the first five ingredients. Bring to a boil over medium heat, stirring occasionally. Reduce heat and simmer 10 minutes. Add cherries. Cook for 2 minutes. Serve over pancakes, waffles or French toast. **Yield:** 1-1/2 cups.

## No-Salt Seasoning

### (Pictured on page 127)

*When you first start on a low-salt diet, everything tastes bland until your taste buds have time to adjust. This seasoning will help overcome that blandness.*
—*Roma Lea Short, Baldwyn, Mississippi*

5 teaspoons onion powder
1 tablespoon garlic powder
1 tablespoon paprika
1 tablespoon ground mustard
1 teaspoon dried thyme
1/2 teaspoon pepper
1/2 teaspoon celery seed

Combine all ingredients in a small jar with a shaker top. Use for seasoning broiled fish, poultry, cooked vegetables, soups and stews, or place it on the table to be used by individuals at mealtime. **Yield:** about 1/3 cup.

— 🥤 🥤 🥤 —

## Herbed Honey Lime Sauce

### (Pictured below)

*The National Honey Board suggests you keep this savory sauce in the refrigerator to serve over a variety of meats. It's quick to prepare and adds a pleasant surprise to your meal.*

1/2 cup chopped onion
1 tablespoon olive *or* vegetable oil
1 cup chicken broth *or* dry white wine
1/4 cup honey

1/4 cup lime juice
2 teaspoons ground mustard
1 teaspoon fresh rosemary, minced *or* 1/4 teaspoon dried rosemary, crushed
1/2 teaspoon salt
Dash pepper
1 tablespoon cornstarch
1 tablespoon water

In a saucepan, saute the onion in oil until tender. Stir in the broth or wine, honey, lime juice, mustard, rosemary, salt and pepper; bring to a boil. Reduce the heat. Combine the cornstarch and water; stir into the sauce. Cook and stir over medium heat until thickened. Serve over turkey, chicken, fish or pork. Cover and refrigerate any leftovers. **Yield:** about 1-1/2 cups.

— 🥤 🥤 🥤 —

## Chivey Potato Topper

*Folks would likely turn away from a plain baked potato. But this cool and creamy topper—featuring fresh chives—adds some spark to spuds!*
—*Ruth Andrewson, Leavenworth, Washington*

1 package (8 ounces) cream cheese, softened
1/3 cup half-and-half cream
1-3 tablespoons snipped fresh chives
1-1/2 teaspoons lemon juice
1/2 teaspoon garlic salt
Baked potatoes

In a small bowl, beat cream cheese and cream. Blend in chives, lemon juice and garlic salt; mix well. Serve on baked potatoes. **Yield:** 1 cup.

— 🥤 🥤 🥤 —

## Creamy Onion Dill Dressing

*I like this dressing because it's creamy and has a great, fresh taste. You don't have to be watching your diet to enjoy it.* —*Jennie Wilburn, Long Creek, Oregon*

✓ Uses less fat, sugar or salt. Includes Nutritional Analysis and Diabetic Exchanges.

1 cup plain reduced-fat yogurt
2 tablespoons reduced-fat mayonnaise
1-1/4 teaspoons fresh dill weed, snipped
1/2 teaspoon dried parsley flakes
1/4 teaspoon garlic powder
1/8 teaspoon pepper
1/2 teaspoon low-sodium beef bouillon granules

1 teaspoon hot water
1 teaspoon dried minced onion

In a small bowl, mix yogurt and mayonnaise. Add dill, parsley, garlic powder and pepper. In another bowl, dissolve bouillon in water. Add onion; add to yogurt mixture and mix well. Refrigerate several hours before serving. **Yield:** 1 cup. **Nutritional Analysis:** One 2-tablespoon serving equals 31 calories, 45 mg sodium, 3 mg cholesterol, 3 gm carbohydrate, 2 gm protein, 1 gm fat. **Diabetic Exchanges:** 1/2 vegetable, 1/2 fat. **Editor's Note:** This dressing also makes a good low-fat vegetable dip.

— 🍵 🍵 🍵 —

## Cherry Honey Relish

*A wonderful accompaniment to cooked chicken or turkey, this colorful relish provides plenty of pizzazz to help make any occasion special. The recipe is provided courtesy of the Cherry Marketing Institute.*

1 can (16 ounces) tart cherries, undrained
1/2 cup raisins
1/2 cup honey
1/4 cup packed brown sugar
1 tablespoon cider vinegar
1/2 teaspoon ground cinnamon
1/8 teaspoon ground cloves
1/2 cup coarsely chopped pecans
1 tablespoon cornstarch
1 tablespoon water

In a saucepan, combine cherries, raisins, honey, brown sugar, vinegar, cinnamon and cloves. Cook, uncovered, over medium heat for 10-15 minutes or until sugar is dissolved and mixture is hot. Remove from heat; stir in pecans. Combine cornstarch and water; mix well. Gradually stir into cherry mixture. Cook, stirring constantly, until mixture thickens. Serve over slices of hot cooked chicken or turkey. **Yield:** 2-1/2 cups.

— 🍵 🍵 🍵 —

## Italian Herb Blend

*I dry the herbs from my garden and prepare my Italian Herb Blend. I store it in airtight containers, then sprinkle it in soups and stews all winter.*
—*Frances Tiocano, Morgan Hill, California*

6 tablespoons dried basil
2 tablespoons dried oregano
1 tablespoon dried marjoram
1 tablespoon dried thyme

Combine all ingredients. Use in stews (plus soups, meat loaf, spaghetti sauce and salad dressings).

## Tomato Chutney

**(Pictured above and on page 127)**

*This flavorful chutney is perfect over slices of ham, turkey or chicken. It dresses up a cracker spread with cream cheese and is an excellent topping for a cheese ball. I like it best spooned into peach halves—it's a real treat!*      —*Mrs. W.C. Tucker, San Antonio, Texas*

2 pounds tomatoes, peeled and coarsely chopped
1 pound tart apples, peeled, cored and chopped
2 medium onions, chopped
1 cup cider vinegar
1 tablespoon salt
1 cup packed brown sugar
1 cup golden raisins
1 garlic clove, minced
1/2 teaspoon ground cinnamon
1/2 teaspoon ground mustard
1/4 teaspoon cayenne pepper
1/8 teaspoon ground allspice
1/8 teaspoon ground ginger
1/8 teaspoon ground cloves

Combine all the ingredients in a large saucepan or Dutch oven; bring to a boil. Reduce heat and simmer, uncovered, for 1-1/2 to 2 hours or until mixture thickens, stirring frequently. Pack hot chutney into hot sterilized jars, leaving 1/4-in. headspace. Adjust caps. Process in a boiling-water bath for 10 minutes. **Yield:** 3 pints.

## Apple Spice Syrup

### (Pictured above)

*This syrup has just the right sweetness to complement your favorite pancakes or waffles. The spicy apple flavor is great for an autumn breakfast or whenever you'd like something a bit different.* —Renae Moncur
*Burley, Idaho*

     1/4 cup packed brown sugar
       2 tablespoons cornstarch
     1/4 teaspoon ground allspice
     1/8 teaspoon ground nutmeg
 1-3/4 cups apple juice *or* cider

In a saucepan, combine brown sugar, cornstarch, allspice and nutmeg; mix well. Add juice or cider. Cook and stir over medium heat until syrup is bubbly and slightly thickened. **Yield:** 1-3/4 cups.

## Cranberry Vinegar

### (Pictured on page 126)

*This rosy vinegar dresses up any favorite holiday salad in a shake. It also makes a pretty present.*
—Lesley Colgan, London, Ontario

   3/4 cup white vinegar
   3/4 cup water
   3/4 cup sugar
     1 cinnamon stick

     1 package (12 ounces) fresh *or* frozen cranberries

In a saucepan, bring all ingredients to a boil. Reduce heat; simmer for 5 minutes or until cranberries burst. Cool. Strain through a fine sieve into bottles or jars. Seal tightly. Discard cranberries and cinnamon stick. Chill until ready to use in your favorite vinegar-and-oil dressing. **Yield:** 1-1/2 cups.

## Chocolate Sauce

### (Pictured on page 126)

*I make different toppings so we can enjoy our favorite dessert—ice cream sundaes. This smooth, creamy sauce is always a big hit.* —Nancy McDonald
*Burns, Wyoming*

   1/2 cup butter *or* margarine
     2 squares (1 ounce *each*) unsweetened chocolate
     2 cups sugar
     1 cup half-and-half cream *or* evaporated milk
   1/2 cup light corn syrup
     1 teaspoon vanilla extract

In a saucepan, melt the butter and chocolate. Add the sugar, cream, corn syrup and vanilla. Bring to a boil, stirring constantly. Boil for 1-1/2 minutes. Remove from the heat. Serve sauce warm or cold over ice cream or pound cake. Refrigerate leftovers. **Yield:** about 3-1/3 cups.

## Pumpkin Butter

*This sweet butter is yummy on toast, biscuits or toasted English muffins. It can be made with pumpkin you've cooked yourself or with canned pumpkin.*
—Kathy Rhoads, Circleville, Ohio

 3-1/2 cups cooked *or* canned pumpkin
     1 tablespoon pumpkin pie spice
     1 package (1-3/4 ounces) powdered fruit pectin
 4-1/2 cups sugar

In a large saucepan, combine pumpkin, pumpkin pie spice and pectin; mix well. Stirring constantly, bring mixture to a boil. Quickly add the sugar. When the mixture returns to a boil, cook for 1 minute. Remove from the heat; skim off any foam. Ladle hot into hot jars, leaving 1/4-in. headspace. Adjust lids. Process in a boiling-water bath for 10 minutes. **Yield:** about 3 pints.

# Violets Perk Up Jam

A FAMILIAR flower is finding its way into more and more foods. The common meadow violet, which grows across most of North America, adds a flash of color and taste to your table.

Also known as Johnny-jump-ups or pansy violets, these petite purple and blue flowers flourish in fields, open woods and even some lawns from Canada to Texas.

The violet blossoms of this plant (fresh or candied) make a lovely edible garnish for salads and desserts, says Jeanne Conte of Columbus, Ohio. They can also be used to make jam or syrup.

The plant's small, heart-shaped leaves are delicious in a mixed-green salad, simmered briefly in soups, brewed as a tea or combined with other cooked greens. Below, Jeanne shares two of her most cherished violet recipes.

— 🏮 🏮 🏮 —

## Candied Violets

*Your surprise ingredient will be the talk of the table if you add beautiful candied-violet garnishes to salads or desserts.*

>      2 egg whites
> Sugar
>      1 large bunch wild violets* (including stems), washed

In a bowl, beat egg whites with a wire whisk just until frothy. Place sugar in another bowl. Taking one violet at a time, pick it up by the stem and dip into egg whites, covering all surfaces. Gently dip into the sugar, again being sure all of the petals, top and bottom, are covered. Place on waxed paper-lined baking sheets; snip off stems. Using a toothpick, open petals to original shape. Sprinkle sugar on any uncoated areas. Dry in a 200° oven for 30-40 minutes or until sugar crystallizes. Gently remove violets to wire racks with a spatula or two-tined fork. Sprinkle again with sugar if violets appear syrupy. Cool. Store in airtight containers with waxed paper between layers. **\*Editor's Note:** If you pick wild purple violets from residential lawns, be sure they haven't been sprayed recently. Do not use African violet varieties like those sold in flower shops or nurseries—and often grown as a houseplant. Those plants are not edible.

— 🏮 🏮 🏮 —

## Violet Jam

*Children, especially, like the taste of this jam. They seem to enjoy helping to make it, too.*

> 1-1/2 cups wild violet blossoms
> 1-1/2 cups water, *divided*
> Juice of 1 medium lime
> 2-1/3 cups sugar
>      1 package (1-3/4 ounces) powdered pectin

Rinse violet blossoms well and place in a blender. Add 3/4 cup water and lime juice; blend well. Gradually add sugar, blending until a smooth paste is formed. In a saucepan, combine pectin and remaining water; bring to a boil and boil for 1 minute. Add to blender and blend for 1 minute. Quickly pour into prepared jars or glasses and seal.

## Mint Jelly

*One whiff is all it takes to tell what we grow on our farm—peppermint! Harvesting 300 acres is hard work, but the invigorating scent keeps our taste buds tuned for minty treats. I use fresh mint or mint oil frequently in my cooking and baking. Try this aromatic jelly on lamb or oven-fresh biscuits.*          —Kandy Clarke
*Columbia Falls, Montana*

>      1 cup packed peppermint leaves
>      2 cups water
> 6-1/2 cups sugar
>      1 cup vinegar
> 1/2 teaspoon butter *or* margarine

>      1 package (6 ounces) liquid fruit pectin
>      3 to 4 drops green food coloring

In a Dutch oven, bring mint and water to a boil. Boil for 1 minute. Remove from the heat and pour through a fine sieve, reserving mint liquid. Discard leaves. Return liquid to Dutch oven. Add sugar, vinegar and butter; bring to a boil, stirring constantly. Quickly add contents of both pouches of pectin; bring to a full boil. Boil for 1 minute, stirring constantly. Remove from the heat; skim off any foam. Add food coloring. Immediately fill sterilized jars, leaving 1/4-in. headspace. Adjust caps. Refrigerate or process in a boiling-water bath for 5 minutes. **Yield:** about 6 half-pints.

# Potluck Pleasers

*Turn to this chapter for large-quantity favorites—from soups and salads all the way through dessert.*

**GOOD AND PLENTY.** Clockwise from upper left: Garden Bean Salad (p. 145), Gazpacho Salad (p. 138), Sausage and Mushroom Stew (p. 148), Pat's Potato Salad (p. 140), Sauerkraut Salad (p. 143), White Texas Sheet Cake (p. 146), Spicy Rice Casserole (p. 145) and Creamy Mocha Frozen Dessert (p. 149).

## Gazpacho Salad

### (Pictured at right and on page 134)

*Here's a beautiful and tasty way to use garden vegetables. This fresh, colorful salad is great to make ahead and take to a potluck later, after the flavors have had a chance to blend. It's sure to be a success!*
—Florence Jacoby, Granite Falls, Minnesota

　4 medium tomatoes, diced and seeded
　2 medium cucumbers, peeled and diced
　2 medium green peppers, seeded and diced
　1 medium onion, diced
　1 can (2-1/4 ounces) sliced ripe olives, drained
　1 teaspoon salt
1/2 teaspoon pepper
DRESSING:
1/2 cup olive *or* vegetable oil
1/4 cup vinegar
Juice of 1 lemon (about 1/4 cup)
　1 tablespoon chopped fresh parsley
　2 garlic cloves, minced
　2 teaspoons chopped green onions
1/2 teaspoon salt
1/4 teaspoon ground cumin

In a 1-1/2-qt. glass jar or bowl, layer one-third to one-half of the tomatoes, cucumbers, green peppers, onion, olives, salt and pepper. Repeat layers two or three more times. In a small bowl, combine all dressing ingredients. Pour over vegetables. Cover and chill several hours or overnight. **Yield:** 10-12 servings.

———— ♥ ♥ ♥ ————

## Vegetable Pasta Salad

### (Pictured at right)

*This light, multicolored salad is an original. When I serve it at potlucks, I'm always asked for the recipe. It's also a standby for the "snowbirds" who gather with us in Arizona each winter.* —Kathy Crow Cordova, Alaska

　12 ounces rotini pasta, cooked and drained
　6 green onions, thinly sliced
　1 to 2 small zucchini, thinly sliced
　2 cups frozen broccoli and cauliflower, thawed and drained
1-1/2 cups thinly sliced carrots, cooked until crisp-tender
　1 cup thinly sliced celery
1/2 cup frozen peas, thawed
　1 can (2-1/4 ounces) sliced ripe olives, drained
　1 jar (6 ounces) marinated artichoke hearts, drained and quartered

DRESSING:
1/2 cup mayonnaise
1/2 cup prepared Italian salad dressing
1/2 cup sour cream
　1 tablespoon prepared mustard
1/2 teaspoon Italian seasoning

In a large bowl, combine pasta, onions, zucchini, broccoli and cauliflower, carrots, celery, peas, olives and artichoke hearts. In a small bowl, combine dressing ingredients; mix well. Pour over pasta and vegetables and toss. Cover and refrigerate for at least 1 hour. **Yield:** 16-18 servings.

———— ♥ ♥ ♥ ————

## Poppy Seed Bread

### (Pictured at right)

*This moist, rich bread is so delicious—it's very popular in our area. It gets golden brown and looks great sliced for a buffet. I also like to make miniature loaves to give as gifts.* —Faye Hintz, Springfield, Missouri

　3 cups all-purpose flour
2-1/4 cups sugar
1-1/2 tablespoons poppy seeds
1-1/2 teaspoons baking powder
1-1/2 teaspoons salt
　3 eggs, lightly beaten
1-1/2 cups milk
　1 cup vegetable oil
1-1/2 teaspoons vanilla extract
1-1/2 teaspoons almond extract
1-1/2 teaspoons butter flavoring
GLAZE:
3/4 cup sugar
1/4 cup orange juice
1/2 teaspoon vanilla extract
1/2 teaspoon almond extract
1/2 teaspoon butter flavoring

In a large bowl, combine first five ingredients. Add eggs, milk, oil and extracts. Pour into two greased 8-1/2-in. x 4-1/2-in. x 2-1/2-in. loaf pans. Bake at 350° for 60-65 minutes. Cool completely in pans. In a saucepan, bring all glaze ingredients to a boil. Pour over bread in pans. Cool for 5 minutes; remove from pans and cool completely. **Yield:** 2 loaves.

### Poppy Flavor

To keep poppy seeds fresh, store in an airtight container in the refrigerator for up to 6 months. To boost their flavor, toast seeds in a 350° oven just until they start to brown. There's no need to pre-toast seeds that will top baked goods.

**TASTY TRIO.** You're sure to get recipe requests when you serve tempting dishes like Vegetable Pasta Salad, Gazpacho Salad and Poppy Seed Bread (shown above, clockwise from left) at your next big gathering.

**SUPER SERVINGS.** Everyone will enjoy the taste when you bring Pizza Salad, Minestrone Soup and Sauerkraut Salad (shown above, top to bottom) to your next family reunion.

## Pizza Salad

### (Pictured at left)

*A fun summer dish, this is a different salad that tastes as good as it looks. I love to take it to parties—the wonderful zesty flavor really complements a barbecue.*
*—Debbie Jones, California, Maryland*

- 1 pound spiral macaroni, cooked and drained
- 3 medium tomatoes, diced and seeded
- 1 pound cheddar cheese, cubed
- 1 to 2 bunches green onions, sliced
- 3 ounces sliced pepperoni
- 3/4 cup vegetable oil
- 2/3 cup grated Parmesan cheese
- 1/2 cup cider *or* red wine vinegar
- 2 teaspoons dried oregano
- 1 teaspoon garlic powder
- 1 teaspoon salt
- 1/4 teaspoon pepper
- Croutons, optional

In a large bowl, combine macaroni, tomatoes, cheddar cheese, green onions and pepperoni. In a small bowl, combine, oil, Parmesan cheese, vinegar and seasonings; pour over macaroni. Cover and refrigerate for several hours. Top with croutons just before serving if desired. **Yield:** 16 servings.

---

## Minestrone Soup

### (Pictured at left)

*Here's the perfect summertime soup to put all those fresh garden vegetables to good use. It's great for a light meal served with a salad and warm bread.*
*—Lana Rutledge, Shepherdsville, Kentucky*

- 1 beef chuck roast (4 pounds)
- 1 gallon water
- 2 bay leaves
- 2 medium onions, diced
- 2 cups sliced carrots
- 2 cups sliced celery
- 1 can (28 ounces) diced tomatoes, undrained
- 1 can (15 ounces) tomato sauce
- 1/4 cup chopped fresh parsley
- Salt and pepper to taste
- 4 teaspoons dried basil
- 1 teaspoon garlic powder
- 2 packages (9 ounces *each*) frozen Italian *or* cut green beans
- 1 package (16 ounces) frozen peas
- 2 cans (15-1/2 ounces *each*) kidney beans, rinsed and drained

- 2 packages (7 ounces *each*) shell macaroni, cooked and drained
- Grated Parmesan cheese

Place roast, water and bay leaves in a Dutch oven; bring to a boil. Reduce heat; cover and simmer until meat is tender, about 3 hours. Remove meat; cool. Add onions, carrots and celery to broth; cook for 20 minutes or until vegetables are tender. Cut meat into bite-size pieces; add to broth. Add tomatoes, tomato sauce, parsley, seasonings, beans, peas and kidney beans. Cook until vegetables are done, about 10 minutes. Add macaroni; heat through. Remove bay leaves. Ladle into bowls; sprinkle with cheese. **Yield:** 40 servings (10 quarts).

---

## Sauerkraut Salad

### (Pictured at left and on page 134)

*I got this tangy recipe from my sister-in-law in Michigan. It always gets raves at potlucks. It's easy to prepare and can be made a day or two before the get-together.*
*—Diane Thompson, Nutrioso, Arizona*

- 1 can (16 ounces) sauerkraut, drained
- 1 cup grated carrots
- 1 cup chopped celery
- 1 cup chopped green pepper
- 1 cup chopped onion
- 1 jar (4 ounces) diced pimientos, drained
- 3/4 cup sugar
- 1/2 cup vegetable oil

In a large bowl, mix sauerkraut, carrots, celery, green pepper, onion and pimientos. In a jar or small bowl, combine sugar and oil. Pour over vegetables and mix well. Cover and refrigerate for at least 8 hours. **Yield:** 10-12 servings.

---

## Quick Fruit Salad

*I used to own a restaurant, so I'm used to cooking in big quantities. This salad is easy to make yet delicious.*
*—Ruth Andrewson, Leavenworth, Washington*

- 10 cans (20 ounces *each*) pineapple chunks, drained
- 10 cans (21 ounces *each*) peach pie filling
- 10 cans (11 ounces *each*) mandarin oranges, drained
- 10 cups green grapes
- 10 cups sliced bananas

Combine first four ingredients. Chill. Just before serving, fold in bananas. **Yield:** 100 servings.

## Kodiak Casserole

### (Pictured at right)

*Because it packs a little kick and has an interesting and tasty mix of ingredients, this is the perfect potluck for fall—or anytime. One of my husband's favorites, it's an Alaskan recipe I found in the early 1950s.*
—Kathy Crow, Cordova, Alaska

- 2 pounds ground beef
- 4 cups diced onions
- 2 garlic cloves, minced
- 3 medium green peppers, diced
- 4 cups diced celery
- 1 jar (5-3/4 ounces) stuffed green olives, undrained
- 1 can (4 ounces) mushroom stems and pieces, undrained
- 1 can (10-3/4 ounces) condensed tomato soup, undiluted
- 1 jar (8 ounces) picante sauce
- 1 bottle (18 ounces) barbecue sauce
- 2 tablespoons Worcestershire sauce
- 3 to 4 cups medium egg noodles, cooked and drained
- 1 cup (4 ounces) shredded cheddar cheese

In a Dutch oven, brown ground beef with onions and garlic; drain. Add remaining ingredients except cheese; mix well. Cover and bake at 350° for 1 hour or until hot and bubbly. Sprinkle with the cheese just before serving. **Yield:** 16-20 servings.

— 🍷 🍷 🍷 —

## White Texas Sheet Cake

### (Pictured at right and on page 134)

*This cake gets better the longer it sits, so I try to make it a day ahead. My mother-in-law introduced this deliciously rich cake to me. No one can stop at just one piece!* —Joanie Ward, Brownsburg, Indiana

- 1 cup butter *or* margarine
- 1 cup water
- 2 cups all-purpose flour
- 2 cups sugar
- 2 eggs, beaten
- 1/2 cup sour cream
- 1 teaspoon almond extract
- 1 teaspoon salt
- 1 teaspoon baking soda

FROSTING:
- 1/2 cup butter *or* margarine
- 1/4 cup milk
- 4-1/2 cups confectioners' sugar
- 1/2 teaspoon almond extract
- 1 cup chopped walnuts

In a large saucepan, bring butter and water to a boil. Remove from the heat; stir in flour, sugar, eggs, sour cream, almond extract, salt and baking soda until smooth. Pour into a greased 15-in. x 10-in. x 1-in. baking pan. Bake at 375° for 20-22 minutes or until cake is golden brown and tests done. Cool for 20 minutes. Meanwhile, for frosting, combine butter and milk in a saucepan. Bring to a boil. Remove from the heat; add sugar and extract and mix well. Stir in walnuts; spread over warm cake. **Yield:** 16-20 servings.

— 🍷 🍷 🍷 —

## Three Cheese Chicken Bake

### (Pictured at right)

*This is a hearty, comforting casserole that's always a crowd pleaser. The combination of flavors and interesting colors ensures I come home with an empty dish!*
—Vicky Raatz, Waterloo, Wisconsin

- 1/2 cup chopped onion
- 1/2 cup chopped green pepper
- 3 tablespoons butter *or* margarine
- 1 can (10-3/4 ounces) condensed cream of chicken soup, undiluted
- 1 can (8 ounces) sliced mushrooms, drained
- 1 jar (2 ounces) chopped pimientos, drained
- 1/2 teaspoon dried basil
- 1 package (8 ounces) noodles, cooked and drained
- 3 cups diced cooked chicken
- 2 cups Ricotta *or* cottage cheese
- 2 cups (8 ounces) shredded cheddar cheese
- 1/2 cup grated Parmesan cheese
- 1/4 cup buttered bread crumbs

In a skillet, saute onion and green pepper in butter until tender. Remove from the heat. Stir in the soup, mushrooms, pimientos and basil; set aside. In a large bowl, combine noodles, chicken and cheeses; add mushroom sauce and mix well. Transfer to a greased 13-in. x 9-in. x 2-in. baking dish. Bake, uncovered, at 350° for 40-45 minutes or until bubbly. Sprinkle with crumbs. Bake 15 minutes longer. **Yield:** 12-15 servings.

### *Cooking with Cheese*

Cheese can turn stringy or grainy when exposed to high heat. To avoid this, shred or cut cheese into small pieces, then stir it into the sauce or other mixture toward the end of the cooking process. Cook over low heat just until the cheese melts. Processed cheeses are not as flavorful as natural cheeses, but they melt easier because they contain emulsifiers.

**HARVEST HELPINGS.** Kodiak Casserole, Three Cheese Chicken Bake and White Texas Sheet Cake (shown above, top to bottom) are perfect for autumn potlucks.

# Cooking for One or Two

**The quantity of servings is small, but these dishes are big on flavor.**

**JUST THE RIGHT SIZE.** Clockwise from upper left: Garlic Chicken on Rice (p. 156), Apple Chicken Salad (p. 153), Cheesy Potato Cassserole (p. 153), Autumn Pork Chop Dinner (p. 155) and Chocolate Bread Pudding (p. 154).

In a bowl, combine bread, egg, carrot, onion, green pepper, celery, seasonings and 2 tablespoons chili sauce or ketchup. Add beef; mix well. Form into a loaf in an ungreased 5-3/4-in. x 3-in. x 2-in. loaf pan. Spoon remaining chili sauce or ketchup over loaf. Bake, uncovered, at 350° for 45-50 minutes or until meat is no longer pink. Serve with baked potatoes topped with shredded cheddar cheese if desired. **Yield:** 2 servings.

## Lime Cream Dessert

*A friend shared this recipe with me many years ago. I love the tart and sweet combination. It's so cool and refreshing on summer days.* —Peggy Burdick
Burlington, Michigan

> 1 egg, beaten
> 1/4 cup sugar
> 1/4 cup butter *or* margarine
> 1/4 cup lime juice
> 1 teaspoon grated lime peel
> 2 drops green food coloring
> 2/3 cup whipped cream

In the top of a double boiler, combine the egg and sugar. Cut the butter into tablespoons; add to double boiler. Add lime juice and peel; cook and stir over boiling water for 8-10 minutes or until thick. Remove from the heat; add food coloring. Cool. Fold in whipped cream. Chill for at least 1 hour. **Yield:** 1 serving.

## Vegetable Meat Loaf

### (Pictured above)

*I hate the thought of making too much and having leftovers for a week, so I've pared down my recipes. This one is simple and quick to prepare, plus the carrot, green pepper and celery make it nutritious and colorful. It's great served with cheddar-topped baked potatoes.* —Judi Brinegar, Liberty, North Carolina

> 1 slice bread, torn into small pieces
> 1 egg, beaten
> 1/4 cup shredded carrot
> 2 tablespoons finely chopped onion
> 2 tablespoons finely chopped green pepper
> 2 tablespoons finely chopped celery
> 1/2 teaspoon salt
> Dash *each* pepper and garlic powder
> 5 tablespoons chili sauce *or* ketchup, *divided*
> 1/2 pound ground beef
> 2 baked potatoes, optional
> Shredded cheddar cheese, optional

## Chocolate Bread Pudding

### (Pictured at right and on page 150)

*This is a fun recipe because the chocolate makes it different from traditional bread pudding. It's a rich, comforting dessert.* —Mildred Sherrer, Bay City, Texas

> 2 squares (1 ounce *each*) semisweet chocolate
> 1/2 cup half-and-half cream
> 1 egg
> 2/3 cup sugar
> 1/2 cup milk
> 1 teaspoon vanilla extract
> 1/4 teaspoon salt
> 4 slices day-old bread, crusts removed and cut into cubes (about 3 cups)
> Confectioners' sugar *or* whipped cream, optional

In a saucepan, melt the chocolate over low heat. Remove from the heat and stir in the cream until smooth; set aside. In a large bowl, beat the egg. Add the sugar, milk, vanilla and salt; mix well. Stir in the chocolate mixture. Add the bread cubes and toss to coat. Let stand for 15 minutes. Spoon into two greased 2-cup souffle dishes. Bake at 350° for 30-35 minutes or until a knife inserted near the center comes out clean. If desired, sprinkle with confectioners' sugar or top with a dollop of whipped cream. **Yield:** 2 servings.

—— 🍵 🍵 🍵 ——

## Autumn Pork Chop Dinner

**(Pictured below right and on page 150)**

*I like to cook for two and try to make just the right amount so I don't have leftovers. With its golden pork chops, tasty green beans and tangy cabbage, this meal-in-one is a favorite of my husband, William.*
—Cecelia Wilson, Rockville, Connecticut

**1 tablespoon vegetable oil**

**2 loin pork chops (1 inch thick)**
**2 cups shredded cabbage**
**1 tablespoon chopped fresh parsley**
**2 tablespoons brown sugar**
**2 medium potatoes, peeled and sliced 1/4 inch thick**
**1 cup fresh *or* frozen green beans**
**1 to 1-1/2 teaspoons lemon-pepper seasoning**
**3/4 cup apple juice**
**1/4 cup seasoned bread crumbs**
**1 tablespoon butter *or* margarine, melted**

In a large skillet, heat the oil over high. Brown chops on both sides; remove and set aside. Toss cabbage with parsley and brown sugar; place in an 11-in. x 7-in. x 2-in. baking dish. Top with potatoes and beans. Arrange chops over vegetables. Sprinkle with lemon-pepper. Pour apple juice over all. Cover and bake at 350° for 45 minutes or until the pork chops and vegetables are tender. Combine the bread crumbs and butter; sprinkle on top. Bake 15 minutes longer. **Yield:** 2 servings.

**FALL HARVEST.** Autumn Pork Chop Dinner and Chocolate Bread Pudding make a comforting combination.

# 'My Mom's Best Meal'

*No one cooks like Mom. Love is the common ingredient in these five delicious dinners that your family is sure to enjoy.*

**COOKING UP MEMORIES.** Clockwise from upper left: Palate-Pleasing Pot Roast (p. 176), A Timeless Chicken Supper (p. 164), Favorite Birthday Dinner (p. 168) and Grandma's Family Tradition (p. 172).

## Mom's farm kitchen was always filled with mouth-watering aromas, good, home-cooked food and lots of love.

*By Rosemary Pryor, Pasadena, Maryland*

AH, THE PRECIOUS memories of youth. I can still see the kitchen table in the farmhouse where I grew up as though it were yesterday. The table is meticulously set, and the glorious scent of baking ham fills the kitchen and spills into the rest of the house.

In reality, the 150-year-old house where I spent my childhood is long gone. But wonderful memories of the many meals our family spent together gathered 'round our huge kitchen table remain fresh in my mind.

I grew up believing my mom was the best cook in the world, and I haven't changed my mind over these many years.

Mom hardly ever used a recipe—she'd add a dash of this or a dab of that and end up with a delectable work of art. Nothing was as fabulous as Mom's Sunday dinners.

How I remember the aroma of her Old-Fashioned Baked Ham baking…her Glazed Sweet Potatoes cooking…her Sauerkraut Casserole brewing. Waiting for dinner to be ready, I felt suspended between bliss and agony. It all smelled so good, it was nearly impossible to hold off. I wanted to sneak at least a bite or two, but, of course, I didn't.

Pineapple and cloves added sweet flavor to the canned ham. Apples and sausage made the sauerkraut special, so that it blended perfectly with the ham. The maple glaze over the sweet potatoes was pure heaven.

And, oh, Mom's Hot Milk Cake! That was the ultimate ending to a perfectly wonderful meal.

I can't bring back those days, but I can keep the memories alive every time I make Mom's special Sunday dinner. She started a tradition of making family time special—with good, home-cooked food and lots of love—and I'm proud to say I've carried on the tradition with my own family. She's helped me do it.

— 🍷 🍷 🍷 —

**PICTURED AT LEFT:** Old-Fashioned Baked Ham, Sauerkraut Casserole, Glazed Sweet Potatoes and Hot Milk Cake (recipes are on the next page).

## Chicken dinner brings back warm memories of childhood days on the Nebraska homestead.

*By Peter Baumert, Jameson, Missouri*

AS THE YOUNGEST of six children, I didn't have a lot of patience. I always rushed through the blessing because I was in a hurry to eat one of Mom's great home-cooked meals.

Afterward, Mom (Mary Lou Baumert) would *finally* pass the food. It seemed like an eternity. It always smelled so good and I was so hungry. My brothers and I ate quickly so we'd be sure to get seconds. Of course, there wasn't any real danger. Mom always made plenty…but we weren't willing to take any chances.

Of all Mom's tasty meals, this has always been my favorite: Chicken and Rice Dinner, Carrot Raisin Salad, Homemade Bread and Lemon Bars. It reminds me of spring and summer on our family homestead, 160 acres of fertile farmland in Nebraska. My folks still live there.

When I left home as a bachelor, Mom sent along that chicken recipe, knowing it was my favorite. For years, it was my *only* recipe card.

It's not a really difficult recipe, but it sure is good. The chicken browns up nicely, and it tastes so good with the fluffy and flavorful rice.

I passed the card along to my wife, Denise, and she's since gotten many more recipes from my mom's fabulous collection. Denise fixes this old-time dinner often for me and our family.

The carrot salad is one of mom's favorites from many years ago. It hasn't lost its appeal, even after all this time.

I remember Mom's bread always tasted heavenly. You'd know how good it was going to be just by the aroma wafting through the kitchen.

Her Lemon Bars are a wonderful dessert. They're both tart and sweet at the same time. Boy, I could eat a handful of those back then. In fact, I still can today. I guess it's true the more things change, the more they stay the same.

— 🍳 🍳 🍳 —

**PICTURED AT LEFT:** Chicken and Rice Dinner, Carrot Raisin Salad, Homemade Bread and Lemon Bars (recipes are on the next page).

## Chicken and Rice Dinner

*My family always lines up for seconds of this hearty main dish when my wife, Denise, makes my mother's recipe. In this easy but tasty entree, the chicken bakes to a beautiful golden brown.*

> 1 broiler/fryer chicken (2 to 3 pounds), cut up
> 1/4 to 1/3 cup all-purpose flour
> 2 tablespoons vegetable oil
> 1-1/2 cups uncooked long grain rice
> 1 teaspoon poultry seasoning
> 1 teaspoon salt
> 1/2 teaspoon pepper
> 1 cup milk
> 2-1/3 cups water
> Chopped fresh parsley

Dredge chicken pieces in flour. In a skillet, heat oil on medium and brown chicken on all sides. Meanwhile, combine rice, poultry seasoning, salt, pepper, milk and water. Pour into a greased 13-in. x 9-in. x 2-in. baking pan. Top with chicken. Cover tightly with foil and bake at 350° for 55 minutes or until rice and chicken are tender. Sprinkle with parsley before serving. **Yield:** 4-6 servings.

## Carrot Raisin Salad

*This colorful traditional salad is one of my mother's favorites. It's fun to eat because of its crunchy texture, and the raisins give it a slightly sweet flavor. Plus, it's easy to prepare, which everyone appreciates.*

✓ Uses less fat, sugar or salt. Includes Nutritional Analysis and Diabetic Exchanges.

> 4 cups shredded carrots (about 4 to 5 large)
> 3/4 to 1-1/2 cups raisins
> 1/4 cup mayonnaise *or* salad dressing
> 2 tablespoons sugar
> 2 to 3 tablespoons milk

Place carrots and raisins in a bowl. In another bowl, mix together mayonnaise, sugar and enough milk to reach a salad dressing consistency. Pour over carrot mixture and toss to coat. **Yield:** 8 servings. **Nutritional Analysis:** One serving (prepared with fat-free milk and 1 cup raisins) equals 110 calories, 80 mg sodium, 2 mg cholesterol, 24 gm carbohydrate, 1 gm protein, 2 gm fat. **Diabetic Exchanges:** 1 fruit, 1 vegetable, 1/2 fat.

### Keeping Raisins

- Store raisins in a tightly sealed plastic bag at room temperature for several months. Raisins stored in the refrigerator or freezer will keep up to 1 year.
- If raisins clump together, put them in a strainer and spray hot, running water over them. Or pop them in the microwave on high for 15 seconds.

## Homemade Bread

*On more than one occasion while I was growing up, I stayed home sick from school, napped on the couch and woke to the aroma of my mother's freshly baked bread. That's enough to make anyone feel better!*

    **2 packages (1/4 ounce *each*) active dry yeast**
    **2 cups warm water (105° to 115°)**
  **2/3 cup nonfat dry milk powder**
    **2 tablespoons butter *or* magarine, melted**
    **2 tablespoons sugar**
    **1 tablespoon salt**
  **6 to 7 cups all-purpose flour**

In a large bowl, dissolve yeast in warm water. Stir in milk, butter, sugar, salt and enough flour to form a stiff dough. Turn out onto a floured surface; knead until smooth and elastic, about 10-12 minutes. Place in a greased bowl, turning once to grease top. Cover and let rise in a warm place until doubled, about 1 hour. Punch down and divide in half. Shape into two loaves and place in greased 8-in. x 4-in. x 2-in. pans. Cover and let rise until doubled, about 1 hour. Bake at 400° for 30 minutes or until golden brown. **Yield:** 2 loaves.

## Lemon Bars

**(Also pictured on front cover)**

*Memorable family meals were complete when these tangy bars were served when I was a child. That's still true today for my own family. The bars' sweetness rounds out the meal, but the lemony flavor keeps them light. Don't expect any leftovers!*

**CRUST:**
    **1 cup all-purpose flour**
  **1/3 cup butter *or* margarine, softened**
  **1/4 cup confectioners' sugar**
**TOPPING:**
    **1 cup sugar**
    **2 eggs**
    **2 tablespoons all-purpose flour**
    **2 tablespoons lemon juice**
  **1/2 teaspoon lemon extract**
  **1/2 teaspoon baking powder**
  **1/4 teaspoon salt**
**Confectioners' sugar**

Combine the crust ingredients and pat into an 8-in. square baking pan. Bake at 375° for 15 minutes. Meanwhile, for topping, combine the sugar, eggs, flour, lemon juice, extract, baking powder and salt in a mixing bowl. Mix until frothy; pour over crust. Bake at 375° for 18-22 minutes or until light golden brown. Dust with confectioners' sugar. **Yield:** 9 servings.

*Remembering those days when a special meal was part of the birthday present Mom gave to each child.*

*By Deborah Amrine, Grand Haven, Michigan*

WHEN we were growing up, Mom let us kids choose our favorite meal on our birthday, and then she'd prepare it for us. Oh, how I'd count the days until my turn!

It might seem like it would be a tough decision, because Mom made lots of great meals, but it wasn't. My brother, my two sisters and I each had our favorite.

I always picked Breaded Pork Chops, Cheese Potatoes, Chunky Applesauce and Chocolate Mayonnaise Cake. Today, that same meal is a favorite with our three sons. When I make it, I'm reminded of my childhood back in Columbus, Ohio.

We were always underfoot as Mom cooked. Using recipes she'd received from her mother, Mom made down-home food using simple ingredients—with extraordinary results.

The pork chops sizzling in the pan really teased your senses. Not only could you hear them, they made the whole house smell so good that it was very hard to wait until dinner!

Homemade applesauce has so much more flavor than canned bought at the store. This recipe has just the right amount of sweetness and cinnamon.

Mom's Cheese Potatoes are pure bliss, with melted cheddar cheese on top. I can't think of another potato dish I enjoy as much.

The Chocolate Mayonnaise Cake was always light and tasty with its rich brown sugar frosting. Sometimes I could talk Mom into giving "the birthday girl" an extra little piece.

Even today, whenever my husband, our boys and I visit Mom, I still request this meal. Absolutely nothing compares to Mom's home cooking made with her very own hands—and love.

—— 🥄 🥄 🥄 ——

**PICTURED AT LEFT:** Breaded Pork Chops, Cheese Potatoes, Chunky Applesauce and Chocolate Mayonnaise Cake (recipes are on the next page).

## Cheese Potatoes

*Don't let the basic ingredients fool you—this recipe has anything but ordinary taste. The hearty potatoes have a wonderful cheesy flavor and practically melt in your mouth. They're simple to prepare and impressive to serve.*

- 3 tablespoons butter *or* margarine
- 6 large potatoes, peeled and thinly sliced
- 1 teaspoon salt
- 1/4 teaspoon pepper
- 1 cup milk
- 2 cups (8 ounces) shredded cheddar cheese

Chopped fresh parsley

Melt butter in a large nonstick skillet. Cook potatoes until almost tender and lightly browned. Sprinkle with salt and pepper. Pour milk over all; cook gently until milk is absorbed. Sprinkle with cheese and allow to melt. Stir; sprinkle with parsley and serve immediately. **Yield:** 6 servings.

## Breaded Pork Chops

*These traditional pork chops have a wonderful home-cooked flavor like the ones Mom used to make. The breading makes them crispy outside and tender and juicy inside. Why not treat your family to them tonight?*

- 1/2 cup milk
- 1 egg, lightly beaten
- 6 pork chops (1 inch thick)
- 1-1/2 cups crushed saltines (about 45 crackers)
- 1/4 cup vegetable oil

In a shallow pan, combine the milk and beaten egg. Dip each pork chop in the mixture, then coat with cracker crumbs, patting to make a thick coating. Heat the oil in a large skillet. Cook pork chops, uncovered, for about 8-10 minutes per side or until browned and no pink remains inside. **Yield:** 6 servings.

## Chunky Applesauce

*There's just something extra special about homemade applesauce. This simple recipe is tart and not too sweet. It makes the perfect side dish, especially with pork chops or a pork roast.*

8 cups chopped peeled tart apples
(about 3-1/2 pounds)
1/2 cup packed brown sugar
2 teaspoons vanilla extract
1 teaspoon ground cinnamon

Place all ingredients in a large saucepan or Dutch oven. Cover and cook over medium-low heat for 30-40 minutes or until apples are tender. Remove from the heat; mash apples (a potato masher works well) until sauce is desired consistency. Serve warm or cold. **Yield:** 6 servings (about 3-1/2 cups).

### Applesauce Alternatives

Add color and texture to applesauce by leaving the peel on the fruit. For even more color and flavor, mix cranberry or cranapple juice into the sauce.

## Chocolate Mayonnaise Cake

*Mom always made this special cake for my birthday meal. It's very moist and has a nice, light chocolate taste. The flavorful frosting is the perfect topping.*

2 cups all-purpose flour
1 cup sugar
3 tablespoons baking cocoa
2 teaspoons baking soda
1 cup water
1 cup mayonnaise*
1 teaspoon vanilla extract
**BROWN SUGAR FROSTING:**
1/4 cup butter *or* margarine
1/2 cup packed brown sugar
2 tablespoons milk
1-3/4 cups sifted confectioners' sugar

In a large mixing bowl, combine flour, sugar, cocoa and baking soda. Add water, mayonnaise and vanilla; beat at medium speed until thoroughly combined. Pour into a greased 9-in. square or 11-in. x 7-in. x 2-in. baking pan. Bake at 350° for 30-35 minutes or until cake tests done. Cool completely. For frosting, melt butter in a saucepan. Stir in brown sugar; cook and stir until bubbly. Remove from the heat and stir in milk. Gradually add confectioners' sugar; beat by hand until frosting is of spreading consistency. Immediately frost cake. **Yield:** 9-12 servings. **\*Editor's Note:** Light or low-fat mayonnaise should not be substituted for regular mayonnaise in this recipe.

**Her grandmother's favorite birthday foods are still the core of a cherished family tradition.**

*By Julianne Johnson, Grove City, Minnesota*

YEARS AGO, my grandmother invited family and friends over on her birthday, and then she made the meal herself! Grandma always served this hearty Chicken Macaroni Casserole and family-favorite Picnic Baked Beans. Everyone gobbled up every bite as we celebrated this special woman's day.

Eventually, my mom—also a wonderful cook—took over the tradition, adding her own special Garden Potato Salad. I consider this to be a key ingredient to the menu. The crunchy radishes and creamy home-made dressing add an extra-special touch.

This tempting salad wasn't reserved for birthday parties, however. Mom would make it for summer picnics as well. No matter the gathering, this savory salad was always one of the first dishes to disappear.

Through the years, Mom also added Peanut Butter Pie to the menu. Everyone agrees that traditional birthday cake just can't hold a candle to this cool and creamy dessert. (And you'll be pleasantly surprised by its simple preparation!)

We loved a similar pie served at a local restaurant, but the cook wouldn't share the recipe with Mom. So she was determined to come up with her own version. She did, and we all thought it was as good as or even better than the restaurant version. Of course, it required a few taste tests to be sure!

With some special additions to Grandma's original menu, this mouth-watering meal has become a tradition I now serve for all the birthdays in my family.

**PICTURED AT LEFT:** Chicken Macaroni Casserole, Garden Potato Salad, Picnic Baked Beans and Peanut Butter Pie (recipes are on the next page).

## Chicken Macaroni Casserole

*My favorite main dish recipe passed on by Grandma and Mom, this casserole is considered "birthday food" because we often requested it for our birthdays. Hearty and flavorful, it's a real family pleaser.*

- 2 tablespoons butter *or* margarine
- 1/4 cup all-purpose flour
- 2 cups half-and-half cream
- 1-1/2 to 2 cups chicken broth
- 3/4 pound process American cheese, cubed
- 2 packages (7 ounces *each*) elbow macaroni, cooked and drained
- 3 cups cubed cooked chicken
- 1 jar (2 ounces) diced pimientos, drained
- 1 teaspoon salt
- 1/2 teaspoon pepper

Minced fresh parsley, optional

In a large saucepan, melt butter. Stir in flour until combined. Add cream and 1-1/2 cups of the broth all at once; stir until smooth. Cook and stir until thickened and bubbly; cook and stir 2 minutes more. Remove from the heat; add the cheese and stir until melted. Stir in macaroni, chicken, pimientos, salt and pepper. Add additional broth if needed. Pour into a 3-qt. baking dish. Bake, uncovered, at 350° for 40 minutes or until heated through. Sprinkle with parsley if desired. **Yield:** 6-8 servings.

## Garden Potato Salad

*The tasty dressing on this potato salad makes it special. A great combination of flavors is a real treat and gives a traditional recipe a whole new twist. It's perfect for almost any occasion, and I consider it a key part of my "Mom's Best Meal".*

- 6 large potatoes (about 3 pounds), cooked, peeled and cubed
- 4 hard-cooked eggs, sliced
- 2 celery ribs, diced
- 6 green onions with tops, sliced
- 6 radishes, sliced
- 1 teaspoon salt
- 1/2 teaspoon pepper

DRESSING:
- 3 eggs, beaten
- 1/4 cup vinegar
- 1/4 cup sugar
- 1/2 teaspoon ground mustard
- 1/2 teaspoon salt
- 1 cup mayonnaise *or* salad dressing

In a large bowl, combine potatoes, eggs, celery, green onions, radishes, salt and pepper; set aside. For dressing, combine eggs, vinegar, sugar, ground mustard and salt in a saucepan. Cook and stir over medium heat until thickened. Cool. Stir in mayonnaise; mix well. Pour over potato mixture; toss to coat. Refrigerate for several hours before serving. **Yield:** 8 servings.

## Picnic Baked Beans

*I loved it when my mom made these classic beans...
now I make them for my own family. They have great
old-fashioned flavor and are a real crowd pleaser. I
like to fix them for potlucks, picnics or as part of a summertime dinner.*

      3 cups dry navy beans (about 1-1/2 pounds)
      4 quarts cold water, *divided*
      1 medium onion, chopped
      1 cup ketchup
      1 cup packed brown sugar
      2 tablespoons molasses
      1 tablespoon salt
      2 teaspoons ground mustard
   1/4 pound bacon, cooked and crumbled

Rinse beans; place in a Dutch oven with 2 qts.
water. Bring to a boil; reduce heat and simmer for
3 minutes. Remove from the heat and let stand for
1 hour. Drain and rinse. Return beans to Dutch
oven with remaining water; bring to a boil. Reduce
heat; simmer for 1 hour or until beans are tender.
Drain, reserving cooking liquid. In the Dutch
oven or a 3-qt. baking dish, combine beans, 1
cup cooking liquid, onion, ketchup, brown sugar,
molasses, salt, mustard and bacon; mix well. Cover and bake at 300° for 2 to 2-1/2 hours or until
beans are as thick as desired. Stir occasionally
and add more of the reserved cooking liquid if
needed. **Yield:** 16 servings.

## Peanut Butter Pie

*This smooth creamy pie with a big peanut butter taste
reminds me of Mom. It's sure to be a hit around your
house, too. I like to make it in the summer because
it's simple to prepare and the kitchen stays cool.*

      4 cups milk
      2 packages (3 ounces *each*) cook-and-serve
         vanilla *or* chocolate pudding
   1/2 cup creamy peanut butter
   3/4 cup confectioners' sugar
      1 pie pastry (9 inches), baked
Whipped cream

In a saucepan, cook milk and pudding over medium heat until thickened and bubbly. Remove
from the heat and cool slightly. Meanwhile, in a
bowl, cut peanut butter into confectioners' sugar
until small crumbs form. (Peanut butter consistency may vary; add additional confectioners' sugar
if necessary.) Set aside about 2 tablespoons of
crumbs; sprinkle remaining mixture into pie shell.
Pour pudding over crumbs. Chill until set. Top with
whipped cream; sprinkle reserved crumbs on top.
**Yield:** 6-8 servings.

### Portable Pie Pans

Lightweight foil pie pans are usually smaller than
regular pans, so you may end up with extra filling.
If so, pour in custard cups for snacks.

*Mom's palate-pleasing pot roast recipe was often requested by family, friends and even customers.*

*By Adeline Piscitelli, Sayreville, New Jersey*

MY MOTHER simply loved to cook. She was well-known for her delicious everyday dinners for our family. Plus, it seemed she was always cooking for a wedding reception or some other party. My sister and I liked to help her whenever we could, and I certainly learned my way around the kitchen thanks to Mom.

Her delicious Old-Fashioned Pot Roast is a recipe she made often when I was growing up. It simmers slowly on the stove, so every mouth-watering bite of beef is moist and delicious. And we would gobble up the accompanying carrots in no time.

Sliced fresh mushrooms and simple seasonings are the secrets of success to Garlic-Buttered Green Beans. After all these years, this is still my favorite way to prepare garden-fresh green beans.

The recipe for Parsley Potatoes is simple, but the flavor is anything but plain. It's nice to have a tried-and-true recipe like this that pairs well with a variety of main dishes.

Years later, I served these same dishes in the family restaurant my husband and I ran. Our customers raved about the tasty beef, potatoes and beans—all recipes I got from Mom, prepared many times and never tired of. I was always pleased to bring a taste of my home to their table.

I'm retired from the restaurant business now, but I still like to do some catering. This pot roast meal, along with my own Peach Bavarian mold, is often requested by family, friends and customers.

I hope you enjoy this comforting meal as much as me and my family. It has a look and aroma that just say "home cooking"!

**PICTURED AT LEFT:** Old-Fashioned Pot Roast, Garlic-Buttered Green Beans, Parsley Potatoes and Peach Bavarian (recipes are on the next page).

simmer 45-60 minutes longer or until meat is tender. Remove meat and carrots to a serving platter and keep warm. Strain cooking juices; set aside. In the same Dutch oven, melt remaining butter. Stir in remaining flour; cook and stir until bubbly. Add 2 cups of the cooking juices and blend until smooth. Cook and stir until thickened; add additional cooking juices until gravy has reached desired consistency. **Yield:** 6-8 servings.

## Garlic-Buttered Green Beans

*These dressed-up beans are simple to make but look and taste special. They're a perfect side dish for nearly any meal.*

>     1 pound fresh *or* frozen green beans
>   1/2 cup sliced fresh mushrooms
>     6 tablespoons butter *or* margarine
>     2 to 3 teaspoons onion powder
>     1 to 1-1/2 teaspoons garlic powder
> **Salt and pepper to taste**

Cook green beans in water to cover until crisp-tender. Meanwhile, in a skillet, saute mushrooms in butter until tender. Add onion powder and garlic powder. Drain beans; add to skillet and toss. Season with salt and pepper. **Yield:** 6 servings.

## Old-Fashioned Pot Roast

*My sister, dad and I loved it when Mom made her pot roast. She was such a great cook! Later, I served this dish in our restaurant for many years. It's a recipe that just says "home cooking".*

>     1 boneless beef chuck roast (about 3 pounds)
>     6 tablespoons all-purpose flour, *divided*
>     6 tablespoons butter *or* margarine, *divided*
>     3 cups hot water
>     2 teaspoons beef bouillon granules
>     1 medium onion, quartered
>     1 celery rib, cut into pieces
>     1 teaspoon salt
>   1/2 teaspoon pepper
>     4 medium carrots, cut into 2-inch pieces

Sprinkle the roast with 1 tablespoon flour. In a Dutch oven, brown the roast on all sides in half of the butter. Add the water, bouillon, onion, celery, salt and pepper; bring to a boil. Reduce heat; cover and simmer for 1 hour. Add carrots; cover and

## Peach Bavarian

*Fruit molds are my specialty, and I enjoy making and serving them. This one, with its refreshing peach taste, makes a colorful salad or dessert.*

> 1 can (15-1/4 ounces) sliced peaches
> 2 packages (3 ounces *each*) peach *or* apricot gelatin
> 1/2 cup sugar
> 2 cups boiling water
> 1 teaspoon almond extract
> 1 carton (8 ounces) frozen whipped topping, thawed

**Additional sliced peaches, optional**

Drain peaches, reserving 2/3 cup juice. Chop peaches into small pieces; set aside. In a bowl, dissolve gelatin and sugar in boiling water. Stir in reserved syrup. Chill until slightly thickened. Stir extract into whipped topping; gently fold into gelatin mixture. Fold in peaches. Pour into a 6-cup mold coated with nonstick cooking spray. Chill overnight. Unmold; garnish with additional peaches if desired. **Yield:** 8-10 servings.

## Parsley Potatoes

*The fresh flavor of parsley is perfect with hot buttered potatoes—it adds a little extra zip. I used this recipe when I did all the cooking at our restaurant, and customers loved it.*

> 2 pounds potatoes, peeled and cut into 2-inch pieces
> 1/2 cup butter *or* margarine, melted
> 1/4 cup minced fresh parsley

**Salt and pepper to taste**

In a saucepan, cook potatoes in water to cover until tender; drain. Combine butter and parsley; pour over the potatoes and toss to coat. Season with salt and pepper. **Yield:** 6-8 servings.

## String-Free Beans

Green beans are also called string beans or snap beans. Wax beans are the pale yellow variety. Select beans with firm, smooth, brightly colored pods. Most fresh beans today do not require stringing because the fibrous string has been bred out of the species. If you have beans that do need stringing, simply snap off the stem end and use it to pull the string down and off the pod.

# *Editors' Meals*

**Taste of Home magazine is edited by 1,000 cooks across North America. On the following pages, you'll "meet" five of those editors and hear about their favorite meals.**

— 🍶 🍶 🍶 —

**FAMILY FAVORITES.** Clockwise from upper left: Southern-Style Thanksgiving (p. 198), Easter Lamb Dinner (p. 186), Grilled Summertime Supper (p. 190) and Easy Entertaining (p. 194).

*The glorious aroma of barbecued chicken welcomes her family home from Sunday morning church services.*

*By Esther Shank, Harrisonburg, Virginia*

MY HUSBAND, Rawley, and I grew up on dairy farms and operated one of our own for 20 years, raising our three daughters there. So for most of my life I've cooked big meals for a hungry family, farmhands and others who sat around our table. And I've enjoyed doing it.

Since moving from the farm, I've kept busy teaching a cooking class for young homemakers, doing volunteer work and helping at church. I've also published a cookbook based on my recipe collection.

I especially like make-ahead recipes and oven dishes that let me do something else while they're cooking. The main dish here, Oven Barbecued Chicken, is my Sunday standby. It goes into the oven before we leave for church, and its appetizing aroma welcomes us back home.

The chicken goes well with Mexican Corn Bread. Peppers and cheese give the bread zip, and buttermilk keeps it moist and pleasantly textured.

I use my crunchy, colorful Favorite Broccoli Salad as a garden-fresh accompaniment to this menu or just about any other meal. This salad has an unbeatable blend of vegetables, bacon and hard-cooked eggs.

It was difficult to choose my favorite dessert because there are so many! I finally decided on Deluxe Chocolate Marshmallow Bars, a longtime family favorite. These chewy, layered bars are always a hit at potlucks, church events and parties. I can't think of another recipe in my collection that's had so many requests.

I sure hope you enjoy this taste of my country cooking. Like most enthusiastic cooks, collecting and sharing great recipes has been a hobby I've enjoyed immensely over the years.

▼ ▼ ▼

**PICTURED AT LEFT:** Oven Barbecued Chicken, Favorite Broccoli Salad, Mexican Corn Bread and Deluxe Chocolate Marshmallow Bars (recipes are on the next page).

ing ingredients. Simmer, uncovered, for 15 minutes. Pour over chicken. Bake at 350° for 1 hour or until meat juices run clear, basting occasionally. **Yield:** 6-8 servings.

— ☕ ☕ ☕ —

## Favorite Broccoli Salad

*"Fresh tasting...so colorful...delicious dressing" are some of the compliments I get whenever I serve this broccoli salad with a meal or take it to a church dinner. Although I have many other good salad recipes, I'm especially fond of this one.*

      1 **bunch broccoli, separated into florets**
      1 **head cauliflower, separated into florets**
      8 **bacon strips, cooked and crumbled**
  1/3 **cup chopped onion**
      1 **cup chopped seeded tomatoes**
      2 **hard-cooked eggs, sliced**
      1 **cup mayonnaise *or* salad dressing**
  1/3 **cup sugar**
      2 **tablespoons vinegar**

In a large salad bowl, combine broccoli, cauliflower, bacon, onion, tomatoes and eggs; set aside. In another bowl, combine mayonnaise, sugar and vinegar; mix until smooth. Just before serving, pour dressing over salad and toss. **Yield:** 6-8 servings.

## Oven Barbecued Chicken

*Chicken and Sunday dinner go together in my mind. During my 20 years of married life on a dairy farm, I'd often brown the chicken and mix up the sauce while my husband milked, then pop it in the oven when we left for church. It was ready when we came home.*

**Vegetable oil**
      3 **to 4 pounds chicken pieces**
  1/3 **cup chopped onion**
      3 **tablespoons butter *or* margarine**
  3/4 **cup ketchup**
  1/3 **cup vinegar**
      3 **tablespoons brown sugar**
  1/2 **cup water**
      2 **teaspoons prepared mustard**
      1 **tablespoon Worcestershire sauce**
  1/4 **teaspoon salt**
  1/8 **teaspoon pepper**

Heat a small amount of oil in a large skillet; fry chicken until browned. Drain; place chicken in a 13-in. x 9-in. x 2-in. baking dish. In a saucepan, saute onion in butter until tender; stir in remain-

## Deluxe Chocolate Marshmallow Bars

*I'd have to say that I've been asked to share this chocolaty layered bar recipe more than any other recipe in my collection. It's a tried-and-true favorite of our three daughters. How many times we've all made these, I couldn't even count!*

    3/4 cup butter *or* margarine, softened
1-1/2 cups sugar
    3 eggs
    1 teaspoon vanilla extract
1-1/3 cups all-purpose flour
    1/2 teaspoon baking powder
    1/2 teaspoon salt
    3 tablespoons baking cocoa
    1/2 cup chopped nuts, optional
    4 cups miniature marshmallows
**TOPPING:**
1-1/3 cups (8 ounces) chocolate chips
    3 tablespoons butter *or* margarine
    1 cup peanut butter
    2 cups crisp rice cereal

In a mixing bowl, cream butter and sugar. Add eggs and vanilla; beat until fluffy. Combine flour, baking powder, salt and cocoa; add to creamed mixture. Stir in nuts if desired. Spread in a greased 15-in. x 10-in. x 1-in. pan. Bake at 350° for 15-18 minutes. Sprinkle marshmallows evenly over cake; bake 2-3 minutes longer. Using a knife dipped in water, spread the melted marshmallows evenly over cake. Cool. For topping, combine chocolate chips, butter and peanut butter in a small saucepan. Cook over low heat, stirring constantly, until melted and well blended. Remove from heat; stir in cereal. Spread immediately over bars. Chill. **Yield:** about 3 dozen.

## Mexican Corn Bread

*This tasty corn bread is easy to mix up. I serve it often with a meal or hearty bowl of soup as an alternative to rolls. Cheddar cheese makes it especially flavorful, and the diced peppers add nice color.*

    1 cup yellow cornmeal
    1/3 cup all-purpose flour
    2 tablespoons sugar
    1 teaspoon salt
    2 teaspoons baking powder
    1/2 teaspoon baking soda
    2 eggs, beaten
    1 cup buttermilk
    1/2 cup vegetable oil
    1 can (8-3/4 ounces) cream-style corn
    1/3 cup chopped onion
    2 tablespoons chopped green pepper
    1/2 cup shredded cheddar cheese

In a mixing bowl, combine the first six ingredients. Combine the remaining ingredients; add to the dry ingredients and stir just until moistened. Pour into a greased 9-in. square baking pan or 10-in. ovenproof skillet. Bake at 350° for 30-35 minutes or until bread is golden brown and tests done. **Yield:** 8-10 servings.

*Leg of lamb in a tempting purple plum and garlic glaze stars in this special family Easter dinner.*

*By Ann Eastman, Greenville, California*

OUR HOME is perched a mile high in the Sierra Nevada Mountains. My husband, Ken, and I discovered the area years ago while vacationing in our RV. Later we retired here on 6 beautiful, forested acres with a creek running along one edge.

Remodeling the old "barn house" that stood on the property was a challenge—especially the kitchen. We gutted it and started from scratch to build the most efficient kitchen I've ever had.

These days, I cook mostly for just the two of us, but I love to prepare special meals for family and friends. One of my favorite meals (and theirs, too, I'm told) is especially appropriate for springtime. Plum-Glazed Lamb is the centerpiece of a wonderful Easter dinner or an elegant meal for company.

Check with your butcher in advance about ordering a fresh leg of lamb—it may take a day or so to get it. Use fresh garlic in the glaze rather than garlic powder or garlic salt. You'll be glad you did!

To complement the flavorful lamb, I serve Minted Rice Casserole, which gets its crunch from almonds. My method for preparing the rice casserole—adding raw rice to boiling salted water, then rinsing it after 3 minutes—may seem odd. But it softens the rice just enough to really absorb the seasoning. Also, adding the mint to the rice for only the last 10 minutes of baking gives the casserole its delicate flavor.

To add a festive look to Grandmother's Orange Salad, I sometimes arrange mandarin oranges in the bottom of the mold and hold them in place with a bit of gelatin/sherbet mixture. (Chill it before adding the rest of the mixture.)

The Cherry Crumb Dessert is quick to make and tastes great topped with whipped cream or ice cream. You can substitute another fruit filling if you prefer.

— ▭ ▭ ▭ —

**PICTURED AT LEFT:** Plum-Glazed Lamb, Grandmother's Orange Salad, Minted Rice Casserole and Cherry Crumb Dessert (recipes are on the next page).

## Plum-Glazed Lamb

*Fruity and flavorful, this wonderful glaze is simple to prepare, and its hint of garlic really complements the leg of lamb. The recipe makes enough glaze to baste the lamb during roasting and leaves plenty to pass when serving.*

 1 **leg of lamb (4 to 5 pounds)**
**Salt and pepper to taste**
 2 **cans (16-1/2 ounces *each*) purple plums, pitted**
 2 **garlic cloves**
 1/4 **cup lemon juice**
 2 **tablespoons soy sauce**
 2 **teaspoons Worcestershire sauce**
 1 **teaspoon dried basil**

In a shallow baking pan, place lamb, fat side up, on rack. Season with salt and pepper. Roast at 325° for 2-1/2 to 3 hours or until meat thermometer reads 160° (medium) or meat reaches desired doneness. Meanwhile, drain plums, reserving 1/2 cup syrup. In a food processor or blender, place plums, reserved syrup, garlic, lemon juice, soy sauce, Worcestershire sauce and basil. Cover and process until smooth. Using half of the plum sauce, baste lamb every 15 minutes during the last hour of roasting. Simmer remaining sauce for 5 minutes and serve with meat. **Yield:** 10-12 servings.

## Grandmother's Orange Salad

*Perfect for spring, this gelatin salad is slightly sweet and tangy, too. It adds beautiful color to any meal and appeals to folks of all ages. When the weather starts turning warm, this cool, fruity salad is just right. Grandma knew what she was doing when she created this one!*

 1 **can (11 ounces) mandarin oranges**
 1 **can (8 ounces) crushed pineapple**
**Water**
 1 **package (6 ounces) orange gelatin**
 1 **pint orange sherbet, softened**
 2 **medium firm bananas, sliced**

Drain oranges and pineapple, reserving juices. Set oranges and pineapple aside. Add water to juices to measure 2 cups. Place in a saucepan and bring to a boil; pour over gelatin in a large bowl. Stir until gelatin is dissolved. Stir in sherbet until smooth. Chill until partially set (watch carefully). Fold in oranges, pineapple and bananas. Pour into a 6-cup mold coated with nonstick cooking spray. Chill until firm. **Yield:** 8-10 servings.

## Minted Rice Casserole

*The mild, minty flavor and almond crunch make this a nice side dish for a meal with lamb. People will likely be impressed when you prepare this different and palate-pleasing rice casserole.*

> **2 cups water**
> **2 teaspoons salt**
> **1 cup uncooked long grain rice**
> **1/4 cup butter *or* margarine**
> **Dash garlic salt**
> **1 can (14-1/2 ounces) chicken broth**
> **1/2 teaspoon dried mint leaves**
> **1/4 cup slivered almonds, toasted**

In a saucepan, bring water and salt to a boil. Remove from the heat; add rice. Cover and let stand for 3 minutes. Drain. Rinse rice with cold water; drain well. In a skillet, melt butter. Add rice and cook over medium heat, stirring frequently, until butter is almost absorbed, about 5 minutes. Turn into a 1-qt. casserole; sprinkle with garlic salt. Pour chicken broth over rice. Cover and bake at 325° for 35-40 minutes or until most of liquid is absorbed. Add mint and fluff with a fork. Sprinkle almonds over top. Bake, uncovered, 5-10 minutes more. **Yield:** 6 servings.

## Cherry Crumb Dessert

*This dessert is a sweet treat, especially when garnished with a dollop of whipped cream or a big scoop of ice cream! The crust and crumb topping have a wonderful nutty flavor, and the smooth fruit filling looks beautiful when served.*

> **1/2 cup cold butter *or* margarine**
> **1 package (18-1/2 ounces) yellow cake mix**
> **1 can (21 ounces) cherry *or* blueberry pie filling**
> **1/2 cup chopped walnuts**
> **Whipped cream *or* ice cream, optional**

In a mixing bowl, cut cold butter into cake mix as for pastry dough. Set aside 1 cup. Pat remaining crumbs onto the bottom and 1/2 in. up the sides of a greased 13-in. x 9-in. x 2-in. baking pan. Spread pie filling over crust. Combine the walnuts with reserved crumbs; sprinkle over the top. Bake at 350° for 30-35 minutes. Serve warm with whipped cream or ice cream if desired. **Yield:** 12-16 servings.

---

### *Getting Gelatin to Gel*

Pineapple contains an enzyme—bromelain—that prevents gelatin from setting properly. Since heat destroys the enzyme, cooked pineapple sets fine.

*When it's "cooking" outside, so is this Carolina mom. She heads to the grill when suppertime nears.*

*By Sharon Bickett, Chester, South Carolina*

FAMILY and friends are used to seeing me wrapped in an apron, standing beside our outdoor grill with tongs in hand. It's one of my favorite ways to cook—and something I learned from my two brothers when we were growing up in the quaint little village of Lockhart in the South Carolina Piedmont.

A wonderfully innovative cook, Mother was always in the kitchen preparing meals for the family or food for church socials, plus canning vegetables from her summer garden and baking all our favorite desserts. When it came time to fire up the grill, my brothers took over the dinnertime chores.

Since good home cooking played such an important role in my childhood, it seems only natural that cooking is a favorite activity around my home, too.

Being co-owner of the local hardware store keeps me busy, so my summertime meals need to be quick and easy yet satisfying for my husband, Al, and our son, Bert. They agree that Peppered Rib Eye Steaks and Hawaiian Kabobs fill the bill deliciously!

I'm proud to say that my steaks were featured in the 1992 National Beef Cook-Off. They start out with a quick herb rubdown called a dry marinade. Applied an hour before grilling, the herb flavors and zesty cayenne are absorbed by the beef. The kabobs have a sweet-tart taste that complements the meat. Conveniently, the kabobs also marinate for an hour.

My family loves the bacon and water chestnuts and the tangy dressing on my Crunchy Spinach Salad.

We usually save dessert to enjoy later in the evening when we're sitting in our rockers on the screened-in back porch. Nothing tastes as good as a piece of Sour Cream Apple Pie when we're looking out at the fields and woods that surround our place and enjoying a cool summer breeze.

**PICTURED AT LEFT:** Peppered Rib Eye Steaks, Crunchy Spinach Salad, Hawaiian Kabobs and Sour Cream Apple Pie (recipes are on the next page).

## Crunchy Spinach Salad

*A fresh salad is the perfect complement to any summer meal, like my grilled rib eye steaks. This salad, with its tangy dressing and crisp, crunchy ingredients, has become one of our very favorites.*

  8 cups fresh torn spinach
  1 can (14 ounces) bean sprouts, drained *or*
  2 cups fresh bean sprouts
  1 can (8 ounces) sliced water chestnuts, drained
  4 hard-cooked eggs, chopped
  6 bacon strips, cooked and crumbled
  1 small onion, thinly sliced
**DRESSING:**
  1/2 cup packed brown sugar
  1/2 cup vegetable oil
  1/3 cup vinegar
  1/3 cup ketchup
  1 tablespoon Worcestershire sauce

In a large bowl, combine spinach, bean sprouts, water chestnuts, eggs, bacon and onion. In a bottle or jar, combine all dressing ingredients. Cover and shake well to mix. Just before serving, pour dressing over salad and toss. **Yield:** 8 servings.

## Peppered Rib Eye Steaks

*A true Southerner to the core, I love to cook—especially on the grill. This recipe is one of my favorites! The seasoning rub makes a wonderful marinade, and nothing beats the summertime taste of these flavorful grilled steaks.*

  4 beef rib eye steaks (1-1/2 inches thick)
  1 tablespoon olive *or* vegetable oil
  1 tablespoon garlic powder
  1 tablespoon paprika
  2 teaspoons dried thyme
  2 teaspoons dried oregano
1-1/2 teaspoons pepper
  1 teaspoon salt
  1 teaspoon lemon-pepper seasoning
  1 teaspoon cayenne pepper
**Orange slices, optional**
**Parsley sprigs, optional**

Brush steaks lightly with oil. In a small bowl, combine all seasonings. Sprinkle seasonings over steaks and press into both sides. Cover and chill for 1 hour. Grill steaks, turning once, over medium-hot heat 14-18 minutes for rare; 18-22 minutes for medium; 24-28 minutes for well-done. Place on a warm serving platter; cut across the grain into thick slices. Garnish with orange slices and parsley if desired. **Yield:** 8 servings.

for 20 minutes or until vegetables are tender, turning and basting with marinade frequently. Serve over rice if desired. **Yield:** 8 servings.

— 🏆 🏆 🏆 —

## Sour Cream Apple Pie

*A cool, creamy version of a traditional apple pie, this delicious dessert is the perfect finish to a satisfying summer meal. Its crumbly topping and smooth apple filling are real crowd pleasers! Be prepared to serve seconds.*

>     2 eggs
>     1 cup (8 ounces) sour cream
>     1 cup sugar
>     6 tablespoons all-purpose flour, *divided*
>     1 teaspoon vanilla extract
>   1/4 teaspoon salt
>     3 cups chopped peeled tart apples
>     1 unbaked pie shell (9 inches)
>   1/4 cup packed brown sugar
>     3 tablespoons cold butter *or* margarine

In a large bowl, beat eggs. Add sour cream. Stir in sugar, 2 tablespoons flour, vanilla and salt; mix well. Stir in apples. Pour into pie shell. Bake at 375° for 15 minutes. Meanwhile, combine brown sugar and remaining flour. Cut in butter until mixture is crumbly. Sprinkle over top of pie. Bake 20-25 minutes longer or until the filling is set. Cool completely on a wire rack. Serve or cover and refrigerate. **Yield:** 8 servings.

## Hawaiian Kabobs

*Fun and different, these kabobs are a treat exclusively from the grill! The pineapple gives ordinary summer vegetables a fresh, tropical taste. They're colorful and always a hit with family or at a get-together.*

>     1 can (20 ounces) unsweetened pineapple chunks
>     2 large green peppers, cut into 1-inch pieces
>     1 large onion, quartered, optional
>   12 to 16 medium fresh mushrooms
>   16 to 18 cherry tomatoes
>   1/2 cup soy sauce
>   1/4 cup olive *or* vegetable oil
>     1 tablespoon brown sugar
>     2 teaspoons ground ginger
>     1 teaspoon garlic powder
>     1 teaspoon ground mustard
>   1/4 teaspoon pepper
> Hot cooked rice, optional

Drain pineapple, reserving 1/2 cup juice. Place pineapple chunks and vegetables in a large bowl; set aside. In a saucepan, combine reserved pineapple juice with soy sauce, oil, brown sugar and seasonings; bring to a boil. Reduce heat and simmer, uncovered, for 5 minutes. Pour over vegetable mixture; cover and refrigerate for at least 1 hour, stirring occasionally. Remove pineapple and vegetables from marinade and reserve marinade. Alternate pineapple, green pepper, onion if desired, mushrooms and tomatoes on skewers. Grill kabobs

*This Iowa cook's
tasty menu
is great for
easy-on-the-hostess
entertaining
in summertime.*

*By Sharon Mensing, Greenfield, Iowa*

MY HUSBAND, Keith, and I raise hogs, cattle, corn and soybeans in partnership with Keith's brother and his family. As you might imagine, our meal schedule can be as changeable as our Iowa weather. That's why recipes that can be prepared ahead or take just minutes to make appeal to me.

Summertime outdoor living for our family means lots of grilling and backyard entertaining, which we enjoy. When we do have guests, this is the meal I often prepare.

My hearty Grilled Ham Steak makes quite an impression even before I serve it. Everyone's eyes widen and their mouths water as I turn the thick ham slice on the grill and baste it with a zippy mustard sauce. The fabulous aroma just sort of drifts by. Grilling is a great way to cook ham—the seared pattern gives it an appealing look.

Party Potatoes can be made a day ahead and stored in the refrigerator. I'll often prepare a batch and divide it into two casseroles—one for guests and one to freeze for later.

Likewise, I mix up my Whole Wheat Refrigerator Rolls the day before I plan to serve them. The dough rises overnight in the refrigerator, and I make up the rolls in the morning.

My Hidden Pear Salad became a family favorite even before Keith and I were married—I made it for him and his parents while we were dating. And it's still requested often all these years later!

To round out my favorite meal, I usually add summer-fresh green beans or peas from my garden, plus a fruit pie or other refreshing dessert.

With so much prepared ahead of time and the ham ready to put on the grill, I can enjoy visiting with guests and still serve a hearty meal.

**PICTURED AT LEFT:** Grilled Ham Steak, Whole Wheat Refrigerator Rolls, Party Potatoes and Hidden Pear Salad (recipes are on the next page).

*Southern traditions and the tang of citrus abound in this Florida cook's memorable and tasty Thanksgiving spread.*

*By Norma Poole, Auburndale, Florida*

JUST LIKE ME, husband Buck was raised in Tignall, a small country town in northeast Georgia. Now that we're in Florida, we have orange and lemon trees growing abundantly right in our backyard.

So it's no wonder that my favorite Thanksgiving spread includes many down-home Southern recipes and the wonderful flavor of citrus. It's also a feast for the eyes—with warm, golden colors.

When I was a child, my mom always made Corn Bread Dressing with our Thanksgiving turkey, and I've since passed on this flavorful accompaniment to both my daughter and granddaughter.

My crumbled homemade corn bread, along with the sage and poultry seasoning, gives the dressing its down-home good taste. It doesn't take long for this dressing to disappear from the table.

My family agrees that rice is a nice change from the more traditional mashed potatoes as a side dish.

To the sweet potatoes Mom always served, I've added orange juice to make my own "Florida special" Creamy Sweet Potatoes. It's another dish the family has come to expect at Thanksgiving!

My Herbed Rice Pilaf is really very basic and easy to fix. The celery adds a pleasant crunch, and dashes of soy sauce and Worcestershire sauce add enough zip to give it character.

Did you expect pie for dessert? My Lemon Orange Cake may be a departure from most folks' idea of a Thanksgiving dessert, but we love this special sweet treat. Our son always offers to take home leftovers—if there are any!

I often give thanks for my blessings, including my wonderful husband, our precious family and the bountiful food that I love to cook!

— 🍴 🍴 🍴 —

**PICTURED AT LEFT:** Turkey with Corn Bread Dressing, Herbed Rice Pilaf, Creamy Sweet Potatoes and Lemon Orange Cake (recipes are on the next page).

## Turkey with Corn Bread Dressing

*Nothing gets family hanging around the kitchen like the aroma of a turkey stuffed with savory dressing roasting in the oven.*

    2 cups chopped celery
    1 cup chopped onion
  1/2 cup butter *or* margarine
    6 cups cubed day-old corn bread
    2 cups fresh bread crumbs
    1 tablespoon rubbed sage
    1 tablespoon poultry seasoning
    2 eggs, lightly beaten
    1 cup chicken broth
    1 turkey (10 to 12 pounds)
Melted butter *or* margarine

In a skillet, saute celery and onion in butter until tender. Place in a large bowl with corn bread, crumbs, sage and poultry seasoning. Combine eggs and chicken broth; add to corn bread mixture, stirring gently to mix. Rinse and dry turkey. Just before baking, stuff the body cavity and inside of the neck with dressing. Skewer or fasten openings. Tie the drumsticks together. Place on a rack in a roasting pan. Brush with melted butter. Bake at 325° for 3-1/2 to 4 hours. When turkey begins to brown, cover lightly with a tent of aluminum foil. When turkey is done, allow to stand for 20 minutes. Remove all dressing to a serving bowl. **Yield:**

8-10 servings. **Editor's Note:** Dressing may be prepared as above and baked in a greased 2-qt. casserole dish. Cover and bake at 400° for 20 minutes. Uncover and bake 10 minutes longer or until lightly browned. Dressing yields 8 cups.

— 🍺 🍺 🍺 —

## Herbed Rice Pilaf

*The zesty flavor of onion is great with the crunch of celery in this light dish. It's tasty for a holiday meal.*

✓ Uses less fat, sugar or salt. Includes Nutritional Analysis and Diabetic Exchanges.

    2 cups uncooked long grain rice
    1 cup chopped celery
  1/2 cup chopped onion
  1/4 cup butter *or* margarine
    4 cups chicken broth
    1 teaspoon Worcestershire sauce
    1 teaspoon soy sauce
    1 teaspoon dried oregano
    1 teaspoon dried thyme

In a skillet, saute rice, celery and onion in butter until the rice is lightly browned and the vegetables are tender. Spoon into a greased 2-qt. casserole. Combine all remaining ingredients; pour over rice mixture. Cover and bake at 325° for 50 minutes or until the rice is done. **Yield:** 8 servings. **Nutritional Analysis:** One serving (prepared with margarine) equals 124 calories, 65 mg sodium, 0 cholesterol, 21 gm carbohydrate, 2 gm protein, 3 gm fat. **Diabetic Exchanges:** 1 starch, 1 vegetable, 1/2 fat.

## Creamy Sweet Potatoes

*I took my mother's delicious sweet potato casserole recipe and gave it a new twist by adding the tempting taste of orange—a fruit very abundant in our state. The flavors are wonderful together and make this dish a family favorite.*

```
   5 pounds medium sweet potatoes, peeled
        and cooked
   4 eggs, lightly beaten
 1/2 cup orange juice
 1/2 cup butter or margarine, softened
 1/2 cup sugar
   1 teaspoon vanilla extract
 1/2 teaspoon ground nutmeg
Dash salt
Marshmallows
```

In a large bowl, mash sweet potatoes. Add eggs, orange juice, butter, sugar, vanilla, nutmeg and salt; mix well. Transfer to a greased 3-qt. baking dish. Bake at 350° for 35-40 minutes or until set. Top with marshmallows; bake 5-10 minutes longer until they just begin to puff and melt. **Yield:** 10-12 servings.

— 🥄 🥄 🥄 —

## Lemon Orange Cake

*I love to bake this lovely three-layer cake instead of a more traditional pie for Thanksgiving. It has that tangy Florida citrus flavor and isn't any more difficult to make than a two-layer cake.*

```
   1 cup butter or margarine, softened
 1/4 cup shortening
   2 cups sugar
   5 eggs
   3 cups all-purpose flour
   1 teaspoon baking powder
 1/2 teaspoon baking soda
 1/2 teaspoon salt
   1 cup buttermilk
   1 teaspoon vanilla extract
 1/2 teaspoon lemon extract
FROSTING:
 1/2 cup butter or margarine, softened
   3 tablespoons orange juice
   3 tablespoons lemon juice
   1 to 2 tablespoons grated orange peel
   1 to 2 tablespoons grated lemon peel
   1 teaspoon lemon extract
5-1/2 to 6 cups confectioners' sugar
```

In a mixing bowl, cream butter, shortening and sugar until light and fluffy. Add eggs, one at a time, beating well after each addition. Combine dry ingredients; add to creamed mixture alternately with buttermilk, beginning and ending with dry ingredients. Stir in extracts. Pour into three greased and floured 9-in. cake pans. Bake at 350° for 25-30 minutes or until cakes test done. Cool for 10 minutes in pans before removing to wire racks to cool completely. For frosting, beat butter in a mixing bowl until fluffy; add the next five ingredients and mix well. Gradually add confectioners' sugar; beat until frosting has desired spreading consistency. Spread between layers and over the top and sides of cake. **Yield:** 10-12 servings.

# Meals in Minutes

*In a hurry? These five
tasty meals are ready to eat
in 30 minutes or less. For more
menu options, just mix and match.*

**FAST FIXINGS.** Clockwise from upper left:
Spanish Rice Supper Hits the Right Spot (p. 206),
Grilled Beef Makes Summer Dinner a Breeze
(p. 208), Any Way You Slice It, Sandwiches Satisfy
(p. 212) and Rise-and-Shine Fare Jump-Starts
Your Day (p. 210).

# Italian-Style Dinner Comes Together in a Jiffy

TAKING THE TIME to prepare an elaborate dinner can be a pleasure—if you enjoy cooking and have the time to do it.

Sometimes, though, even the most accomplished cook has to make a speedy meal to feed a hungry, on-the-go family. There's no time for fuss—just good food. The time-saving dinner here has a tangy Italian taste that's both hearty and satisfying.

Quick Italian Spaghetti has been a standby for Ruth Peterson of Jenison, Michigan for more than 40 years. "I can make it in a snap," says Ruth, "and there's no other spaghetti recipe my husband is even interested in trying!"

Norma Erne of Albuquerque, New Mexico shares her recipe for Celery Seed Bread. "This quick, easy bread is a family favorite with just about any Italian meal," she says.

Crunchy Vegetable Salad is colorful and tasty, plus it's a good way to get kids to eat their veggies, says Linda Russell of Exeter, Ontario. "I put it on my dinner table frequently, because the kids just love it!"

Taffy Apple Dip is a fun, speedy dessert. "My mother-in-law gave me this recipe," notes Sue Gronholz of Columbus, Wisconsin. "It's simple to make, and it tastes just like the real thing!"

— 🍶 🍶 🍶 —

## Quick Italian Spaghetti

- 1/2 pound ground beef
- 3/4 cup thinly sliced green onions
- 1/2 teaspoon salt
- 1/8 teaspoon pepper
- 2 teaspoons sugar
- 1 teaspoon Worcestershire sauce
- 3 cans (8 ounces *each*) tomato sauce
- 1 can (2-1/4 ounces) sliced ripe olives, drained

**Hot cooked spaghetti**
**Grated Parmesan *or* Romano cheese**
**Real bacon bits, optional**

In a skillet, brown ground beef and onions. Add next five ingredients; cover and simmer for 10 minutes. Add olives; simmer 5 minutes longer. Spoon over spaghetti; sprinkle with cheese and bacon bits if desired. **Yield:** 4 servings.

## Celery Seed Bread

- 6 tablespoons butter *or* margarine, softened
- 1/2 teaspoon celery seed
- 1/4 teaspoon paprika
- 1/4 teaspoon dried parsley flakes
- 4 hot dog rolls, sliced

In a mixing bowl, combine butter, celery seed, paprika and parsley flakes, stirring well to blend. Spread on cut sides of each roll. Place on baking sheet; broil until golden brown. **Yield:** 4 servings.

— 🍶 🍶 🍶 —

## Crunchy Vegetable Salad

- 2 cups cauliflowerets
- 2 cups broccoli florets
- 2 medium carrots, thinly sliced
- 1 small zucchini, sliced
- 1 small red onion, sliced
- 1 to 1-1/2 cups Italian salad dressing

Combine vegetables in a large mixing bowl. Pour salad dressing over and toss to coat evenly. Refrigerate until serving time. **Yield:** 4-6 servings.

— 🍶 🍶 🍶 —

## Taffy Apple Dip

- 1 package (8 ounces) cream cheese, softened
- 3/4 cup packed brown sugar
- 1 tablespoon vanilla extract
- 1/2 cup chopped peanuts
- 6 medium apples, cut into wedges

In a small bowl, beat cream cheese, brown sugar and vanilla until smooth. Spread mixture on a small serving plate; top with nuts. Serve with apple wedges. **Yield:** 6 servings.

### Softening Sugar

If your brown sugar has hardened, put it in a resealable plastic bag with an apple wedge; seal. Remove the apple in 1 to 2 days, when the sugar is soft.

# Spanish Rice Supper Hits the Right Spot

YOU CAN COUNT ON this casserole, salad, biscuits and pudding dessert to satisfy your hungry clan. It's tasty, filling and quick.

Hamburger Spanish Rice is a favorite busy-day dish for Bernice Morris of Marshfield, Missouri. "I like to have something hearty that I can make in a snap," she says.

Wilted Lettuce Salad comes from Alberta McKay from Bartlesville, Oklahoma. "This salad looks and tastes great," she says. "The bacon drippings become part of the dressing."

Quick Biscuits are unbelievably easy to make, says Diane Hixon of Niceville, Florida. "I'd never even made biscuits until I tried this two-ingredient recipe. Now my husband wants biscuits all the time. And there's no reason for me to say no!"

Ambrosia Pudding is a speedy yet special way to end the meal. "Serving this in a parfait glass showcases the layers," notes Debbie Jones of California, Maryland.

## Hamburger Spanish Rice

1 pound lean ground beef
1 medium onion, chopped
1/2 medium green pepper, chopped
1 cup uncooked instant rice
1 can (15 ounces) tomato sauce
3/4 cup hot water
1 teaspoon prepared mustard
1 teaspoon Worcestershire sauce
1 teaspoon salt
1 teaspoon sugar

In a skillet, brown beef, onion, green pepper and rice. Add remaining ingredients; mix well. Bring to a boil. Reduce heat. Cover and simmer 20-25 minutes or until rice is tender. **Yield:** 4-6 servings.

## Wilted Lettuce Salad

8 cups torn leaf lettuce *or* spinach
1/4 cup sliced green onions
Pepper to taste
3 bacon strips, diced
1 tablespoon cider *or* white wine vinegar
2 teaspoons lemon juice
1/2 teaspoon sugar
1/4 teaspoon salt
1 hard-cooked egg, chopped

Place lettuce or spinach and onions in a large salad bowl. Sprinkle with pepper; set aside. In a large skillet, cook bacon until crisp. Do not drain off drippings. Stir in vinegar, lemon juice, sugar and salt. Pour over lettuce and toss gently until well coated. Top with hard-cooked egg. Serve immediately. **Yield:** 6 servings.

## Quick Biscuits

2 cups self-rising flour*
1 cup whipping cream

In a large bowl, combine the flour and cream. Turn out onto a floured surface; knead for 5 minutes or until no longer sticky. On a floured surface, roll dough to a 1/2-in. thickness. Cut into 3-in. biscuits. Place on a greased baking sheet. Bake at 450° for 8-10 minutes. **Yield:** 9 biscuits. *Editor's Note:** As a substitute for each cup of self-rising flour, place 1-1/2 teaspoons baking powder and 1/2 teaspoon salt in a measuring cup. Add all-purpose flour to measure 1 cup.

## Ambrosia Pudding

2 cups cold milk
1 package (3.4 ounces) instant vanilla pudding mix
1/4 cup honey
2 teaspoons grated orange peel
1/4 teaspoon vanilla extract
1 cup whipping cream, whipped
1 medium firm banana, sliced
1 can (11 ounces) mandarin orange sections, drained
1/4 cup flaked coconut
1/4 cup sliced almonds

In a bowl, blend milk and pudding mix according to package directions. Add honey, orange peel and vanilla. Fold in the whipped cream. In individual dessert dishes, layer half of the pudding, banana slices, orange sections, coconut and almonds. Repeat the layers. Chill. **Yield:** 4-6 servings.

# Grilled Beef Makes Summer Dinner a Breeze

COOL DOWN during warm weather with this tasty just-off-the-grill main dish and its two refreshing chilled-in-the-fridge accompaniments.

Even if you have a full schedule, you can squeeze in this flavor-packed dinner in a mere 30 minutes. And there's no time spent slaving over a hot stove. The menu is made up of family-favorite recipes contributed by fellow cooks and combined in our test kitchen.

Mardi Gras Beef, shared by Lucy Meyring from Walden, Colorado, tastes great, and cleanup is a breeze. Sauteed vegetables and seasonings are served over a juicy sirloin steak, providing a wonderful summertime twist to grilling.

Broccoli Salad comes from Jane Hale of Desert Hot Springs, California. "This is a great make-ahead salad," Jane notes. "If you keep frozen broccoli in your freezer, you'll always have the fixings for a quick, delicious salad when company drops in—or if you want to treat your family to a different kind of salad with dinner."

Creamy Pineapple Pie is a light dessert that's a snap to make and impressive to serve, says Sharon Bickett of Chester, South Carolina. "This is one of our favorite ways to complete a summer meal."

## Mardi Gras Beef

- 1 medium onion, chopped
- 1 small green pepper, cut into strips
- 1 teaspoon dried thyme
- 2 teaspoons garlic powder, *divided*
- 2 tablespoons vegetable oil
- 1 to 1-1/2 pounds sirloin steak (1 inch thick)
- 1 can (14-1/2 ounces) stewed tomatoes
- 2 teaspoons cornstarch
- Salt and pepper to taste

In a skillet, saute the onion, green pepper, thyme and 1/2 teaspoon garlic powder in oil until the vegetables are crisp-tender. Meanwhile, sprinkle the steak with the remaining garlic powder. Grill or broil steak 5 in. from the heat for 6-8 minutes (for medium-rare), turning once, or until desired doneness is reached. Drain the tomatoes, reserving juice. Add the tomatoes to skillet. Combine the reserved tomato juice and cornstarch; add to the vegetable mixture. Cook and stir until thickened. Season to taste with salt and pepper. Thinly slice meat; top with vegetables. **Yield:** 4 servings.

## Broccoli Salad

- 1/4 cup mayonnaise
- 1/4 cup sweet pickle relish
- 1 teaspoon sugar
- Salt and pepper to taste
- 1 cup chopped celery
- 1 cup sliced green onions with tops
- 2 packages (10 ounces *each*) frozen cut broccoli, thawed and drained

In a bowl, combine mayonnaise, relish, sugar, salt and pepper. Add celery and green onions; mix well. Add broccoli and toss gently to coat. Chill until serving. **Yield:** 6-8 servings.

## Creamy Pineapple Pie

- 1 can (14 ounces) sweetened condensed milk
- 1 can (8 ounces) crushed pineapple, undrained
- 1/4 cup lemon juice
- 1 carton (8 ounces) frozen whipped topping, thawed
- 1 prepared graham cracker crust (9 inches)

In a bowl, mix milk, pineapple and lemon juice. Fold in whipped topping. Pour into the crust. Chill until serving. **Yield:** 8 servings.

### Pineapple Pointer

If you prefer fresh pineapple over canned, choose fruit that's slightly soft to the touch, with strong color and no sign of greening. Look for crisp, green leaves. Avoid fruit with soft or dark skin.

# Rise-and-Shine Fare Jump-Starts Your Day

THE BEST WAY to start out the day is with a hearty, scrumptious breakfast. But if you have a busy morning planned, you don't want to spend half of it in the kitchen.

This fast-to-fix meal was put together in our test kitchen using tried-and-true recipes from country cooks. It's sure to get your gang off to a good start.

Zucchini Scramble, shared by Betty Claycomb of Alverton, Pennsylvania, has garden-fresh taste. "I like this recipe because I can change it through the year as other fresh vegetables become available. It also makes a tasty light lunch or dinner," Betty notes.

Pork Patties come from Lois Fetting of Nelson, Wisconsin. They provide a taste-bud wake-up call with a variety of herbs and spices and are quick to put together. To some save time, combine all the spices and herbs the night before, then stir in the ground pork just before frying in the morning.

Bran Muffins can bake while you're preparing your other menu items. Shared by Amber Sampson of Somonauk, Illinois, these muffins are a nutritious and hearty addition to the meal. Serve warm with butter or jam for an irresistible morning treat.

— 🍶 🍶 🍶 —

## Zucchini Scramble

**2 to 3 small zucchini (about 1 pound),
   sliced
1 medium onion, chopped
2 tablespoons butter *or* margarine
Salt and pepper to taste
6 to 8 eggs, beaten
1/2 cup shredded cheddar cheese
Tomato wedges, optional**

In a skillet, saute zucchini and onion in butter until tender. Season with salt and pepper. Add the eggs; cook and stir until set. Sprinkle with cheese. Remove from the heat; cover until cheese is melted. Serve with tomato wedges if desired. **Yield:** 4-6 servings.

— 🍶 🍶 🍶 —

## Pork Patties

**1-1/2 teaspoons salt
1/2 teaspoon rubbed sage
1/4 teaspoon pepper
1/4 teaspoon ground nutmeg
1/4 teaspoon dried thyme
Pinch ground ginger
2 tablespoons water
1 pound lean ground pork**

In a bowl, combine the first seven ingredients. Add pork; mix well. Shape into six patties. Fry in a skillet until meat is browned and cooked throughout. **Yield:** 6 servings.

— 🍶 🍶 🍶 —

## Bran Muffins

☑ Uses less fat, sugar or salt. Includes Nutritional Analysis and Diabetic Exchanges.

**1-1/4 cups all-purpose flour
1 tablespoon baking powder
1/3 cup sugar
1/2 teaspoon salt
1 cup 100% bran cereal
1 cup milk
1 egg
1/4 cup vegetable oil**

Combine the flour, baking powder, sugar and salt; set aside. In a mixing bowl, combine the bran cereal and milk; let stand for 2 minutes. Add the egg and oil; mix well. Add the dry ingredients, stirring just until combined. Spoon into 12 greased muffin cups. Bake at 400° for 18-20 minutes or until muffins are golden brown. Serve warm. **Yield:** 1 dozen. **Nutritional Analysis:** One serving (prepared with fat-free milk) equals 116 calories, 299 mg sodium, 18 mg cholesterol, 23 gm carbohydrate, 4 gm protein, 2 gm fat. **Diabetic Exchanges:** 1-1/2 starch, 1/2 fat.

### Mess-Free Muffins

Nonstick cooking spray takes the work out of greasing muffin tins. If you prefer shortening, avoid messy fingers by dipping a paper towel into the shortening before spreading it. Don't grease unused cups; the grease will burn. Instead, add 3 tablespoons water so the pan doesn't warp.

# Any Way You Slice It, Sandwiches Satisfy!

WHEN you're in a pinch to put food on the table quickly for your famished family, why not serve up a sure-to-please menu?

This sandwich and salad standby is comprised of recipes from three different cooks and combined in the *Taste of Home* test kitchen. You can have everything ready to serve in under half an hour.

"My mouth waters just thinking of these Reuben Sandwiches. I adapted the recipe from one my mother found years ago," says Kathy Jo Scott of Hemingford, Nebraska.

"Now my family requests them often," she adds. "That's all right with me…these tasty sandwiches are also one of *my* favorites because of their fantastic flavor and ease of preparation."

Hot Potato Salad is a hearty side dish with old-fashioned flair from Alpha Wilson of Roswell, New Mexico. "This potato salad is so appealing and tasty, your hungry bunch will think you spent hours in the kitchen preparing it."

Sue Gronholz of Columbus, Wisconsin shares her Fruited Pistachio Pudding. "It's a quick dessert with broad appeal and it's so easy to make," she says. "This tasty, creamy pudding is not only perfect for everyday family meals, it's a flavorful dessert to feed unexpected guests. Don't be surprised if you're asked to share the recipe, too!"

## Hot Potato Salad

 6 bacon strips
 1 medium onion, chopped
 2 tablespoons all-purpose flour
 2 tablespoons sugar
1-1/2 teaspoons salt
 1/2 teaspoon celery seed
 1/8 teaspoon pepper
 3/4 cup water
 1/2 cup vinegar
 5 medium potatoes (about 2 pounds), peeled, cooked and sliced

In a skillet, cook the bacon strips until crisp. Remove bacon to paper towel to drain; crumble and set aside. In the bacon drippings, saute the onion until tender. Remove from the heat. Combine the flour, sugar, salt, celery seed and pepper; stir into the onion mixture. Add the water and vinegar. Return the mixture to the heat; cook, stirring constantly, until it comes to a boil. Boil for 1 minute. Place the potatoes and bacon in a large bowl; pour the sauce over and toss gently. Serve warm. **Yield:** 4-6 servings.

## Reuben Sandwiches

12 ounces thinly sliced canned *or* fully cooked corned beef
 8 slices light *or* dark rye bread
 1 can (8 ounces) sauerkraut, drained
1/2 cup Thousand Island dressing
 4 slices Swiss cheese
Butter *or* margarine

Arrange corned beef on four slices of bread. Top each with a quarter of the sauerkraut, 2 tablespoons of dressing and a slice of cheese. Top with remaining bread slices. In a skillet over medium heat, melt 2-3 tablespoons butter. Toast sandwiches until bread is lightly browned on one side. Turn sandwiches and brown other side, adding more butter if necessary. Cook until cheese is melted and meat is heated through. **Yield:** 4 servings.

## Fruited Pistachio Pudding

1 package (3.4 ounces) instant pistachio pudding mix
1 carton (8 ounces) frozen whipped topping, thawed
2 tablespoons salad dressing *or* mayonnaise
1 can (16 ounces) fruit cocktail, undrained
1 can (8 ounces) crushed pineapple, undrained
2 medium firm bananas, sliced
1 cup miniature marshmallows

In a large bowl, combine pudding mix, whipped topping and salad dressing; mix well. Fold in remaining ingredients. Leave in bowl or spoon into individual serving dishes. Serve immediately or chill. **Yield:** 6-8 servings.

# Meals on a Budget

*These five frugal meals show you how to feed your family well without spending big bucks at the grocery store.*

**BUDGET CHECKERS.** Clockwise from upper left: Broccoli Soup and Curried Egg Salad (p. 218); Teriyaki Chicken, Scalloped Pineapple Casserole and French Dressing (p. 224); Tangy Fruit Salad and Western Beef and Cornmeal Pie (p. 220); Tuna Burgers and Summer Apple Salad (p. 222).

# Feed Your Family for 90¢ a Plate!

MAKING a nutritious dinner for your family doesn't have to cost a bundle every night.

With protein-packed red beans and a nice blend of Southern spices, this dinner will satisfy your family without taking a big bite out of your grocery budget. The meal was put together by Marcia Salisbury, an Extension home economist for Waukesha County, Wisconsin. She figured the cost at just 90¢ per plate.

"The Red Beans and Rice recipe originated with my sister-in-law," says Marcia. "I changed it around a bit to suit the tastes of my family.

"I chop and freeze garden peppers in individual packets so they're ready any time I want them. If you don't grow your own, it makes sense to buy in season at a farmer's market or grocery store and then freeze them. That way you can enjoy their flavor later without paying out-of-season prices!"

For a slightly different flavor, Marcia adds leftover ham, sausage or ham bones (whichever is on hand) to the original recipe. "If you'd like a little more spice, simply add salsa," she suggests.

Corn Bread Squares make a nice accompaniment for a wholesome, low-cost meal.

## Red Beans and Rice

1/2 **pound dry kidney beans, rinsed**
1/2 **pound dry pinto beans, rinsed**
4 **cups water**
4 **cups chicken broth**
2 **garlic cloves, minced**
2 **bay leaves**
1 **can (14-1/2 ounces) diced tomatoes, undrained**
1 **jar (4 ounces) diced pimientos, drained**
1 **large green pepper, chopped**
1 **large sweet red pepper, chopped**
1 **large onion, chopped**
1 **cup chopped celery**
1 **can (4 ounces) diced green chilies**
1 **teaspoon paprika**
1 **teaspoon salt**
1 **tablespoon vinegar**
1/4 **cup snipped fresh parsley**
1/4 to 1/2 **teaspoon crushed red pepper flakes**
1/4 to 1/2 **teaspoon ground cumin**
1/4 to 1/2 **teaspoon hot pepper sauce**
**Hot cooked rice**

Place beans in a Dutch oven with water. Bring to a boil; simmer 2 minutes. Remove from the heat. Cover and let stand 1 hour. Drain and rinse beans. Return to Dutch oven with broth, garlic and bay leaves; bring to a boil. Reduce heat; cover and sim-

mer for 1-1/4 hours. Stir in the next 14 ingredients. Cover and simmer for 1 hour or until beans and vegetables are tender and gravy is thick. Remove bay leaves. Serve over hot cooked rice. **Yield:** 12 servings.

———— 🍳 🍳 🍳 ————

## Corn Bread Squares

1 cup all-purpose flour
1 cup yellow cornmeal
1/4 cup sugar
  2 teaspoons baking powder
3/4 teaspoon salt
  2 eggs, beaten
  1 cup milk
1/4 cup vegetable oil

In a mixing bowl, combine the flour, cornmeal, sugar, baking powder and salt. Add the eggs, milk and oil. Beat just until moistened. Spoon into a greased 8-in. square baking pan. Bake at 400° for 20-25 minutes or until the corn bread tests done. **Yield:** 9 servings.

# Feed Your Family for $1.08 a Plate!

FRUGAL but flavorful are the words to describe this extra-economical yet quick meal.

The soup and sandwich combination comes from Joyce McDowell, an Extension home economist in Adams County, Ohio. She and her husband, Gary, an agriculture teacher, raise registered Polled Hereford cattle on their farm in Winchester. They have two sons, Chad and Chris, who work up an appetite helping their mom and dad.

"Creamy Broccoli Soup and hearty Curried Egg Salad make a satisfying and nutritious meal, and all of the ingredients can be purchased at any basic grocery store," explains Joyce.

"After a full day of work, I like to make a supper that is easy and quick," she says. "I know many other people feel the same way."

To round out this pleasing, penny-pinching meal, Joyce suggests a favorite dessert that can be made ahead of time, such as cookies or brownies.

## Broccoli Soup

**2 cans (14-1/2 ounces *each*) chicken broth**
**1 large bunch broccoli, chopped (about 5 cups)**
**1-1/2 cups chopped onion**
**3 bay leaves**
**6 tablespoons butter *or* margarine**
**7 tablespoons all-purpose flour**
**3 cups milk**
**Salt and pepper to taste**

In a saucepan, bring chicken broth to a boil. Add broccoli, onion and bay leaves. Reduce heat and simmer until broccoli is tender; remove bay leaves. Meanwhile, in another saucepan, melt butter. Stir in flour to make a smooth paste. Gradually stir in milk. Cook over medium heat until mixture is hot and thickened, stirring occasionally. Add 1 cup of broccoli stock to milk mixture; stir until well blended. Gradually add remaining broccoli stock to milk mixture. Heat and stir until well blended. Season with salt and pepper. **Yield:** 6 servings.

## Curried Egg Salad

**1/2 cup mayonnaise**
**1/2 teaspoon honey**
**1/2 teaspoon ground curry**
**Dash ground ginger**
**6 hard-cooked eggs, coarsely chopped**
**3 green onions, sliced**

**6 slices whole wheat bread**
**Sliced tomato, optional**

In a bowl, blend the mayonnaise, honey, curry and
ginger. Stir in the chopped eggs and green onions.
Divide the mixture among bread slices and spread
to cover. Top with a tomato slice if desired. **Yield:**
6 servings.

### Broccoli Basics

Buy broccoli with a deep, strong color—green or
greenish purple. Buds should be tightly closed;
leaves should be crisp. Store, unwashed, in an airtight plastic bag in the fridge for up to 4 days.

# Feed Your Family For $1.65 a Plate!

WHEN you're checking out at the grocery store, it may seem like there's no such thing as a good meal that's not expensive. This is not so.

You can feed your family well *and* economically. The frugal but flavorful meal here comes from Darlene Alexander of Nekoosa, Wisconsin. It costs only $1.65 per serving.

"With this hearty main-dish recipe, the bread is baked right in the casserole," says Darlene. "The meal covers all four food groups, and it's a guaranteed family pleaser."

Along with Western Beef and Cornmeal Pie, Darlene serves Tangy Fruit Salad as a sweet and refreshing side dish or light dessert.

"I got these recipes from dear friends many years ago, and they've been a mainstay at my house ever since," she says. "Besides being great family meals, they're both perfect for church potlucks, reunions and other group functions."

— 🍴 🍴 🍴 —

### Tangy Fruit Salad

  1 **can (20 ounces) pineapple chunks**
  1 **package (3.4 ounces) instant vanilla pudding mix**
1/4 **cup dry orange-flavored instant breakfast drink**
  1 **can (11 ounces) mandarin oranges, drained**
  1 **can (16 ounces) fruit cocktail, drained**
  2 **medium firm bananas, sliced**
  2 **medium apples *or* pears, cut into chunks**
  1 **cup sliced fresh strawberries, optional**

Drain pineapple, reserving juice. In a small bowl, combine reserved pineapple juice, pudding mix and breakfast drink; set aside. In a large bowl, combine all the fruit. Fold juice mixture into fruit. Refrigerate before serving. **Yield:** 8 servings.

### Western Beef and Cornmeal Pie

**FILLING:**
  1 **pound ground beef**
  1 **can (11 ounces) Mexican-style corn, drained**
  1 **can (6 ounces) tomato paste**
  1 **cup (4 ounces) shredded cheddar cheese**
3/4 **cup barbecue sauce**
1/2 **teaspoon salt**
1/2 **teaspoon chili powder**

**CRUST:**
- **1 cup all-purpose flour**
- **1/2 cup cornmeal**
- **1/2 cup milk**
- **1/4 cup butter *or* margarine, softened**
- **1 egg**
- **2 tablespoons sugar**
- **1 teaspoon baking powder**
- **1 teaspoon salt**
- **1 cup (4 ounces) shredded cheddar cheese, *divided***

In a large skillet, brown the ground beef; drain. Stir in the corn, tomato paste, cheddar cheese, barbecue sauce, salt and chili powder. Set aside. In a large bowl, combine all the crust ingredients except 1/2 cup cheddar cheese; mix well. Spread on the bottom and up the sides of a greased 2-1/2-qt. baking dish or a 10-in. ovenproof skillet. Pour the beef filling into the prepared pie crust. Sprinkle with the remaining cheese. Bake, uncovered, at 400° for 25-30 minutes. **Yield:** 8 servings.

# Feed Your Family for $1.02 a Plate!

TAKING THE FAMILY out for a burger can break your budget just as much as a fancy sit-down dinner.

So when Kim Stoller's clan in Smithville, Ohio is craving a satisfying sandwich, she knows it makes "cents" to serve this featured meal in her own kitchen instead. Our test kitchen estimates the cost of this hearty lunch or light supper at just $1.02 a setting!

"My family was hesitant to try these Tuna Burgers when I first prepared them. They were so accustomed to the typical beef burger," Kim says. "But any skepticism they had disappeared after one bite.

"These savory seafood burgers are tasty inside and cook up golden brown and crispy on the outside. They're also simple and quick to make," she adds.

Lettuce and tomato are fresh, tasty toppings, but you can also serve these sandwiches with your favorite tartar sauce.

Kim frequently pairs her burgers with Summer Apple Salad, a great-tasting, colorful side dish that contains a mixture of ingredients.

"It's a good thing this recipe serves 12 because my family can't get enough of it," she says. "Tossing fruits and vegetables with a sweet dressing is a deliciously different idea."

—— 🍴 🍴 🍴 ——

## Tuna Burgers

**1 can (6 to 7 ounces) tuna, drained and flaked**
**1/2 cup dry bread crumbs**
**1/2 cup finely chopped celery**
**1/3 cup mayonnaise**
**1/4 cup finely chopped onion**
**2 tablespoons chili sauce**
**1 egg, beaten**
**2 tablespoons butter *or* margarine**
**4 hamburger buns, split and toasted**
**Lettuce, optional**
**Sliced tomatoes, optional**

In a bowl, combine tuna, bread crumbs, celery, mayonnaise, onion, chili sauce and egg. Shape into four patties. Melt butter in a skillet; cook patties for about 4-5 minutes per side or until lightly browned. Serve on buns with lettuce and tomatoes if desired. **Yield:** 4 servings.

—— 🍴 🍴 🍴 ——

## Summer Apple Salad

**3 medium tart red apples, cored and diced**
**1 can (8 ounces) pineapple tidbits, drained**

**1-1/2 cups sliced celery**
**1 cup grape halves**
**1 medium carrot, shredded**
**1/2 cup coarsely chopped almonds**
**3/4 cup sour cream**
**1 tablespoon sugar**
**1/2 teaspoon lemon juice**

In a large salad bowl, combine apples, pineapple, celery, grapes, carrot and almonds. In a small bowl, combine sour cream, sugar and lemon juice; mix well. Add to apple mixture and toss to coat. Chill.
**Yield:** 12 servings.

### Money-Saving Tuna Tips

Stock up on canned tuna when it goes on sale. It comes in three grades, the best being solid or fancy (large pieces), followed by chunk (smaller pieces) and flaked (bits and pieces). If you're making tuna burgers or sandwiches, don't spend money on solid- or chunk-style tuna, since the mixture will be broken up anyway. Water-packed tuna has fewer calories than oil-packed and tastes like you splurged on fresh fish.

# Feed Your Family For $1.47 a Plate!

FOR THIS cost-conscious chicken dinner, three great country cooks prove you don't have to sacrifice flavor to be frugal. Our test kitchen estimates a cost of just $1.47 per serving.

Moist and delicious Teriyaki Chicken comes from Jean Clark of Albion, Maine. "These drumsticks get their great flavor and golden color from the tasty, easy-to-prepare marinade," she explains. "During hurried work weeks, it's convenient to marinate the chicken overnight and then bake it the next day."

Don't shy away from Judy Howle's Scalloped Pineapple Casserole. "My family can't get enough of this sweet and satisfying side dish," Judy shares from her Columbus, Mississippi kitchen. "This casserole disappears quickly whenever I prepare it."

Instead of turning to store-bought salad dressings that lack freshness and flavor, why not sample French Dressing from Mrs. Robert Lieske of Ripon, Wisconsin? This simple homemade topping adds tangy flavor to an ordinary lettuce salad. The price of this meal includes the head of lettuce plus 2 tablespoons of dressing per person.

Add whatever garden-fresh vegetables you have on hand to the salad to complete an inexpensive meal that's sure to become a favorite in your family.

— ▽ ▽ ▽ —

## Teriyaki Chicken

- 3/4 **cup soy sauce**
- 1/4 **cup vegetable oil**
- 3 **tablespoons brown sugar**
- 2 **tablespoons sherry, optional**
- 1/2 **teaspoon ground ginger**
- 1/2 **teaspoon garlic powder**
- 12 **chicken drumsticks (about 2-1/2 pounds)**

In a large glass dish, combine the soy sauce, oil, brown sugar, sherry if desired, ginger and garlic powder; mix well. Add drumsticks; turn to coat. Cover and refrigerate for 1 hour or overnight, turning occasionally. Drain and discard marinade. Place chicken in a single layer on a foil-lined baking sheet. Bake at 375° for 35-45 minutes or until chicken is no longer pink. **Yield:** 6 servings.

— ▽ ▽ ▽ —

## Scalloped Pineapple Casserole

- 3/4 **cup butter *or* margarine**
- 1-1/4 **cups sugar**
- 3 **eggs**

**1 can (20 ounces) crushed pineapple, well drained**
**1-1/2 teaspoons lemon juice**
**4 cups firmly packed cubed white bread (crusts removed)**

In a mixing bowl, cream butter and sugar. Add eggs, one at a time, beating well after each addition. Stir in the pineapple and lemon juice. Gently fold in bread cubes. Spoon into a greased 2-qt. baking dish. Bake, uncovered, at 350° for 40-45 minutes or until top is lightly golden. Serve warm. **Yield:** 6 servings.

## French Dressing

**1 cup vegetable oil**
**2/3 cup ketchup**
**2/3 cup sugar**
**1/2 cup vinegar**
**2 teaspoons paprika**
**2 teaspoons salt**
**1 small onion, quartered**

Combine all ingredients in a blender container. Cover and blend at medium-high until well mixed. Chill before serving. Store in a covered container in the refrigerator. **Yield:** 3 cups.

# Substitutions & Equivalents

## Equivalent Measures

| | | | | | |
|---|---|---|---|---|---|
| 3 teaspoons | = | 1 tablespoon | 16 tablespoons | = | 1 cup |
| 4 tablespoons | = | 1/4 cup | 2 cups | = | 1 pint |
| 5-1/3 tablespoons | = | 1/3 cup | 4 cups | = | 1 quart |
| 8 tablespoons | = | 1/2 cup | 4 quarts | = | 1 gallon |

## Food Equivalents

### Grains

| | | | |
|---|---|---|---|
| Macaroni | 1 cup (3-1/2 ounces) uncooked | = | 2-1/2 cups cooked |
| Noodles, Medium | 3 cups (4 ounces) uncooked | = | 4 cups cooked |
| Popcorn | 1/3 to 1/2 cup unpopped | = | 8 cups popped |
| Rice, Long Grain | 1 cup uncooked | = | 3 cups cooked |
| Rice, Quick-Cooking | 1 cup uncooked | = | 2 cups cooked |
| Spaghetti | 8 ounces uncooked | = | 4 cups cooked |

### Crumbs

| | | | |
|---|---|---|---|
| Bread | 1 slice | = | 3/4 cup soft crumbs, 1/4 cup fine dry crumbs |
| Graham Crackers | 7 squares | = | 1/2 cup finely crushed |
| Buttery Round Crackers | 12 crackers | = | 1/2 cup finely crushed |
| Saltine Crackers | 14 crackers | = | 1/2 cup finely crushed |

### Fruits

| | | | |
|---|---|---|---|
| Bananas | 1 medium | = | 1/3 cup mashed |
| Lemons | 1 medium | = | 3 tablespoons juice, 2 teaspoons grated peel |
| Limes | 1 medium | = | 2 tablespoons juice, 1-1/2 teaspoons grated peel |
| Oranges | 1 medium | = | 1/4 to 1/3 cup juice, 4 teaspoons grated peel |

### Vegetables

| | | | | | | | |
|---|---|---|---|---|---|---|---|
| Cabbage | 1 head | = | 5 cups shredded | Green Pepper | 1 large | = | 1 cup chopped |
| Carrots | 1 pound | = | 3 cups shredded | Mushrooms | 1/2 pound | = | 3 cups sliced |
| Celery | 1 rib | = | 1/2 cup chopped | Onions | 1 medium | = | 1/2 cup chopped |
| Corn | 1 ear fresh | = | 2/3 cup kernels | Potatoes | 3 medium | = | 2 cups cubed |

### Nuts

| | | | | | | | |
|---|---|---|---|---|---|---|---|
| Almonds | 1 pound | = | 3 cups chopped | Pecan Halves | 1 pound | = | 4-1/2 cups chopped |
| Ground Nuts | 3-3/4 ounces | = | 1 cup | Walnuts | 1 pound | = | 3-3/4 cups chopped |

## Easy Substitutions

| When you need... | | Use... |
|---|---|---|
| Baking Powder | 1 teaspoon | 1/2 teaspoon cream of tartar + 1/4 teaspoon baking soda |
| Buttermilk | 1 cup | 1 tablespoon lemon juice *or* vinegar + enough milk to measure 1 cup (let stand 5 minutes before using) |
| Cornstarch | 1 tablespoon | 2 tablespoons all-purpose flour |
| Honey | 1 cup | 1-1/4 cups sugar + 1/4 cup water |
| Half-and-Half Cream | 1 cup | 1 tablespoon melted butter + enough whole milk to measure 1 cup |
| Onion | 1 small, chopped (1/3 cup) | 1 teaspoon onion powder *or* 1 tablespoon dried minced onion |
| Tomato Juice | 1 cup | 1/2 cup tomato sauce + 1/2 cup water |
| Tomato Sauce | 2 cups | 3/4 cup tomato paste + 1 cup water |
| Unsweetened Chocolate | 1 square (1 ounce) | 3 tablespoons baking cocoa + 1 tablespoon shortening *or* oil |
| Whole Milk | 1 cup | 1/2 cup evaporated milk + 1/2 cup water |

# *Cooking Terms*

HERE'S a quick reference for some of the cooking terms used in *Taste of Home* recipes:

**Baste**—To moisten food with melted butter, pan drippings, marinades or other liquid to add more flavor and juiciness.

**Beat**—A rapid movement to combine ingredients using a fork, spoon, wire whisk or electric mixer.

**Blend**—To combine ingredients until *just* mixed.

**Boil**—To heat liquids until bubbles form that cannot be "stirred down". In the case of water, the temperature will reach 212°.

**Bone**—To remove all meat from the bone before cooking.

**Cream**—To beat ingredients together to a smooth consistency, usually in the case of butter and sugar for baking.

**Dash**—A small amount of seasoning, less than 1/8 teaspoon. If using a shaker, a dash would comprise a quick flip of the container.

**Dredge**—To coat foods with flour or other dry ingredients. Most often done with pot roasts and stew meat before browning.

**Fold**—To incorporate several ingredients by careful and gentle turning with a spatula. Used generally with beaten egg whites or whipped cream when mixing into the rest of the ingredients to keep the batter light.

**Julienne**—To cut foods into long thin strips much like matchsticks. Used most often for salads and stir-fry dishes.

**Mince**—To cut into very fine pieces. Used often for garlic or fresh herbs.

**Parboil**—To cook partially, usually used in the case of chicken, sausages and vegetables.

**Partially set**—Describes the consistency of gelatin after it has been chilled for a small amount of time. Mixture should resemble the consistency of egg whites.

**Puree**—To process foods to a smooth mixture. Can be prepared in an electric blender, food processor, food mill or sieve.

**Saute**—To fry quickly in a small amount of fat, stirring almost constantly. Most often done with onions, mushrooms and other chopped vegetables.

**Score**—To cut slits partway through the outer surface of foods. Often used with ham or flank steak.

**Stir-Fry**—To cook meats and/or vegetables with a constant stirring motion in a small amount of oil in a wok or skillet over high heat.

# *Guide to Cooking with Popular Herbs*

| HERB | APPETIZERS SALADS | BREADS/EGGS SAUCES/CHEESE | VEGETABLES PASTA | MEAT POULTRY | FISH SHELLFISH |
|---|---|---|---|---|---|
| BASIL | Green, Potato & Tomato Salads, Salad Dressings, Stewed Fruit | Breads, Fondue & Egg Dishes, Dips, Marinades, Sauces | Mushrooms, Tomatoes, Squash, Pasta, Bland Vegetables | Broiled, Roast Meat & Poultry Pies, Stews, Stuffing | Baked, Broiled & Poached Fish, Shellfish |
| BAY LEAF | Seafood Cocktail, Seafood Salad, Tomato Aspic, Stewed Fruit | Egg Dishes, Gravies, Marinades, Sauces | Dried Bean Dishes, Beets, Carrots, Onions, Potatoes, Rice, Squash | Corned Beef, Tongue Meat & Poultry Stews | Poached Fish, Shellfish, Fish Stews |
| CHIVES | Mixed Vegetable, Green, Potato & Tomato Salads, Salad Dressings | Egg & Cheese Dishes, Cream Cheese, Cottage Cheese, Gravies, Sauces | Hot Vegetables, Potatoes | Broiled Poultry, Poultry & Meat Pies, Stews, Casseroles | Baked Fish, Fish Casseroles, Fish Stews, Shellfish |
| DILL | Seafood Cocktail, Green, Potato & Tomato Salads, Salad Dressings | Breads, Egg & Cheese Dishes, Cream Cheese, Fish & Meat Sauces | Beans, Beets, Cabbage, Carrots, Cauliflower, Peas, Squash, Tomatoes | Beef, Veal Roasts, Lamb, Steaks, Chops, Stews, Roast & Creamed Poultry | Baked, Broiled, Poached & Stuffed Fish, Shellfish |
| GARLIC | All Salads, Salad Dressings | Fondue, Poultry Sauces, Fish & Meat Marinades | Beans, Eggplant, Potatoes, Rice, Tomatoes | Roast Meats, Meat & Poultry Pies, Hamburgers, Casseroles, Stews | Broiled Fish, Shellfish, Fish Stews, Casseroles |
| MARJORAM | Seafood Cocktail, Green, Poultry & Seafood Salads | Breads, Cheese Spreads, Egg & Cheese Dishes, Gravies, Sauces | Carrots, Eggplant, Peas, Onions, Potatoes, Dried Bean Dishes, Spinach | Roast Meats & Poultry, Meat & Poultry Pies, Stews & Casseroles | Baked, Broiled & Stuffed Fish, Shellfish |
| MUSTARD | Fresh Green Salads, Prepared Meat, Macaroni & Potato Salads, Salad Dressings | Biscuits, Egg & Cheese Dishes, Sauces | Baked Beans, Cabbage, Eggplant, Squash, Dried Beans, Mushrooms, Pasta | Chops, Steaks, Ham, Pork, Poultry, Cold Meats | Shellfish |
| OREGANO | Green, Poultry & Seafood Salads | Breads, Egg & Cheese Dishes, Meat, Poultry & Vegetable Sauces | Artichokes, Cabbage, Eggplant, Squash, Dried Beans, Mushrooms, Pasta | Broiled, Roast Meats, Meat & Poultry Pies, Stews, Casseroles | Baked, Broiled & Poached Fish, Shellfish |
| PARSLEY | Green, Potato, Seafood & Vegetable Salads | Biscuits, Breads, Egg & Cheese Dishes, Gravies, Sauces | Asparagus, Beets, Eggplant, Squash, Dried Beans, Mushrooms, Pasta | Meat Loaf, Meat & Poultry Pies, Stews & Casseroles, Stuffing | Fish Stews, Stuffed Fish |
| ROSEMARY | Fruit Cocktail, Fruit & Green Salads | Biscuits, Egg Dishes, Herb Butter, Cream Cheese, Marinades, Sauces | Beans, Broccoli, Peas, Cauliflower, Mushrooms, Baked Potatoes, Parsnips | Roast Meat, Poultry & Meat Pies, Stews & Casseroles, Stuffing | Stuffed Fish, Shellfish |
| SAGE | | Breads, Fondue, Egg & Cheese Dishes, Spreads, Gravies, Sauces | Beans, Beets, Onions, Peas, Spinach, Squash, Tomatoes | Roast Meat, Poultry, Meat Loaf, Stews, Stuffing | Baked, Poached & Stuffed Fish |
| TARRAGON | Seafood Cocktail, Avocado Salads, Salad Dressings | Cheese Spreads, Marinades, Sauces, Egg Dishes | Asparagus, Beans, Beets, Carrots, Mushrooms, Peas, Squash, Spinach | Steaks, Poultry, Roast Meats, Casseroles & Stews | Baked, Broiled & Poached Fish, Shellfish |
| THYME | Seafood Cocktail, Green, Poultry, Seafood & Vegetable Salads | Biscuits, Breads, Egg & Cheese Dishes, Sauces, Spreads | Beets, Carrots, Mushrooms, Onions, Peas, Eggplant, Spinach, Potatoes | Roast Meat, Poultry & Meat Loaf, Meat & Poultry Pies, Stews & Casseroles | Baked, Broiled & Stuffed Fish, Shellfish, Fish Stews |

# General Recipe Index

*This handy index lists every recipe by food category, major ingredient and/or cooking method, so you can easily locate recipes to suit your needs.*

*✓ Recipe includes Nutritional Analysis and Diabetic Exchanges*

*✓ Recipe includes Nutritional Analysis and Diabetic Exchanges*

*✓ Recipe includes Nutritional Analysis and Diabetic Exchanges*

*✓ Recipe includes Nutritional Analysis and Diabetic Exchanges*

*✓ Recipe includes Nutritional Analysis and Diabetic Exchanges*

✓ *Recipe includes Nutritional Analysis and Diabetic Exchanges*

*✓ Recipe includes Nutritional Analysis and Diabetic Exchanges*

*✓ Recipe includes Nutritional Analysis and Diabetic Exchanges*

# Alphabetical Recipe Index

*This handy index lists every recipe in alphabetical order
so you can easily find your favorite recipes.*

*✓ Recipe includes Nutritional Analysis and Diabetic Exchanges*

✓ *Recipe includes Nutritional Analysis and Diabetic Exchanges*

✓ *Recipe includes Nutritional Analysis and Diabetic Exchanges*